#MenToo

BETTINA ARNDT

Published by:
Wilkinson Publishing Pty Ltd
ACN 006 042 173
Level 4, 2 Collins Street
Melbourne, Vic 3000
Ph: 03 9654 5446
www.wilkinsonpublishing.com.au

Copyright © 2018 Bettina Arndt
Reprint January 2019

A catalogue record for this
book is available from the
NATIONAL
LIBRARY   National Library of Australia
OF AUSTRALIA

Planned date of publication: 12-2018

Title: #MenToo

ISBN(s): 978-1-925642-65-0 : Printed - Paperback

Design by Spike Creative Pty Ltd
Ph: (03) 9427 9500
spikecreative.com.au

Printed in Australia by Griffin Press

Bettina Arndt trained as a clinical psychologist before becoming well known as one of Australia's first sex therapists. She then became a respected social commentator appearing regularly on television and radio and writing about gender issues. She's now making YouTube videos campaigning to end the demonisation of men. She is the author of *Private Lives* (1986), *All About Us* (1989), *Taking Sides* (1995), *The Sex Diaries* (2009) and *What Men Want — In Bed* (2012).

CONTENTS

INTRODUCTION

Last year I found myself at the cricket surrounded by men in pink. It was a yearly event for our Australian team which every year devotes the five days of a cricket test to raising funds for breast cancer, in honour of the late spouse of one of our famous cricketers, Glenn McGrath whose young wife Jane died of the disease.

Everywhere you looked there was a sea of pink, with the largely male audience decked out in pink shirts, jackets and silly hats. Yet this great display of men's natural chivalry and kindness left me frustrated. I spent the whole day recording interviews for a YouTube tube video[1] asking men in pink why men's lives don't matter.

Fifty-seven per cent of cancer deaths are male. The risk of dying from cancer before the age of 85 is one in four for males and one in six for females, according to the 2017 Australian Institute of Health and Welfare Cancer in Australia Report. Why then don't we see men dressed in blue, raising money to prolong the lives of their fathers, brothers, friends?

Yes, it's probably true we should be wearing blue today, I was told by two brightly-dressed men in blushing hues. "It's mother nature to look after the women," explained the younger man who admitted it was proof that women's lives matter more than men. And was that fair? "That's the way it is," he said. He and his mate boasted they were allowed by their wives to go away once a year to spend a week at the cricket — so there's no way these two were complaining.

My concern wasn't just losing more men to cancer than women — I realise it's usually older men who are dying compared to some very much younger women. My real beef was that I've spent decades lobbying for more help for men dealing with the devastating consequences on their sex lives of prostate cancer treatments. It is just appalling how few men receive proper advice on the penile rehabilitation needed to have any hope of enjoying normal sexual functioning.

It just didn't make sense for all these men in pink to raise money for more breast cancer nurses when at that time there were hundreds working across the country compared to 28 prostate cancer nurses. Given the squeamishness of most urologists to educate their clients on this issue, the need for prostate nurses is dire. Cancer Council research reveals many prostate cancer patients have life-long problems with erections due to this poor treatment.

That's why, some years ago, a rather embarrassed group of journalists at our National Press Club found themselves listening to me talking about why a breast shouldn't be worth more than a penis, as I explained the inequities of funding for cancer recovery. I've written articles about this for newspapers, given talks across the country. The funniest was a ball in Queensland raising money for prostate cancer support services. I assumed this would attract an older audience but since it is pretty young things and their partners who most enjoy dressing up in fancy gear, it was a very surprised group of twenty-somethings who found themselves learning all about rejuvenating wilting erections.

I've learnt that it is not just talk of men's nether regions that makes these audiences squirm. It's talk about men's issues, men's rights. We live in a society where women's wants and needs receive constant attention, a society which frowns on any discussion of men missing out. Just look at what happened to Cassie Jaye's documentary, *The Red Pill.*

In November 2016, this controversial movie was due to have its first screening in Melbourne when feminist protestors persuaded the cinema to pull out. The protestors hadn't even seen the film, they simply believed social media stories alleging it promoted violence against women. In fact, Cassie Jaye was a young feminist who originally planned to make a movie attacking the Men's Rights movement but after listening to what these men had to say, she ended up focussing on how feminists silence debate on men's issues. And what happened? For months feminists in Australia strenuously tried to ban the movie. It was the ultimate irony.

But it didn't surprise me. I've been writing about the issues raised in *The Red Pill* for over thirty years — battles in the family court, false abuse accusations, paternity fraud, education pitched to favour girls, unequal health funding, the distorted debate over domestic violence. I've long been speaking out about the tilting of laws, practises and regulations to unfairly advantage women at the expense of men.

I'd started my career as a proud feminist, determined to help women achieve equality. My background was clinical psychology, but my passion was teaching people to be comfortable talking about sex. As one of Australia's first sex therapists it was thrilling to help women overcome their embarrassment and gain more pleasure from their love lives. I rejoiced in those heady times for the feminist movement as more opportunities opened up for women and girls.

But even as I celebrated these achievements, I was starting to listen to men. Everywhere I went men reached out to me, keen to talk about sex. But inevitably sharing such intimate revelations lead to them opening up about other aspects of their lives. I heard devastating stories of divorced fathers' hopeless fights to see their children as they battled a family law system which enabled mothers to just shut these men out of their children's lives. I started to write about all this only to receive a surprising letter from a retiring family law judge.

"You're quite right" he said. "We've made a huge mistake. We've given too much power to the custodial parent... [then always almost women] and that power is often abused," he said describing common patterns of mothers breaching orders to deny fathers contact with children, moving wherever they liked, and making false accusations of abuse to weaken the man's case.

At the time we were lucky enough to have a Prime Minister, John Howard, who was concerned about the role of fathers. I ended up being appointed to various government committees to reform family law, a most instructive experience particularly as I was there representing men because the femocrats running the show insisted on appointing men to the committees who didn't do their side many favours.

Howard's people included me to even things up a little. I quickly learnt that while the women's lobby groups attract large numbers of outstanding professional women, most well-educated professional men shun involvement in men's groups, choosing instead to fight individual battles using highly paid lawyers. It became clear that one reason feminists are winning all the battles is that the powerful men in our society are reluctant to associate themselves with a group of men they see as losers.

A classic example was a very senior male bureaucrat who took me aside between committee meetings. He admitted he'd always dismissed men's complaints about bias in family law until the day he came home to find the locks on his home had been changed — his wife had decided to throw him out. His attempt to break in to pick up a few clothes led to him being arrested, issued with a protection order and facing hundreds of thousands in legal bills and years of struggle to even see his children. How tragic that men like him are only willing to see what's going on when they are victims of the process.

Howard was able to introduce reforms which included some real breakthroughs such as the presumption of shared parental responsibility and a new child support formula which at least made some attempt, however flawed, to account for the costs of the non-custodial parent. Yet many of these changes were wound back by the next Labor government when feminists played the violence card to frighten politicians into pulling back on the legislative changes. Claiming shared care put children at risk from being exposed to violent men proved a very effective means of undermining the Howard reforms and that opened the floodgates to the current situation where across the country false allegations of violence are being used to have men removed from their homes and denied contact with their children.

It's been alarming watching our legal system gradually shifting to favour women as feminists gain control over key institutions. "We prefer to err on the side of the victim," pronounced one of our state Police Ministers, unashamedly acknowledging new domestic laws are designed to make it easier for women to obtain protection orders with no evidence of violence. Now simply a fear of violence is enough to obtain such an order.

As I started to write about these issues many people weren't happy. Two friends, both prominent journalists, took me out to lunch, suggesting that it wasn't a good idea to be seen as an apologist for men. I needed more balance in my articles, they argued. It was an absurd suggestion. The notion that my articles should include the female perspective was foolish given that the cultural dialogue had been entirely captured by the feminist narrative. It was mainly female journalists who were writing about social issues, almost always from their own perspective, with female editors acting as gatekeepers. And when men's experiences clashed with the female view of the world, male opinions were silenced.

A man once told me he'd sat with tears rolling down to his cheeks as he heard me on the radio talking about husbands being constantly sexually rejected. My research on sexual desire, published in my book *The Sex Diaries*, was based on 98 couples keeping diaries about how they negotiated their sex supply and the howl of anguish that emerged from men was truly moving. But in a world where women's right to say "no" to sex is now sacrosanct, men's sexual frustrations have become a taboo topic.

I've been lucky. For most of my long career in journalism I worked full-time for some of our major newspapers. Being well-known gave me extra clout which meant I could write features and opinion pieces — many included in this book — which challenged the feminist narrative dominating mainstream media. One example was research regularly released on housework, who does what around the home. Inevitably this would lead to a rash of headlines talking about the huge load on women and how little men do to help around the house. But what was always missing from the news stories was the total hours worked — combining paid plus unpaid work — which show men work just as hard overall as women do. Australian men average twice as many hours of paid work as women.

So, I was able to write about the Australian research which showed that most women are happy with the deal over housework because they are aware that their partners' long working hours buy them choice about spending more time with their children — a point of view many of my female editors weren't keen to promote.

I once ran into Bruce Baird, father of Julia Baird, then the opinion editor of my paper, the *Sydney Morning Herald*[2]. At the time I was writing opinion pieces which were to be published in both *The Age* and the *Sydney Morning Herald*. *The Age* was giving me a great run, often running my articles as the main opinion piece whilst the *SMH* never gave the same pieces any prominence. Baird told me he loved my work but confessed his daughter, my editor, "hated it". He admitted to heated discussion with his feminist daughter who confessed she did everything she could to bury my work.

It must have been galling that my writing was popular with the readers, and not just with males. It's hardly surprising to me that most ordinary woman are fed up with the male-bashing that has come to dominate the public agenda. Survey after survey has shown less than thirty per cent of Australians are willing to call themselves "feminist"[3] — the only way that number reaches a majority is when feminism is defined as "achieving equality."[4]

Ordinary women write to me — mothers of sons, women worried about the men in their lives, or simply fed up with fainting-couch feminists treating women as victims always in need of special protection. A successful young musician wrote to complain about discrimination policies taking over Australia's music organisation aiming at more women winning prizes. She'd made it mainly through talent and hard work, although she admits affirmative action probably worked in her favour. She strongly believes everyone should be judged on their merits rather than gender.

Most women are appalled by the #MeToo attacks where unproven allegations are being used to destroy men's careers. They are fed up with trivial issues being blown up as sexism and once proud, independent women endlessly demanding special treatment such as lower entry standards into the police-force or armed forces.

Mothers write about schools where boys are filling the remedial reading classes, disengaged and dropping out whilst the girls win all the prizes. We had a parliamentary commission about boys' education some years ago which attracted record numbers of submissions from the community. The government introduced all manner of programmes to try to engage boys and for a while Australia led the world in tackling the boys' education problem. But here too a change in government meant the conservatives were out and the boys' education initiatives lost their funding.

Naturally that had the activists celebrating. One of the scariest letters I have ever received starts by slagging off at my fat poodle face, goes on to commiserate with my daughter for the shame of having such a mother and concludes that "girls today are far beyond needing equality. They need compensation for two thousand years of being repressed, mutilated, enslaved, raped and treated as inferiors."

That compensation is what's driving our domestic violence industry — a blatant disregard for equity but blind adherence to a feminist script which is all about seeking funding for women and denying any possibility of men as victims. We see a totally one-sided debate on domestic violence in this country which refuses to acknowledge the forty years of international research showing most family violence is two-way, involving both male and female perpetrators. Governments pay for television campaigns featuring violent men and boys, they pour money into propaganda organisations which tell porkies about this important social issue.

Earlier this year a young male Perth counsellor was forced out of his job at Relationship Australia for posting on his private Facebook page my ground-breaking article summarising key domestic violence research and statistics — as described in chapter 17. I find it just extraordinary that this government-funded organisation proudly promotes a one-sided feminist policy on domestic violence and pushes out their only male counsellor when he doesn't toe the line.

Domestic violence is all about respect for women, intones our Prime Minister Malcolm Turnbull when he knows full well that underpinning the problem is a range of complexities, from poverty and mental illness, to drug and alcohol abuse. I used to hand out how to vote pamphlets for this man, who once spent months trying to persuade me to run the Liberal's Menzies

Research Institute. He knows all about the complexities of social research yet this most powerful of men prefers to kow-tow to the feminists, assuming that will win him votes.

But he's wrong. There are signs that people have had enough. A woman at the pink cricket test told me that her father, who died of prostate cancer, would have been outraged to see the men in pink selling out other men. Anti-male grandstanding by men in power is increasingly being called out. Earlier this year I made a video about the push to allow women to join Men's Sheds[5]. The Men's Sheds Movement is all about providing men with a place to get away, enjoy male company and provide support for one another. My video revealed that the chairman of the Men's Sheds Association, who had a background in promoting equity in the workplace, didn't believe there was anything special about male culture and was all for having women in sheds. Boy, did he feel the heat when my video was published.

Here in Australia, as elsewhere, people are turning away from mainstream media seeking more balanced views elsewhere. Since I pulled out of journalism to make videos about men's issues a year ago, I've discovered a thriving new world on what people are calling the "intellectual dark web", with people like Canadians Jordan Peterson and Karen Straughan raising all manner of challenging issues, including demanding fairer treatment for men and boys. Huge numbers are involved in serious conversations about gender, relationships, family life — tackling questions which really matter.

That includes properly addressing what's happening to men. I've been blessed by the men in my life, a brilliant, inspiring father, two loving, extraordinary sons and wonderful partners who have brought so much to my life: love, laughter and great sex. This collection of writing is meant a celebration of all the good men who do so much to contribute to our society.

I've included some key articles dating back twenty years, adding footnotes to provide updates on critical issues. There are lengthy chapters based on my feature writing and many short opinion pieces where I vent about whatever madness inspired me that week. Reading it now I am struck by how often I was a voice in the wilderness, expressing views that I knew most people believed but were hardly ever heard.

So, here's #MenToo — to tell the other side of the story.

SECTION ONE

#MeToo and the male chastity crusade

CHAPTER 1

#MeToo – the latest attempt to crush male sexuality

First published 2018

Canadian writer Margaret Atwood whose book *The Handmaid's Tale* led to a hit television series has spelt out the risks of "guilt by accusation" where lynch-mobs "throw justice out the window".

"In times of extremes, extremists win. Their ideology becomes a religion," Atwood warned. Ironically her *Handmaid's Tale* is all about a dystopian future with men brutally regaining control yet the lynch-mobs she is now denouncing are privileged young women controlling men's lives by claiming the victim role.

Next, we heard from Germaine Greer arguing women should take direct and immediate action against the men preying on them. They should simply outwit them or slap them down, she suggested bluntly, pointing out that's what women used to do to leering men in the old British *Carry On* comedies. Greer acknowledged it is different when a man like Harvey Weinstein has economic power over the women: "But if you spread your legs because he said 'be nice to me and I'll give you a job in a movie' then I'm afraid that's tantamount to consent, and it's too late now to start whingeing about that."

Good to see the original saucy feminist encouraging women to consider their role in perpetuating the casting couch. Back in 1971 Germaine featured on the cover of *Life* magazine in pink lipstick and a clinging knit dress as the "Saucy feminist that even men like", happily rebutting many of the sisterhood's claims that women could do without men in their sex lives.

A decade later she was attacking the sexualised Western culture's "genital dabbling" in her book *Sex and Destiny* and telling *Rolling Stone* journalists Steve Chapple and David Talbot that she was exhausted by the tension and jealousies of sexual love. Yet still male sexuality held a certain appeal. "I would love to lose interest altogether in the penis. I don't know what's the matter with me that I still think it's so fascinating."

But by then many of her feminist sisters saw male sexuality and male bodies as anything but appealing. Ferocious American anti-pornography campaigner Andrea Dworkin was in full flight, engaged in her mighty battle to close down video shops and adult sex shops. "Violence is male: the male is the penis, violence is the penis," she wrote in her book *Pornography: Men possessing women*. She saw intercourse as consorting with the enemy, pornography as "Dachau brought into the bedroom and celebrated."

That's what's so odd about all the excitement around #MeToo, the idea that this is some kind of revelatory moment, a breakthrough in women's march towards liberation. Those of us who have been around for a while have seen it all before.

#MeToo is simply the latest salvo in a long crusade by feminists to crush male sexuality — as I've explained in my YouTube video discussion with Men's Rights activist Karen

Straughan[6]. It's a very long campaign, dating back to 19th century suffragettes whose slogan — "Votes for Women. Chastity for Men!" — linked the political equality of women to controlling men's sex drive. Along with the vote, the suffragettes sought an end to their sexual subjugation to men, control over their bodies. They decided that required reining men in, putting an end to their tomcatting ways and keeping them on a very tight leash.

That was just the beginning. Second wave feminists were quick to hop on board. Kate Millet's 1970 book, *Sexual Politics,* known as the "bible of women's liberation", denounced raunchy male novelists like Norman Mailer and Henry Miller, slamming their depictions of sex as all about subordination of women. Sex was the expression of men's misogyny wrote Millet: "Women have very little idea of how much men hate them."

Ongoing feminist campaigns saw male sexuality increasingly publicly reviled. Men were endlessly in trouble over sex. Men in trouble for not keeping their trousers zipped, for groping and harassing women, for looking at pornography, or gazing at women in the wrong way. Shame-faced men were paraded in front of jeering chat show audiences and forced to atone for their sins.

It left men reeling and silenced: "Like a man who sullenly withdraws to his tool shed to escape his wife's temper and misery, American men simply opted out of the cultural dialogue," said Chappie and Talbot in their book *Burning Desires,* explaining that men became so far removed from the field of battle that the term "sex war" seemed a misnomer.

Today the suffragettes' crusade is succeeding beyond their wildest dreams. It's not just the public display of male sexuality which is being so effectively curtailed. In private many heterosexual married men are living lives of sexual deprivation, with sex doled out to them only very occasionally or not at all. There's research showing the desire gap between men and women is increasing, with most married women ending up going off sex.

Growing numbers of women are happily living celibate lives and forcing their husbands to just cop it sweet. Men who visit prostitutes are reviled — the push is now on to criminalise the customers of prostitutes, a campaign that has already succeeded in Nordic countries, Canada, and a bunch of European countries. Men know risking an affair could mean the end of their marriages and loss of their families. Even the man who resorts to masturbation is in trouble, particularly if he turns to the Internet for fantasy material to make the process more enjoyable.

So #MeToo is nothing new. Rather it is simply the latest round in this relentless crusade to demonise male sexuality — as Catherine Deneuve and the 100 prominent French women spelt out in their letter denouncing the campaign as all about "hatred of men and of sexuality."

The ongoing campaign finds a very receptive audience in a society with increasing numbers of sexually indifferent women. And then there's the new generation of young women, raised by a culture which paints a sexual joke as an attack on women, which teaches women that a lusty gaze is sexual violence, which manufactures a fake campus rape crisis. The resulting fragile, wilting wallflowers are ideal fodder for the #MeToo campaign, eager to claim victimhood and tell tales of scary encounters with the dangerous sexual predator they believe lurks in every man.

"Leaving sex to the feminists is like letting your dog vacation at the taxidermist," said Camille Paglia. But that's just what we have done.

CHAPTER 2

Men in trouble over sex – the constant refrain

First published 2011

The 71-year-old virgin was a surprising volunteer for the sexuality project. As he expected, he didn't have that much to contribute to my research on male sexuality, but his story was intriguing. Here was a man who hadn't planned to miss out on sex and marriage but so wanted his first experience to be special that he'd waited for years hoping to meet the right woman. Despite plenty of dating, she never showed up. Hence, he'd ended up on his own, spending his whole life struggling with his strong sexual urges.

Yet he now wonders whether he has missed out on all that much. He wrote eloquently about watching his friends go through the pain of marriage break-up or struggling to cope without much sex in their marriages. "I'm not complaining. I've had a good life. There are no arguments in my household," he said chirpily. Certainly, no arguments about sex.

From the outside, life as a hot-blooded married heterosexual man doesn't look much fun. America's best-known sex guru, Dan Savage, reaches much the same conclusion. The wildly popular advice columnist is currently in the news as a result of a thoughtful profile published in

The New York Times that focused largely on Savage's attack on America's obsession with fidelity.

Openly gay Savage, whose sex advice column is syndicated across the world in more than 70 newspapers and attracts millions more followers online, started off jokingly offering heterosexuals sex advice but quickly attracted a huge following with his hard-hitting, provocative take on bedroom manners and responsibilities.

He promotes mutual care-taking, suggesting both men and women adhere to his famous acronym GGG — all lovers should be good, giving and game. He writes at length about the relationship between low libido and monogamy. "You can have strict monogamy, or you can have low libido, Ladies, but you can't have both." But then he adds. "Oh, and guys? You need to accept those tide-you-over blowjobs and hand-jobs just as cheerfully as she gives them." That's if she gives them.

When *New York Times* interviewer Mark Oppenheimer suggested Savage's views are tainted by the American gay male view of the sexual world, with its tolerance for pornography, fetishes and a variety of partnered arrangements, Savage responded that the male gay world simply expresses what men are really like when they don't have women reining them in. "Women, straight women, are in relationships with men. Doesn't it help to know what we're really like? Women can go on marrying and pretending that their boyfriends and husbands are Mr Darcy or some rom-com dream man. But where's that going to get them? Besides divorce court?"

That's where he is wrong. Faced with the misery of a lifetime spent dealing with the frustrations of monogamous sex-starved marriage, most men don't leave. On my website forum, I once had a letter titled "Do I stay or do I go" from a 40-year-old married man who'd gone for years without any sex in his marriage. The letter attracted hundreds of responses, many from men urging him to go. He left, for a while, but then came back and struggled on, trying to make his marriage work. Like most men who write to me, he loves his wife and children and feels he has too much to lose if he leaves.

Dan Savage is right in thinking that many heterosexual men share the same voracious sexual desires that have come to define gay male sexuality. But most are doing an incredibly good job keeping a lid on them. Men come in for constant criticism about sex. We hear endlessly about the men who stray, the men who harass women or make inappropriate sexual remarks, men caught looking at women in the wrong way, or in trouble for gazing at naked bodies on the Internet. But what we never hear about is men's restraint, the remarkable stoicism of current generations of heterosexual men who cop it sweet, despite their immense frustrations.

Some time ago *The Sunday Age* published a sweetly amusing story about men's sexual fantasies, written by a man who describes himself as a "respectable, married" man who has spent the last few years taming what he calls his "inner goat". There's no place for hidden sexual yearnings in his proudly reconstructed world — he boasts he keeps his goat firmly locked inside a concrete pen, tethered to a post. Yet he ruefully acknowledges that sometimes it manages to escape and he finds himself mentally undressing a woman as she walks past.

The online responses to his article were intriguing — the men who applauded his courage and the women who condemned him for expressing such thoughts. "Men, you could put your minds to much better use than fantasising about women you are never going to get ... There's something you can do: you can respect women and learn to control your pathetic, primitive minds. Meditation helps," wrote one smug woman.

A male responder hit the nail on the head, summing up what's happened here: "While the feminists and soft men like to kid themselves that they are changing our nature, all they've really done is teach men to keep their mouths shut, while our minds still explore exactly the same topics they always have."

There's an interesting book — *The Testosterone Files* — written by a feminist writer who had a sex change and became a male. The author, Max Wolf Valerio, describes being blown away by the urgency of his newly acquired sexual urges, his constant sexual fantasies — sex is now food, he says. He cringes when he sees female audiences on talk shows pursing their lips, shaking their heads at sheepish male guests who are supposed "porn addicts" or "womanisers". He's shocked by women's ready assumption of moral superiority.

"How to explain this to women?" Valerio ponders. "There is this thing about men that they cannot completely know. Few people want to believe that there could be a real chasm, a chemically induced difference of sexual drive between the sexes. Few want to believe that there might be any difference at all that is not socially constructed.

"Now that I am Max, I see that this rift, this fundamental chasm between men and women's perceptions and experience of sexuality, is one that may never be bridged.

"There certainly can be no hope for understanding as long as society pretends that men and women are really the same, that the culture of male sexuality is simply a conflation of misogyny and dysfunction. That the male libido is shaped and driven primarily by socialisation, that can be legislated or 'psychobabbled' out of existence."

The strong male libido remains, even if the inner goat now must remain firmly tethered. Men live with up to 20 times the testosterone of women and that makes it very tough to cope with decades of monogamous marriage, particularly when sex is offered very reluctantly — "like meaty treats to a dog", as one man put it.

Yet most men are doing a remarkable job remaining true to their women. For all the talk about unfaithful men, most married men succeed at monogamy most of the time. Just look at the statistics. The first Sex in Australia Survey, also known as the Australian Study of Health and Relationships or ASHR1 (2003), sampled almost 20,000 people and found just five per cent of partnered men had strayed in the previous year. Now admittedly, these tiny numbers can add up over a long marriage or relationship, but while there are men who are compulsive philanderers, this wasn't the case for most of the men taking part in my research who admitted to having had an affair.

The overwhelming majority wanted to be faithful and were succeeding, even though there may have been a lapse along the way — a one-night stand at a conference, a few weeks of illicit pleasure, or even an affair lasting months or perhaps a year or two. But nothing compared with the many years of restraint.

In one of Dan Savage's amusing Q&A sessions with college students now available on YouTube, he argues men should get credit for this. "If you are with a guy for 40 years and he cheats on you three or four times, he is GOOD at monogamy! Not BAD at monogamy. We think of monogamy the way we think of virginity — it exists until you f--- someone and then it's gone forever. We need to think of monogamy the way we think of sobriety — you can fall the f--- off the wagon and still get back up."

Men's well-known urge for sexual variety has long been acknowledged by psychologists who refer to it as the "Coolidge effect". The name comes from a story about former US president Calvin Coolidge and his wife visiting a poultry farm. During the tour, Mrs Coolidge noticed roosters mating frequently and inquired how often that happened. The farmer proudly explained that his roosters performed their duty dozens of times each day.

"Perhaps you could point that out to Mr Coolidge," replied the first lady.

On being told, the president asked the farmer, "Does each rooster service the same hen each time?"

"No," replied the farmer, "there are many hens for each rooster."

"Perhaps you could point that out to Mrs Coolidge," replied the president.

All the evidence suggests the urge is hardwired — yet most men find ways of ignoring that itch, or diverting it into harmless pursuits like looking at pornography.

Harmless pursuits? That's not, of course, how porn is presented. We are subject to an endless stream of people, mainly women, warning of the dangers of porn. Witness British sociologist Gail Dines, who appears on television panels and at writers' festivals describing in the most salacious terms the horrors of gonzo porn — gagging women, women whose anuses "literally drop off their bodies because of anal prolapses". She claims that mainstream porn invariably dehumanises women and normalises male sexual cruelty.

Yet the truth is when men sit in the wee hours staring at their flickering computer screens, the big attraction is willing women, eager women, easy women — easy to bed and easy to please. "Images of women hungry for sex with us, possessed by desire for us. Receptive women who greet our sexual desire not with fear or loathing but with appreciation, even gratitude," wrote David Steinberg in an essay relating sexual scarcity to the male attraction for porn.

A research study looking at porn usage in Australia, published in *The Porn Report*, found most (98 per cent) of the best-selling porn videos are pretty white-bread and free of violence — in fact, some of the most popular mainstream Internet sites are DIY amateur sites where thoroughly ordinary couples bonk for their webcams. My research suggests men turn to porn for good reasons: as a harmless outlet for their sexual curiosity; to control a sexual drive causing conflict in their relationships; to relieve sexual boredom; and as relief from the tensions of trying to please women in real-life sex.

There are, of course, high-drive women who struggle to live with their own rampaging inner doe. There are many such single women but far fewer in long-term relationships. There are also those who enjoy watching porn, who cheerfully spend Friday nights with their partners munching take-away and watching R-rated DVDs. Women who happily live in open relationships, or go swinging with their partners, or post their own beaver shots on Internet sites. And there are women genuinely concerned about their partners' frustrations. It's just that these women rarely enter the public debate.

I recently received an email from a 60-year-old woman talking about her "fabulous, amazing, caring, awesome, loving" husband who keeps harassing her to get involved in threesomes and group sex. She's an intelligent, thoughtful woman who is perplexed about how to negotiate this difference in their attitudes. "There is, I believe, a big difference between 'just saying yes' within the confines of a marriage and agreeing to sexual arrangements that simply fly in the face of everything that you believe that sex is about."

Her husband grew up in a very liberal sexual environment and had previously enjoyed open relationships. He's convinced his desire for sexual experimentation is perfectly natural, but it holds no attraction for her. After much persuasion, she participated in a threesome with a male friend yet the pressure continues, with her husband seeking further get-togethers with other males and even sending a photo of her (clothed) to a potential partner. Naturally she was upset by this, but rather than rant about his behaviour, she wrote seeking simply to illustrate the difficulties of negotiating this divide between men and women.

I suggested she post the letter on my website forum, to generate discussion on this difficult issue. It attracted an immediate response from an angry woman: "NOBODY, and I mean NOBODY (not even hubby) has the right to pressure you into doing anything that makes you feel uncomfortable. A person who does this is not respecting OR loving his/her partner," she wrote, tearing strips off the man for his unseemly behaviour. "If that was my husband, and he continued to harass me over this, it would be grounds for separation and divorce. Red flags going off all over the place for me," she added emphatically.

Naturally that served to shut off any real discussion. Few men would dare venture an opinion after such a tirade. That's what happens all the time. Whenever anyone, man or woman, talks openly about how to accommodate male sexual desire, angry women close down the conversation. It strikes me as odd.

Of course, women have a right to say no to such activities, but shouldn't men have freedom to ask? Is it so very different from other areas where women feel perfectly free to try to persuade men into life-changing decisions — like buying a bigger house (involving him in an extra decade or two of mortgage payments) or persuading a new husband, a remarried father, to have more children?

A few years ago, the Australian National University's Women's Studies students held a demonstration protesting about a talk I was giving at their university. They objected to me even raising questions about sexual obligation in marriage, suggesting such talk is dangerous for young women.

What nonsense. Closing down the debate on the vexed business of accommodating male and female sexual needs doesn't solve anything. This is mighty tough stuff but it's a conversation we must continue.

)

CHAPTER 3

The politics of cleavage – women flaunting sexual power

First published 2012

A young man and woman are having a friendly chat after a yoga class. The fresh-faced blonde seems totally relaxed but then she freezes. "Did you just look at my chest," she asks angrily, arms firmly folded.

"Yep," mutters the bloke sheepishly. Her response is fierce. "Can't I go to one yoga class without being ogled by some jerk?"

Instead of being cowed, he takes her on, launching into a passionate defence of his action: "If you really didn't want me to stare at your beautiful breasts, you'd be wearing something other than a purple sports bra covering maybe one-third of your perfect tits," he argues, suggesting, among other things, that he's biologically programmed to scan for life-giving breasts for his future offspring. He's cute, passionate and ultimately convincing. She ends up asking him out for coffee.

This skit, from New York media company The Kloons[7], has attracted more than a million hits on YouTube. The producers say it wasn't just meant as a joke but rather "to investigate the deep chasm between men and women".

That mighty chasm is indeed wide and growing, with so many women now feeling absolutely entitled to dress as they like — bare tits, enticing flesh squeezed into the shortest, tightest clothing. Everywhere you look, women are stepping out dressed provocatively but bristling if the wrong man shows he enjoys the display.

And men — well, they are in a total state of confusion. There are cocky, attractive, successful men, alpha males, revelling in this unexpected bounty, boldly eyeing off the assets of women they fancy.

Sensitive males are wary, not knowing where to look. Afraid of causing offence. And there are angry men, the beta males who lack the looks, the trappings of success to tick these women's boxes. They know the goodies on display are not for them. These are the men most likely to behave badly, blatantly leering, grabbing and sneering. For them, the whole thing is a tease. They know it and resent it.

The state of play was neatly summed up some time ago during the SlutWalks, where scantily dressed women took to the streets, proudly proclaiming their right to dress as they wish, in protest over a Canadian cop, who suggested women shouldn't dress like sluts if they don't want to be raped.

Jamie Lauren Keiles, an organiser of SlutWalk Chicago, explained that a half-naked woman as a form of protest is different from a half-naked lady pandering to the male gaze. It's about "a woman putting herself out there as a 'f--- you' as opposed to a 'f--- me'," Keiles explained. That may be fine in the context of protesting that scantily dressed women aren't asking to be raped. Of course, there's never an excuse for sexual violence or for men to paw or harass women.

But when young women stand in front of mirrors on a Saturday night, adjusting their cleavage, seeking ever greater exposure, maybe they need to think more about what they are doing. While there are women who claim they dress sluttishly just to make themselves feel good, the fact remains that, like the protesters, the main message sent is about flaunting women's sexual power.

It's an "UP YOURS" gesture of the most provocative kind.

Not that all women understand that's how they come across. A mid-40s woman told me about a naive 22-year-old work colleague who had had a breast enlargement. "She is a tiny thing, quite pretty but socially inept and ready to settle for anything that comes along. She went for a breast enlargement to a D cup in the belief it would attract a better type than her current, unsatisfactory bloke."

The older colleague tried to discourage her but she went ahead with the operation. "Now she gets all weird when older men or ugly men or fat men or any men she doesn't see as ideal even glance at her. She reacts with nervous laughter and at the first opportunity runs back to me and says, 'OMG, you won't believe who looked at me,' as if it is unreasonable for these men to take any notice of her.

"And surprise — it hasn't introduced her to a better partner! Now she is talking about having them redone a size larger."

This girl hasn't a clue but plenty of other women know exactly what they are doing, as they make clear in Internet discussions of this issue.

"I luv my 36DDs and show them off. I like to see men drool."

"It's so funny when some men get caught cos they have that 'Am I in trouble?' look on their face!"

"It is a tease thing … men are so weak."

"We have such power over them."

Jean is a 33-year-old, extremely attractive Sydney divorcee completing her PhD in physics. She has a fit body and large breasts, which she likes showing off in revealing clothes. When she "gets the girls out", she enjoys the subtle looks, even a discreet compliment about her body from the right man.

"A quick glance from them, a little moment of recognition, and then back to the conversation. It's part of the dance, hinting at a possible connection," she said.

Are some allowed to look and others not?

"Well, I think there's a sort of sexual food chain and I prefer to engage with people on a similar level as me. Sometimes it feels sleazy when I'm way out of the observer's league, like if they're really old or fat or ugly."

That's the problem. She's advertising her wares to the world, not just her target audience, and somehow men are expected to know when they are not on her page. Jean described at length the subtle dance, based largely on non-verbal behaviour, that she uses to show men when attention is welcome. But as we all know, many men are lousy at that stuff — the language totally escapes them.

Rob Tiller is a Perth counsellor who has run more than 200 men's workshops on communication skills, sex and intimacy. He believes many men are confused about what's going on.

"In one of my workshops, I remember a guy describing women flaunting their bodies as a form of 'biological sexual harassment' towards men, to which most of the group gave a collective nod," Tiller says. "The self-assured, cocky blokes seem to see bare flesh as a green light and often express a 'bring-it-on' attitude but others find it difficult to handle. I think it's a real catch-22 for most men. We really do want to be respectful but that's not always easy with a neon pink G-string staring up at us."

The Internet is bristling with men writing about what they regard as women's sexual arrogance. Provocative female attire is an assault against men, wrote Giovanni Dannato for *In Mala Fide*, an online magazine of heretical ideas. He argued women exposing themselves without intending to reciprocate the attention they attract is impolite and inconsiderate — which, he bizarrely suggested, is rather like schoolchildren who bring something tasty to class that they are not prepared to share. It amounts to "an act of aggression in which they use the power of their sex as a weapon", he wrote.

Dannato may be on to something when he proposed that some of the catcalling these women attract is a "defence mechanism used by low-status men against women flaunting themselves publicly". There certainly are a bunch of men writing about the plight of the beta males — unattractive, low-status guys who don't get to first base with women.

F. Roger Devlin, a political philosopher who has written challenging material on gender issues for *The Occidental Quarterly*, points out these beta males have long been tearing their hair out trying to discover what on earth they have to do to make themselves acceptable to the girl next door. They get the message that what women instinctively want is "for 99 per cent of the men they run into to leave them alone, buzz off, drop dead, while the one to whom they feel attracted makes all their dreams come true".

Of course, there is no excuse for gross behaviour when beta males are told to buzz off, told that the titillation isn't meant for them — plenty of men do manage to control themselves in these circumstances.

But surely men have a right to show what it's like to be on the receiving end. There's a great scene in the animated television comedy *Family Guy* where Peter Griffin, the overweight, ugly, blue-collar dad, lets fly about Lindsay Lohan putting on her little outfits and jumping around on stage throwing "those things" in front of his face. "What am I supposed to do? What do you want from me?" he asks plaintively. But he knows the answer all too well: "I'll tell you what you want. You want NOTHING. We all know no woman anywhere wants to have sex with anyone and to titillate us with any thoughts otherwise is just bogus."

Griffin's howl of protest is based on the simple truth that some men spend their lives in a state of sexual deprivation, dealing with constant rejection. Roy F. Baumeister is a psychology professor, now at the University of Queensland who has extensively researched gender difference in sex drive. "Sexual frustration is almost inevitable for the majority of men and not just occasionally. They won't have enough partners or even enough sex with one partner to satisfy their wishes," Baumeister writes, concluding, "the tragedy of the male sex drive" is men's state of perpetual readiness, which so rarely meets its match.

That's the context that makes the constant just-out-of-reach titillation men now face confusing, irritating and even insulting. Yet many men are still trying hard to get it right, listening to their partners about why they hate men's ogling.

Take these soul-searching words from a 35-year-old Brisbane man.

"When I was first dating my partner, we'd be walking along

the beach through the 'minefield' of tanning lasses and I'd
moan out loud when a particularly sexy beach bunny crossed
our path. My lady would protest my caveman shenanigans to no
avail; not only was she hurt by my overtly disrespectful ogling,
it also deeply impacted her confidence about her body. Over
time, she became much less comfortable with her body at the
beach, as well as the bedroom. Five years later, the scars left by
my clumsy perving are healing but she still struggles with her
body image. Such a shame because, honestly, she's a knockout."

Of course, men are going to want to look — "it feels like
there's a magnet in her chest" one man complained. But there
are men struggling with how to do this in a respectful way.
There's a sweet blog on *The Good Men Project* website — which
promotes enlightened "masculinity" — where Hugo Schwyzer
describes his total humiliation when Jenny Talbot caught him
staring at her boobs in maths class. "You're so perverted,"
she yelled and Hugh cringed with embarrassment. But since
then, he's taken women's studies courses and understands "the
problematic power of the male gaze".

And he's ready to give helpful hints to men about how to
look without making women uncomfortable. Like the Three-
Second Rule: "Few women are going to feel you're undressing
them if your glance lasts so short a time."

There are other blogs where men describe how awkward it is
not to be caught glancing chest height. Spending conversations
looking over women's heads, or straight up at the ceiling. "By
the time the conversation is over, we'll know how many light
bulbs are in every room," joked writer Anslem Samuel Rocque.

It does all have its funny side and there are also plenty of
men who love the passing parade. Some men, particularly

successful, attractive men, enjoy the show — confident that they are in the target audience. Harry is a fit, cute 28-year-old, well launched on his media career, a world where he suggests flirting and flaunting is part of the culture. He's comfortable with women displaying themselves to him: "If she has a great body and she enjoys showing it off, for sure I enjoy looking." He tells the story of a meeting with a young woman wearing a fairly fitted yellow dress, "popping out of the top".

"The conversation was about the rate I was going to charge them for advertising. As I looked down at my notebook and did some basic sums, I realised that she was leaning forward, deliberately showing her tits, presumably to throw my concentration." He called her bluff.

"I started to laugh and made a comment about putting her body on the line for the business!"

She backed off, embarrassed, and he got his deal done.

The young people caught up in all the titillation rarely see any harm in what's going on. I have had many conversations with parents of young women who try to tell their daughters that revealing dress isn't a good idea, only to be rebuffed by statements about women's rights.

Often, the older women will admit they'd been down this road themselves. Here's one: "At 43 years old, I no longer wear revealing outfits as I don't have the body for it, I think women my age look silly flaunting themselves and, frankly, I couldn't be bothered. But when I was young I was always the one to wear outfits that would make a father say, 'You're not going out in that, young lady!'"

She'd yell abuse at guys catcalling from cars at her. "I can wear whatever I want!" Only now does she think about the confused young men she left in her wake, the mixed messages she'd sent them. "Deep down I was much more aware of my power than I actually let on."

That may well still apply to many young women today. But feminists have so successfully shut down proper debate on this issue that women are discouraged from ever considering their own responsibility in flaunting that power and the distain that shows for men.

CHAPTER 4

Flirting is the new harassment

First published 2016

What a joke. West Indies cricketer Chris Gayle laughingly makes a pass on national television during an interview with Network Ten reporter Mel McLaughlin. Predictably, commentators line up to condemn the man's behaviour as yet one more example of vulnerable women needing protection from predatory men.

But the real lesson from this latest media beat-up was a very positive one. It was great seeing McLaughlin so clearly able to handle Gayle's banter — it's a fine example for younger women to see such a confident professional woman able to bat off this type of flirtatious nonsense.

Equally, many people enjoyed watching Maria Sharapova flirting with a male reporter some time back, telling him: "I was just admiring your form."

Such harmless flirtation is not sexual harassment and luckily there are many in our community who resent the constant intrusion into enjoyable male-female interaction by thought police determined to stamp out any hint of what Australian writer Helen Garner famously described as "Eros — the spark that ignites and connects".

There are plenty of women who bristle at the present male-bashing climate where men are forced into tiptoeing around their female colleagues for fear they will be accused of saying or doing the wrong thing.

There are women who regret efforts to brand all compliments about their appearance as inappropriate and who want to retain the right to make their own choices about whether they enjoy male-female sexual banter and what they choose to do if it becomes offensive.

That's the essence of went wrong in the Jamie Briggs affair, where a government minister was forced to step down after flirting with a female public servant on a night out in Hong Kong. The young woman concerned didn't mention harassment, nor did she seek to make a formal complaint. Given the trivial behaviour under discussion — a compliment about her "piercing blue eyes", and a kiss on the cheek or neck — it's not surprising she chose simply to ask Briggs's chief of staff to let him know he had been out of line.

That's exactly the approach recommended in these circumstances. Back in the 1970s when sexual harassment policies were first being framed in Australia, the focus in more trivial matters was all about education — setting up mediation so victims could convey their concerns to the perpetrators and teach them why their behaviour was inappropriate.

The aim was to clearly differentiate minor matters from serious concerns that required a punitive approach involving adjudication and possible criminal sanctions.

How this line has now blurred. What's shocking about the Briggs case was that the woman's sensible desire for a low-key approach was disregarded, with some politicians seeing the issue as a means of forcing Briggs out of the ministry.

This is what led to all the nonsense that followed. Next Malcolm Turnbull jumped on board, bemoaning the impact of all this on the young woman concerned, when it was he and his colleagues who set the whole thing in play.

There's a pattern emerging here as the Prime Minister seems determined to go overboard on such issues — stressing the seriousness of the "inappropriate behaviour" and making endless motherhood statements about "respect for women". He's clearly convinced that playing the gender card wins votes from women.

He shouldn't be so sure. He's ignoring the lesson from our political history where Julia Gillard's misogyny speech ultimately failed to win votes from women who were unimpressed by her blatant effort to use gender politics to salvage her dwindling support. Gender beat-ups may impress social commentators but leave many ordinary women unmoved.

Witness the reaction of many women to some of the high-profile sexual harassment cases that have played out in Australia, where women stand to gain so much by accusing men of unseemly behaviour. We've seen widespread public debate, led by female as well as male commentators, who are extremely cynical about the supposed innocence of many of the accusers. Women know all too well that the truth in many of these situations is often a murky shade of grey.

There's good reason female jurists make it harder to gain convictions in sexual consent cases. Notions of sisterhood often go out the window when it comes to making judgments about the behaviour of other women, precisely because we know that women are capable of matching any man when it comes to manipulative, duplicitous behaviour.

Many women were concerned by Turnbull's first major policy announcement on domestic violence, which whitewashed this complex issue by presenting men as the only villains. When I wrote about research showing the prominent role women played in violence in the home, I received many supportive letters from women, including professionals working with families at risk from violent mothers and other women who had grown up in such homes, or had witnessed brothers, fathers, male friends experiencing violence at the hands of a woman. Many commented how surprised they were that Turnbull made such an offensive, one-sided policy announcement.

Politicians who play gender politics risk antagonising not only men fed up with the constant male-bashing but also women determined not to live their lives as victims, women who want responsibility for aggressive, offensive behaviour to be sheeted home to the true perpetrators — male or female.

CHAPTER 5

Men and pornography – dangers are oversold

First published 2011

"My wife doesn't show much enthusiasm for sex. She will passively let me do things and this annoys me as it is a real turn on to have women really enthusiastic and getting off on giving you pleasure. So when she's asleep I turn to porn where all these young women appear to be totally enthusiastic about pleasing the man. I know it's all acting and they are only doing it for money and that it's not fair to expect my wife to be like these porn actresses but in my fantasy world this is what I love and get off on. I'll do it for up to an hour, slowly, going from video to video on my laptop, while my wife is sound asleep. I can take as long as I want and get lost in my own world."

Late at night in suburban homes, men like this one, hunch over flittering computer screens looking at pornography. Often their partners aren't aware of what they are doing, assuming the poor dears are simply working late or catching up on a missed rugby podcast. Most men keep these viewing habits to themselves, as secret men's business, fearing discovery would mean a solid stint in the doghouse.

Everywhere men look there's another woman banging on about the dangers of porn. British sociologist Gail Dines was recently holding forth on the ABC's *Q&A* programme about the damage done by "body-punishing, brutal, dehumanizing and debasing" pornography.

Then came one of the viewer's video questions, featuring Jeff Poole, a cheerful man with a greying goatee. "Miss Dines, I am one of the third of the Australian population who cheerfully consumes pornography," he said, explaining he had been watching porn for over 30 years. "In all those many thousands of hours of wobbling pink bits I've never seen any of the things you talk about. I've never seen the degradation of women or men for that matter. I've never seen rape, real or simulated. I have never seen violence." Porn, he added, had never harmed his relationships.

He spoke for a huge audience of men who watch constant negative discussion of pornography and wonder why their own experiences are so very different. "What's the problem?" they ask, bewildered at women's outrage at what they see as a harmless outlet for the strong male sex drive. To many men, porn seems a perfectly normal aspect of male sexuality that provides comfort and entertainment and redresses the serious sexual imbalance between male and female desire. (The problem of lost libido in women is well documented — The Sex in Australia survey[8] of almost 20,000 people found 55 per cent of women reported low sexual desire.)

For all the scare-mongering about misogynist, hate-filled porn, the attraction for most men is the antithesis of violence against women. What most men really like watching is fully naked, eager, willing women who look like they are enjoying sex.

Men are often defensive about their use of porn, not understanding what the fuss is all about. "Yes, I have always been interested in pictures of women and of people copulating or whatever. I feel somewhat embarrassed at the thought of being caught watching — by wife or daughter but, what the heck, I am a grown man of 59. I suppose my wife knows I occasionally watch Internet porn (but maybe not how much). I don't think she approves but since we don't have sexual contact I suppose she ignores it."

This is from a man who took part in my project on male sexuality published in the book *What Men Want — in bed*. This was a sequel to my earlier project on sexual desire, *The Sex Diaries*, but this time I had 150 men writing about their sexual joys and frustrations, including how they cope with their strong drives. Like many, the man quoted above had spent years with no sex in his marriage. Pornography provided such men with outlet that helped keep a lid on their frustrations — sometimes with a partner's reluctant consent.

One 37-year-old reported his wife had asked him early in their marriage if he'd be willing to give up watching porn. "I responded by saying yes and then asked her whether she would have sex whenever I felt like it — given that I would not have any pornography. She said no, so to this day I still have my porn. These days my wife accepts it and I think she actually prefers I watch pornography instead of hassling her for sex."

Many men seek out porn rather than pressure a partner for sex. Dale, 25, has a great sex life with his partner of two years but there are times mid-week when he knows she's too stressed for sex. "I don't want to bother her if I know she doesn't want it. Watching porn and wanking means it's done and dusted in five minutes. It's quick and easy and relaxes me — no big deal." Yet it was a pretty big deal when she caught him doing just that some time ago. Her hissy fit wasn't about the porn but the masturbation — she's happy to share a porn movie with him occasionally and it turns them both on. But it took some persuading for her to accept that the occasional hand job didn't mean he wasn't happy with their love life. Watching porn for most men is accompanied by masturbation — and that's something many women still find hard to accept.

The intrigue of pornography is also about men's curiosity about sex and their powerful, visual sexual imagination. There's always been fuel for this — one man reported spending his adolescence pouring over shopping catalogues: "The best ones were when Kmart or Target had a sale on underwear — all these young women in sexy underwear. It was irresistible."

While the older men in my project wrote about pouring over Dad's stolen *Playboy*s, todays' young men grow up with an astonishing Internet sexual smorgasbord. Most report roaming far and wide, from vanilla sex to the "oh my God" offerings. One mentions breakfast conversations at his university college, dominated by boys sharing notes on the latest online "girl shagged by donkey" type video to add to the collection. Throughout history there has been sexual material designed to stir male loins, from Roman frescoes and Japanese screen prints to Victorian "dirty postcards".

Yet other motivations also push men away from real life sex towards the comforts of porn. These complexities were vividly revealed in a couple who wrote diaries for my research. To begin with, Zoe, 38, was fine about her husband Leo, 44, using porn to masturbate: "I'm well aware men like to relax with porn. It's a real boys' club." (Like all my diarists, names were changed to protect their privacy.)

But normal sex presented problems for Leo because his wife was more sexually experienced than he was, contributing to his anxiety about losing erections. Plus he wasn't keen on the sex Zoe really enjoyed. "He doesn't like a lot of foreplay or kissing. He thinks it's all girly crap." This was also a second marriage for them both, complicated by major struggles over stepchildren — the couple wrote more in their diaries about the hassles of a blended family than they did about sex.

As the tensions in their relationship increased, Leo retreated more into the world of porn. "Watching porn gets me aroused which leads to masturbation. This helps me relax and sleep and it is a lot less effort than actual sex. With Zoe some of my anxiety kicks in about losing my erection so in some ways porn is almost better than actual sex as I can watch it for one to two hours and there is an endless supply of beautiful women, all doing stuff most of us guys can only dream of."

Zoe is a volatile woman whose reaction to conflict was often explosive. Leo's response was to retreat, turning more to porn. Tensions then spilt over into their sexual relationship: "He would like me to behave like a porn actress," Zoe complained. Within eight months the couple had split up, leaving Zoe convinced porn had poisoned their marriage. Yet the situation was complicated by Leo's sexual anxiety and his immature sexual attitudes.

That's the problem with the common argument that porn turns men off real-life sex. The reality is real sex can be threatening for men, particularly if they have fears about performance or partners who are hard to please. "Pornography can be a thick emotional buffer zone, separating a man from rejection, masking his insecurities and perceived

55

inadequacies," write Bob and Susan Yager-Berkowitz in their book *He's Just Not Up For It Anymore*.

Most men are sensible enough to avoid retreating into a sexual fantasy world. I've talked to men who cut back on their porn viewing when they felt it was distorting their feelings about normal sex. "One time I was using it a lot and I found sex with my partner wasn't as exciting as it usually was. After that I was careful how I use it. I don't want that to happen," says Joe, a 26-year-old arts student. But lonely men, socially inadequate men, are more vulnerable to the seductive comfort of porn.

Of course, there are men whose upbringing and social experience draws them towards misogynist, violent pornography. Many of the young men I spoke to were aware of other men caught up in this world. One talked of mates he went to school with who'd always had "strange attitudes to women, seeing them as sex objects". Their attraction to particular porn fantasies — "like 50 guys with one woman" — simply reflected the way they'd always seen women. Most men aren't interested in this violent material. "I don't like the mean stuff... that's just not my personality," commented one young man, mentioning that he worries whether women in porn films are being coerced into participating.

The suggestion that porn changes men's attitudes to sex is really questionable. While there's a body of psychology research suggesting exposure to porn has that effect, Professor Catherine Lumby and colleagues in the Australian book *The Porn Report*, published in 2008, found this laboratory-based research to be contradictory and unlikely to reflect real-life situations. "The entire tradition of social science research into pornography has started with the assumption that porn is a major cause of negative attitudes towards women and has set out to prove this," conclude these Australian academics.

These researchers found mainstream porn to be largely free of violence and other degrading material. They noted that the huge growth area online is the DIY amateur porn industry, where ordinary men and women are baring all, grunting and groaning in front of web camera — a far cry from the dark and dangerous world so many warn about.

Many men will admit porn has opened their eyes to new sexual practices. Many use porn to enjoy fantasies they can't get at home. Alex, 65, has always had an interest in anal sex, which his wife won't consider. And that's where porn comes in — seeing women apparently enjoying this taboo activity is very much part of his pleasure. His wife allows him to rub his penis between her butt cheeks. "I find having sex in her bum crack such a turn on. My brain knows one thing but my dick does not have a brain so thinks it is right into her anus," he cheekily explained.

Anal sex is high on the list of porn fantasies that rarely get played out in real life — although in some couples both partners enjoy it. Porn has also revolutionised attitudes to oral sex, shifting it from an experience that 30 years ago most men only dreamt about, to an hors d'oeuvre that for many teens is on offer long before the main course. This shift in oral sex patterns is often mentioned as an example of the negative effects of porn — since it is usually males on the receiving end. Yet there's ample evidence that porn has also taught men that cunnilingus is a great route to women's pleasure. Many men are keen to try it but young women's self-consciousness about their bodies often prevents this from happening.

Porn is giving men new ideas about sex and that can cause tension in relationships. Many young men report trouble over the "money shot" — that peculiar in-her-face finale common in pornography. Unsurprisingly many women aren't keen on "facials" (having a man ejaculate in her face). James, a 35-year-old engineer, found himself back-peddling fast with a very upset young lady reacting badly to this suggestion. "I realised it wasn't appropriate or respectful," he reports and has never tried it since. But other men find women happy to explore this rather strange practice.

So yes, Internet porn is encouraging some men to suggest exotic practices — and some women take offence at that. But others are happy to participate and to watch porn, with or without their partners. The problem comes when men try to bully women into things they don't want to do — but porn has nothing to do with the insensitivity causing men to behave in that way, which stems from their cultural and social backgrounds. For all the sky-is-falling warnings about pornography, the reality is far less frightening. Pornography brings out the worst in some vulnerable men and that's cause for concern. But the real struggle is for women to come to terms with what pornography reveals about men and their relentless, lusty drive. That's what many women just don't want to know.

SECTION TWO

The scary grip of feminism

CHAPTER 6

The demonisation of men – our anti-male society

First published 2015

There was a funny discussion on an ABC's show, *How Not to Behave*. One of the hosts, Gretel Killeen started complaining about "manspreading" — men sitting with their legs apart. "Men sitting with their legs so wide apart you'd think they are about to give birth," quipped Killeen.

The male host, Matt Okine suggested men sit that way simply because it is more comfortable. "For whom?" asked Killeen. "For my balls," responded Okine with a funny explanation involving a grape ending up in a wine making process after being squashed at the apex of two adjoining rulers.

Man spreading has attracted attention on public transport in New York due to men's spread legs sometimes taking up more than their allocated seat space. The city ran a campaign: "Dude, Stop the spread, please. It's a space issue". Fair enough. It makes sense to promote consideration for others in public spaces but as always the public discussion descended into talk about male aggression. It's all about patriarchal men claiming their territory, sneered the feminist commentators.

Hardly a day goes by without some new story appearing which rubbishes men. After being criticised non-stop for about half a century, it's probably time men had a right of reply, wrote

UK journalist Peter Lloyd in his 2016 book *Stand By Your Manhood*. Arguing that men have spent decades as the target in a long line of public floggings, Lloyd comprehensively but with surprising good humour outlined the "dismissive, patronizing and skewed" narrative about heterosexual men that has dominated mainstream media and public policy for so long.

"So why is it that, today, there has there never been a worse time to be a man? Rubbishing the male of the species and everything he stands for is a disturbing — and growing — 21st century phenomenon. It is the fashionable fascism of millions of women — and many, many men, too. Instead of feeling proud of our achievements, we men are forced to spend our time apologizing for them. When people chide us for not being able to multi-task or use a washing machine we join in the mocking laughter — even though we invented the damned thing in the first place," wrote Lloyd.

Lloyd's examples of this skewed public discussion include many that should make any rational woman squirm.

Like his comment on former US Presidential candidate Hillary Clinton: "Hillary Clinton once said — remarkably, with a straight face — that women have 'always been the primary victims of war,' not the men who get their legs blown off in the battlefield in Iraq. Or Libya. Or Sudan."

What I found astonishing was Lloyd's discussion of Nigeria's militant Islamic group Boko Haram who apparently set fire to a school dormitory killing 59 sleeping boys — the third tragedy of its kind in just eight months. There wasn't a peep about this yet two months later when the same terrorist organisation kidnapped a group of schoolgirls the world mounted a viral campaign in minutes. "What gives? Why is a boy's life worth less — or worthless?" queried Lloyd.

Isn't it odd, he asked, that men's health is not given any priority, given that men die five years earlier in a life expectancy gap that's increased 400 per cent since 1920? Lloyd's book included an Australian example of the disparity in health funding. Data from our National Health and Medical Research Council shows a "spectacular gender gap" with "men's health problems being allocated a quarter of the funding women's research gets." LLoyd quoted a News Ltd article showing funding specifically targeting men's health ranks 36th in health research priorities just behind sexually transmissible infections.

Yet where the anti-male bias reaches its zenith is in the current witch hunt over domestic violence. In their determination to promote what is a very serious social problem — some men's violence towards their partners — the zealots controlling public debate on this issue are absolutely determined to allow no muddying of the waters. Violence by women is dismissed as irrelevant, violence against men is routinely ignored or seen as amusing.

Some time ago a promo for a "screwball" comedy *She's Funny That Way* ran in all our major cinemas. It featured three successive scenes showing different women slugging men in the face followed by a woman sniggering "Wham, bam, thank you, ma'am". Audiences found that hilarious and there's been not one word of protest about the promotion.

Anyone speaking out about the circumstances which drive men to violence is quickly reined in. Look what happened to our former Australian of the Year, Rosie Batty. Who could forget this extraordinary woman speaking with such compassion about her mentally ill husband within days of him murdering Luke, their young son. "No one loved Luke more than Greg, his father," she said explaining Greg's mental health had deteriorated after a long period of unemployment and homelessness.

How disappointing then to hear her speech at Malcolm Turnbull's first major policy announcement, the launch of the government's new $100 million Women's Safety Package. "This is a gender issue," she said firmly, mouthing the party line, not one word about mental illness, nothing about the men and children who are victims of female violence.

I suggested at the time that Rosie needed to open her eyes: "The epidemic of violence you are rightly so concerned about isn't just about men. Didn't you notice Melbourne mother Akon Guode who was charged with murder after driving her car with her four small children into a lake? Or Donna Vasyli arrested after her Sydney podiatrist husband was found with seven stab wounds. Why is it that when a woman was charged with murdering her partner in Broken Hill, the story sunk without a trace and domestic violence was never mentioned in the media reports?"

Around the country there are government departments struggling to cope with daily reports of child abuse, most often by their mothers. Yes, it is appalling that so many children grow up in homes terrorised by violent fathers but abuse by mothers is surely part of the story of violence in the home if we are really concerned about protection of children and breaking the cycle of violence.

Our Opposition Leader Bill Shorten's wife Cloe once gave a speech boasting about her husband's commitment to the eradication of violence against women. Funnily enough her talk mentioned a book — *Scream Quietly or the Neighbours Will Hear* — written by the woman who set up the world's first domestic violence refuge, Erin Pizzey. Clearly Ms Shorten's speech writer isn't up on the politics of DV.

In fact Erin Pizzey is now world famous for her strenuous campaign arguing that domestic violence is not a gender issue. "I always knew women can be as vicious and irresponsible as men," she wrote, describing her childhood experience with a mother who beat her with the cord from an iron. She points out that many of the women in her refuge were violent, dangerous to their children and others around them. Pizzey's honesty has attracted constant attacks — she was forced to flee her native England with her children after protests, threats, and violence culminated in the shooting of her family dog.

Pizzey started her own "White Ribbon Campaign" to counter "40 years of lies," the constant male-bashing misinformation that dominates the domestic violence debate. The feminist White Ribbon Campaign which operates both here and overseas is a prime offender. "We must stop demonizing men and start healing the rift that feminism has created between men and women," says Pizzey, arguing that the current "insidious and manipulative philosophy that women are always victims and men always oppressors can only continue this unspeakable cycle of violence."

This brave, outspoken 76-year-old woman is one of a growing number of domestic violence experts and scholars who have struggled to set the record straight about violence in the home. There was Murray Straus, the former professor of sociology from the University of New Hampshire and editor of a number of peer-reviewed sociology journals. Straus died in 2016 but back in 1975 he first published research showing women were just as likely as men to report hitting a spouse. Subsequent surveys showed women often initiated the violence — it wasn't simply self-defence. These findings were confirmed by more than 200 studies of intimate violence summed up in Straus's 2010 paper, *Thirty Years of Denying the Evidence on Gender Symmetry in Partner Violence.*

It's true that physical violence by women may cause fewer injuries on average due to differences in size and strength but it is by no means harmless. Women use weapons, from knives to household objects to neutralise their disadvantage, and men may be held back by cultural prohibitions on using force toward a woman even in self-defence. Straus's review concluded that in the US men sustain about a third of the injuries from partner violence, including a third of the deaths from attacks by a partner (in Australia men made up a quarter of the 1645 partner deaths between 1989-2012). And proportions of non-physical abuse (e.g. emotional abuse) against men are even higher[9]. Women are about as likely as men to kill their children[10] and account for more than half of substantiated child maltreatment perpetrators.

In fact, the bulk of the international research supports Straus' conclusions. The world's largest domestic violence research database published in the peer-reviewed journal *Partner Abuse* summarised 1,700 peer-reviewed studies and found that in large population samples, 58 per cent of intimate partner violence reported involved both the female and male partner[11].

Straus spent much of his working life weathering attacks for publicising these unwelcome truths about violence, regularly being booed from the stage when he tried to present his findings. On two occasions the chair of a Canadian commission into violence against women claimed publicly that he was a wife-beater — after repeated requests she finally was forced to apologise to him.

Straus also received death threats, along with his co-researchers, Richard Gelles and Suzanne Steinmetz, with the latter the subject of a campaign to deny her tenure and attempts made to rescind her grant funding. "All three of us became 'non persons' among domestic violence advocates. Invitations to conferences dwindled and dried up. Librarians publicly stated they would not order or shelve our books," records Gelles.

It would be nice to report more civilised debate over this issue in Australia but sadly here too lies and bullying are par for the course. Look at what happened to Dr Tanveer Ahmed. This Sydney psychiatrist has long written about taboo topics, like reverse racism or denial in the Moslem community, which got up the nose of the Fairfax audience. Some years ago he ended up losing his column over plagiarism charges.

Ahmed had spent six years as a White Ribbon Ambassador but this all came unstuck when he wrote an article for *The Australian* which pointed to the pernicious influence of radical feminists on public debate over domestic violence and suggested that the "growing social and economic disempowerment of men is increasingly the driver of family-based violence."

Boy, did that bring them out in force. Fairfax columnist Clementine Ford condemned his dangerous message which "prioritises men's power over women's safety" adding that she didn't have time for "men's woe-betide-me feelings." After a tirade of attacks on social media, White Ribbon asked him to step down, informing him that in order to be reinstated he would need to undergo a recommitment program. Shades of Stasiland, eh?

There's a fascinating twist to this whole saga. Heading up White Ribbon Australia's Research and Policy Group is Dr Michael Flood[12] who's on the Technical Advisory Group for UN Partners for Prevention which has produced research papers supporting the essential points Ahmed makes about the links between men's social disempowerment and violence towards their partners.

Michael Flood has spent his career milking men's violence, from his early years teaching boys in Canberra schools about date rape, through to alarmist papers suggesting pornography promotes male aggression, to his latest role as pro-feminist sociologist at the University of Wollongong. Despite his years in academia he's happy to play fast and loose with statistics when it comes to demonising men.

"Boys think it's OK to hit girls." Back in 2008 this shocking news about teenager attitudes to violence led to headlines across the country. The source was a press release by White Ribbon Australia reporting on a publication by Michael Flood and Lara Fergus which made the extraordinary claim: "Close to one in three (31 per cent) boys believe 'it's not a big deal to hit a girl'." Politicians jumped on the bandwagon, everywhere there were calls for the re-education of these horrible, violent young men.

Flood and his colleagues had it totally wrong. The research actually found males hitting females was seen by virtually all young people surveyed to be unacceptable. Yet it was quite ok for a girl to hit a boy — 25 per cent of young people agreed with the statement "When a *girl* hits a *guy*, it's really not a big deal".

When the "error" was brought to their attention, White Ribbon finally issued a correction, sent letters to newspapers but, of course, none of these had the impact of the incorrect, misleading media headlines splashed right across the country.

A simple mistake? Well, perhaps, but there's actually been a steady stream of misleading statistics about domestic violence and it's a full-time job trying to get them corrected. The person who has taken on that daunting task is Greg Andresen, the key researcher for the One in Three Campaign which seeks to present an accurate picture of violence in the home. The Sydney man somehow manages to challenge much of the deluge of DV misinformation while also working a day job and raising a young family.

The campaign's reference to "One in Three" refers to the proportion of family violence victims that are male. Our best data on this comes from the ABS Personal Safety Survey in 2012 which found 33 per cent of persons who had experienced violence by a current partner were male[13]. Confusingly, there's another "One in Three" figure constantly bandied about in DV discussions — referring to the proportion of women who have experienced violence during their lifetime. This figure actually refers to all victims of incidents of physical violence, not just violence by partners and about one in two[14] men experience similar violence — as explained in an excellent report[15] released by Australia's National Research Organisation for Women's Safety.

The One in Three website (oneinthree.com.au) opens with

a startling image of a man with battered nose and a shocking shiner plus the slogan "It's amazing what my wife can do with a frypan". That certainly makes the point but the strength of this site is the solid statistical analysis — over twenty pages dissecting misleading statistics aired over Australia's media.

Here's one example from ABC's Radio National: "A recent survey in Victoria found family violence is the leading cause of death and ill health in women of child bearing age." Andresen draws on Australian Institute of Health and Welfare (AIHW) data to show the top five causes of death, disability and illness combined for Australian women aged 15-44 years are anxiety and depression, migraine, type 2 diabetes, asthma and schizophrenia. "Violence doesn't make the list," he concludes.

The same nonsense about DV being the leading cause of death in young women also appeared on Sky News last year, spurring psychologist Claire Lehmann into doing her own analysis which she published on her blog[16] on White Ribbon Day. Lehmann made it very clear she supports the important work of the campaign but "what I do not support, however, are dodgy statistics and false claims which belittle this good cause," she writes.

In great detail she demonstrates how the dodgy statistics stem from misleading analysis of a VicHealth report and presents all the solid Australian data from the Australian Bureau of Statistics and AIHW showing the claim is just totally absurd. Yet the ABC, presented with all the data, still concluded the claim was accurate.

One of the major tactics used by DV campaigners is to only highlight men's violence and leave out any statistics relating to women. "A quarter of Australian children had witnessed

violence against their mother," thundered SA Victims of Crime
Commissioner Michael O'Connell in August 2010. This statistic
came from a Young People and Domestic Violence study which
showed almost an identical proportion of young people was
aware of domestic violence against their fathers or stepfathers.
Yet this barely got any mention in the media coverage.

Whenever statistics are mentioned publicly that reveal the
true picture of women's participation in family violence, they
are dismissed with the DV lobby claiming they are based upon
flawed methodology or are taken out of context. But as Greg
Andresen points out, "We use the best available quantitative
data — ABS surveys, AIC homicide stats, police crime data,
hospital injury databases — all of which show that a third of
victims of family violence are male. The same data sources
are cited by major domestic violence organisations but they
deliberately minimise any data relating to male victims."

An amusing episode of the ABC's satirical comedy *Utopia*
showed public servants who run the "Nation Building
Authority" all in a twit working out how to knock back a
Freedom of Information request. It made for great comedy
watching the twists and turns of the bureaucrats seeking to
refuse the request, assuming it was better to block it "just to be
on the safe side."

Pretty funny considering this fictional FOI request turned
out to relate to a harmless, long-finished multi-story carpark.
The bureaucrats must run around like headless chooks when
they receive the regular FOI requests sent to all government
bodies regarding the long-term cover up of the gender of child
abuse perpetrators.

The one time the relevant national body, the Australian

Institute of Health and Welfare published this data was in 1996
and showed 968 male perpetrators to 1138 women. Since then
FOI requests have only produced data from West Australia
— namely WA Department for Child Protection figures which
showed the number of mothers responsible for "substantiated
maltreatment" between 2005-6 and 2007-8 rose from 312 to
427. In the same period the number of fathers reported for
child abuse dropped from 165 to 155. Easy to see why the
bureaucrats would be nervous of figures like that[17].

Labor premier of Queensland, Annastacia Palaszczuk made
headlines by calling for campaigns against domestic violence
to include male victims. Her comment was met by a barrage of
complaint from domestic violence services warning her not to
recognise male victims at the expense of women. She has been
remarkably quiet about the issue ever since.

According to Erin Pizzey, that's the real issue. It is all
about funding. In a 2011 article for the *Daily Mail* she argued
domestic violence had become a huge feminist industry, "This
is girls-only empire building, and it is highly lucrative at that."

Pizzey has spent most of her life speaking out about the
lies being promoted by this industry in order to protect
their funding base and begging audiences not to create a DV
movement hostile to men and boys. "I failed," she concludes
sadly but she hasn't given up. Her message is clear: "The roots
of domestic violence lie in our parenting. Both mothers and
fathers can be violent — we need to acknowledge this. If we
educate parents about the dangers of behaving violently — to
each other and to their children — we will change the course of
those children's lives."

As Peter Lloyd so eloquently points out, domestic violence

is only one of many issues where men are being demonised, where the exclusive promotion of women's priorities leaves men with a dud deal. His book explores issues such as paternity fraud, schools failing boys, circumcision, becoming a weekend dad, men's sex drive, pornography and the early male death rate.

Ironic considering how often we are told that men still hold all the power. It's about time that those male newspaper editors, politicians, bureaucrats and other powerful men started asking hard questions about the one-sided conversation that leaves so many men missing out. And maybe women who care about their brothers, sons, fathers, partners and male friends might care to join in.

CHAPTER 7

The domestic violence industry – feminism's cash cow

First published 2016

This article, published in August 2016, was one of the most difficult and significant pieces I have ever written. Challenging the misinformation on domestic violence being promoted by our key organisations, it took many months to prepare, with every statistic checked by relevant bodies and experts. The article featured prominently in an unfair dismissal case this year before the Fair Work Commission in Perth after relationship counsellor Rob Tiller was forced out of his job with Relationships Australia for posting it on his private Facebook page.

Eva Solberg is a Swedish politician, a proud feminist who holds an important post as chair of the Moderate Women's party. In 2015 she was presented with her government's latest strategy for combating domestic violence. Like similar reports across the world, this strategy assumes the only way to tackle domestic violence is through teaching misogynist men (and boys) to behave themselves.

The Swedish politician spat the dummy. Writing on the news site Nyheter24, Eva Solberg took issue with her government's "tired gendered analysis" which argues that eradicating sexism is the solution to the problem of domestic violence. She explained her reasoning: "We know through extensive practice and experience that attempts to solve the issue through this kind of analysis have failed. And they failed precisely because violence is not and never has been a gender issue."

Solberg challenged the government report's assumption that there is a guilty sex and an innocent one. "Thanks to extensive research in the field, both at the national and international level, we now know with great certainty that this breakdown by sex is simply not true."

Solberg made reference to the world's largest research database on intimate partner violence, the Partner Abuse State of Knowledge project, (PASK) which summarised over 1700 scientific papers on the topic. She concluded that her government's report was based on misinformation about family violence and that, contrary to the report's one-sided view of men as the only perpetrators, many children are experiencing a very different reality: "We must recognise the fact that domestic violence, in at least half of its occurrence, is carried out by female perpetrators."

One of the key patterns that emerged from the PASK, explained Solberg, is that violence in the family is an inherited generational problem and children learn from watching the violence of both their parents. "To know this and then continue to ignore the damage done to the children who are today subjected to violence is a huge social betrayal," Solberg concluded. "The road to a solution for this social problem is hardly to stubbornly continue to feed the patient with more of the same medicine that has already been tried for decades."

There's a certain irony that this happened in Sweden, the utopia for gender equality which is the last place you'd expect misogyny to be blamed for a major social evil. But despite being world-leaders in gender equality (as shown by the 2014 World Economic Forum's global gender gap index) the Nordic women experience the worst physical or sexual violence in the EU. Given this inconvenient truth it seems quite extraordinary that for decades the gendered analysis of domestic violence has retained its grip on Sweden — as it has in Western countries around the world, including Australia.

No one would deny that it was a great achievement to have men's violence towards women fully acknowledged and take critical steps to protect vulnerable women and ensure their safety. But it has been shocking to watch this morph into a world-wide domestic violence industry determined to ignore evidence showing the complexities of violence in the home and avoid prevention strategies that would tackle the real risk factors underpinning this vital social issue.

Here, too, we are witnessing Solberg's "huge social betrayal" by denying the reality of the violence being witnessed by many Australian children. Just look at the bizarre $30M television campaign which the federal government launched in 2016 which starts with a little boy slamming a door in a little girl's face. A series of vignettes follow, all about innocent females cowering from nasty males. The whole thing is based on the erroneous notion that domestic violence is caused by disrespect for women — precisely the type of "tired gender analysis" that Eva Solberg has so thoroughly discredited. Yet our government spent at least $700,000 funding for research and production of this campaign — just one example of the shocking misuse of the hundreds of millions of dollars that Malcolm Turnbull regularly boasts our government is spending on domestic violence.

Last year, Liberal Democrat Senator David Leyonhjelm repeatedly grilled bureaucrats in Senate Estimates committee, seeking evidence to support the government's claim that addressing gender equity is key to tackling domestic violence. They failed dismally to come up with any such proof[18].

Our key organisations all sing from the same songbook, regularly distorting statistics to present only one part of this complex story. "Up to one quarter of young people in Australia have witnessed an incident of physical or domestic violence against their mother or stepmother," wrote Adam Graycar, a former director of the Australian Institute of Criminology, in an introduction to a 2001 paper, *Young Australians and Domestic Violence*, a brief overview of the much larger Young People and Domestic Violence study.

Somehow Graycar failed to mention that while 23 per cent of young people were aware of domestic violence against their mothers or step-mothers, an almost identical proportion (22 per cent) of young people were aware of domestic violence against their fathers or step-fathers by their mothers or step-mothers — as shown in the same study[19].

This type of deliberate omission is everywhere, with most of our bureaucracies downplaying statistics which demonstrate women's role in family violence and beating up evidence of male aggression.

How often have we been told we face an "epidemic" of domestic violence? It's simply not true. Most Australian women are lucky enough to actually live in a peaceful society where the men in their lives treat them well. The official data from the Australian Bureau of Statistics show violence against women has decreased over the twenty-year period it has been studied, with the proportion of adult women experiencing physical violence from their current male partners in the preceding year down from 2.6 per cent in 1996 to 0.8 per cent in 2012[20]. (Violence from ex-partners dropped from 3.3 to 0.7 per cent[21].)

"There's no evidence that we're in the middle of an epidemic of domestic violence," says Don Weatherburn the well-respected director of the NSW Bureau of Crime Statistics and Research, confirming these figures from national surveys carried out by the ABS provide the best data on domestic violence in the country[22]. (This fact was grudgingly acknowledged by one of the bureaucrats being grilled in Senate Estimates by Leyonhjelm.)

Weatherburn adds that in NSW "serious forms of domestic assault, such as assault inflicting grievous bodily harm, have actually come down by 11 per cent over the last 10 years."

The astonishing and very welcome news is that the 2012 statistics from the ABS Personal Safety Survey show only 1.06 per cent of women are actually physically assaulted by their partner or ex-partner each year in Australia[23]. (This figure is derived from the 2012 PSS and published in this ANROWS Horizons report[24]. The rate is obtained by dividing cell B9 in Table 19 (93,400) by the total female residential population aged 18 years and over [8,735,400].)

One in a hundred women experiencing this physical violence from their partners is obviously a matter of great concern. But this low percentage is very different from the usual figures being trotted out. You'll never find the figure of 1.06 per cent mentioned by any of the domestic violence organisations in this country. Their goal is to fuel the flames, to promote an alarmist reaction with the hope of attracting ever greater funding for the cause.

What we hear from them is one in three women are victims of violence. But that's utterly misleading because it doesn't just refer to domestic violence. These statistics are also taken from the Personal Safety Survey but refer to the proportion of adult women who have experienced any type of physical violence at all (or threat of violence). So, we're not just talking about violence by a partner, or violence in the home but any aggressive incident even involving a perfect stranger. Like an altercation with an aggressive shopping trolley driver or an incident of road rage.

That's partly how the figure inflates to one in three but it also doesn't even refer to what's happening now because these figures include lifetime incidents for adult women — so with our 70-year-olds the violence could have taken place over 50 years ago. And the equivalent figure for men is worse — one in two[25].

As for the most horrific crimes, where domestic violence ends in homicide, we are constantly told that domestic violence kills one woman every week. That's roughly true — according to Australian Institute of Criminology figures, one female is killed by an intimate partner or ex-partner every nine days[26]. One man is killed by his partner approximately every 30 days. So it is important to acknowledge that male violence is more likely to result in injury or death than female violence towards a partner. This is inevitable due the average man's greater size and strength.

But the fact remains that almost a quarter (23.1 per cent) of victims of intimate partner homicide are male[27] — and we hardly ever hear about these deaths. It is not serving our society well to downplay the fact that female violence can also be lethal, towards men and particularly towards children — females account for over half of murders of children (52 per cent).

These are all still alarming statistics but here too there is good news. Domestic homicides are decreasing. The number of victims of intimate partner homicide dropped by almost a third (28 per cent) between 1989–90 and 2010–12[28] [29], according to data supplied by the Australian Institute of Criminology.

Professor Chris Lloyd is one of a growing number of Australian academics concerned at the misrepresentation of domestic violence statistics in this country. An expert in statistics and data management at the Melbourne Business School, Lloyd confirms our best source of data, the ABS's Personal Safety Survey, clearly demonstrates domestic violence is decreasing.

He too says it's wrong to suggest there's an epidemic of domestic violence in this country. "Many of the quoted statistics around domestic violence are exaggerated or incorrect. Contrary to popular belief and commentary, rates of intimate partner violence are not increasing," says Lloyd adding that while he understands the emotional reaction people have to this crime, "emotion is no basis for public policy".

He's concerned that Australia media so often publishes misinformation — like a 2016 *The Age* editorial which repeated the falsehood that domestic violence is the major cause of death or illness for adult women in Victoria. (As I explained in the previous chapter on the demonisation of men, it doesn't even make the list of the top ten such causes.) *The Age* ignored Lloyd's efforts to correct their mistake, ditto his concern about erroneous media reports which inflate domestic violence figures by using police crime statistics — a notoriously unreliable source.

As Don Weatherburn points out, it's very difficult to determine whether swelling numbers of reported incidents to police reflect any increase at all in actual crime. "It may simply be a tribute to the excellent job that has been done to raise awareness of DV, encouraging women to report, and efforts to get the police to respond properly," he says. Weatherburn believes that the slight (5.7 per cent) increase in reports of domestic assault in NSW over the last 10 years could be due to an increase in victim willingness to report domestic assault and points to the 11 per cent drop over that time in serious forms of domestic assault, such as assault inflicting grievous bodily harm, as a more reliable picture of the trend in domestic violence.

Weatherburn adds that valid comparisons of state police figures on assault are impossible because each police force has a different approach to recording assault. But in many states the goal posts have also shifted — the explosion in police records is also due to recent expansions in the definition of family violence to include not just physical abuse but also threats of violence, psychological, emotional, economic and social abuse. Look at Western Australia, where this changed definition was introduced in 2004. That year WA police recorded 17,000 incidents of violence but by 2012 this had almost tripled (45,000). Other states report similar trends due to these expanded definitions.

"If a woman turns up to a police station claiming her man
has yelled at her, the chances are that she'll end up with a
police report and well on her way to obtaining an Apprehended
Violence Order (AVO) which puts her in a very powerful
position," says former WA Law Reform Commissioner Augusto
Zimmermann, who explains that AVOs can be used to force
men to leave their homes and deny them contact with their
children. Often men are caught in police proceedings and
evicted from their homes by orders that are issued without any
evidence of legal wrongdoing.

"It is a frightening reality that here in Australia a perfectly
innocent citizen stands to lose his home, his family, his
reputation, as a result of unfounded allegations. This is
happening to men every day as consequent of domestic
violence laws which fail to require the normal standards of
proof and presumptions of innocence," says Zimmermann,
adding that he's not talking about genuine cases of violent men
who terribly abuse their wives and children, but "law-abiding
people who have lost their parental and property rights without
the most basic requirements of the rule of law."[30]

The growing trend for AVOs to be used for tactical purposes
in Family Law disputes is also pushing up police records of
domestic violence, "Rather than being motivated by legitimate
concerns about feeling safe, a woman can make an application
to AVO simply because she was advised by lawyers to look for
any reason to apply for such an order when facing a family law
dispute," says Zimmermann who served on a WA government
inquiry into legal issues and domestic violence.

A survey of NSW magistrates found 90 per cent agreed that
AVOs were being used as a divorce tactic. Research by Family

Law Professor Patrick Parkinson and colleagues from the University of Sydney revealed lawyers suggesting that clients obtain AVOs, explaining to them that verbal and emotional abuse was enough to do the trick.

The bottom line is police reports tell us little and the ABS Personal Safety Survey remains our best source of data showing the true picture of domestic violence. But there's one more vital fact revealed by that survey that rarely ever surfaces — that men accounted for one in three victims of current partner violence[31].

You'll never find this figure mentioned on OurWatch, one of our major domestic violence organisations, annually attracting government grants of up to two million. In 2016 when Lucy Turnbull became an ambassador to OurWatch she was welcomed by OurWatch's CEO Mary Barry thanking the ambassadors for "engaging Australians to call out disrespect and violence towards women and advocating for gender equality" which she said was "exactly what the evidence says is needed to end the epidemic."

OurWatch staff spend their time writing policy documents and running conferences all firmly locked into the gender equity framework. The site's facts and figures pages include lists of cherry-picked statistics about violence against women but male victims are dismissed by simply stating that the "overwhelming majority of acts of domestic violence are perpetrated by men against women".

There's an interesting parallel here. As it happens this one-in-three ratio is very similar to the proportions of women to men committing suicide. In males 2.8 per cent of all deaths in 2014 were attributed to suicide[32], while the rate for females was

0.9 per cent. Imagine the public outcry if the smaller number of female suicides was used to justify committing the entire suicide prevention budget to men. So how come all our government organisations are getting away with doing just that with the hundreds of millions being spent on domestic violence?

According to one of Australia's leading experts on couple relationships, Kim Halford, a professor of clinical psychology at the University of Queensland, most family violence does not fit the picture most of us think of when we imagine domestic violence — a violent man severely beating up his partner in order to control her. Such violence makes up less than one per cent of family violence.

The vast majority of family violence is two-way aggression with international research showing about a third of couples having a go at each other — pushing, slapping, shoving or worse. Given the shame and stigma associated with being a male victim of family violence it is not surprising that men downplay these experiences in victim surveys such as Australia's PSS. It's only when men and women are asked about *perpetrating* violence that the two-way violence emerges, with women readily admitting to researchers that they are very actively involved and often instigate this type of "couple violence". "Thirty years of international research consistently shows that women and men are violent towards each other at about the same rate," confirms Halford.

As one example, two major meta-analysis studies by psychology professor John Archer from the University of Central Lancashire found that women were more likely than men to report acts like pushing, slapping or throwing something at their partner. Archer pointed out that women are more likely to be injured as a result of the couple violence although there was still a substantial minority of injured male victims.

This two-way violence wasn't what most researchers expected to find, admits a leading researcher in this area, Professor Terrie Moffit from Duke University. "We asked the girls questions like 'Have you hit your partner?' 'Have you thrown your partner across the room?' 'Have you used a knife on your partner?' I thought we were wasting our time asking these questions but they said yes, and they said yes in just the same numbers as the boys did." Terrie Moffit's work with young people was part of the world-renowned Dunedin longitudinal study back in the 1990s which recently featured on the SBS series *Predict My Future*. The Dunedin researchers like Moffit are no longer willing to speak publicly about their important research after receiving such a hostile reception to their findings[33].

It is telling that Australia has not conducted any of the large-scale surveys focussing on perpetrating violence likely to reveal the two-way pattern shown elsewhere. But gender symmetry did emerge in violence studies by Professor Kim Halford which focussed on couples at the start of their relationships, newly-wed couples and couples expecting a child together. Even with these early relationships about a quarter of the women admit they have been violent towards their partners — just as many as the men.

Halford suggests that perhaps three quarters of a million children every year in Australia are witnessing both parents engaged in domestic violence. Only small numbers see the severe violence we hear so much about, what the feminists call "intimate terrorism" where a perpetrator uses violence in combination with a variety of other coercive tactics in order to take control over their partner, but as Halford points out, even less severe couple violence is not trivial. "Children witnessing any form of family violence, including couple violence suffer high rates of mental health problems and the children are more likely to be violent themselves. Couple violence is also a very strong predictor of relationship break up, which has profound effects on adults and their children," he says.

The 2001 Young People and Domestic Violence study mentioned earlier was national research involving 5,000 young Australians between 12 and 20. This found ample evidence that children are witnessing this two-way parental couple violence with 14.4 per cent witnessing "couple violence", nine per cent witnessing male to female violence only, and 7.8 per cent witnessing female to male violence only — which means about one in four young Australians have this detrimental start to their lives. The report found the most damage to children occurred when they witnessed both parents involved in violence.

It is often claimed that women only hit in self-defence in response to male violence but Halford points out the evidence shows that is just not true. "In fact, one of the strongest risk factors for a woman being hit by a male partner is her hitting that male partner. It's absolutely critical that we tackle couple violence if we really want to stop this escalation into levels of violence which cause women serious injury," he says. Of course, the impact on children is the other important reason to make couple violence a major focus.

Naturally none of this is mentioned in the section on "what drives violence against women" in the official government framework[34] promoted by all our key domestic violence bodies. Nor is there any proper attention paid to other proven, evidence-based risk factors like alcohol and drug abuse, poverty, mental illness. The only officially sanctioned risk factor for domestic violence in this country is gender inequality. "Other factors interact with or reinforce gender inequality to contribute to increased frequency and severity of violence against women, but do not drive violence in and of themselves," is the only grudging acknowledgement in the framework that other factors might be at play.

During hearings of the Victorian Royal Commission into Domestic Family Violence in 2016, Australian experts in alcohol abuse and mental illness spoke out about this blatant disregard of the forty years of research which speaks to these complexities. "It is simplistic and misleading to say that domestic violence is caused by patriarchal attitudes," said Professor James Ogloff, a world-renowned mental health expert.

"A sole focus on the gendered nature of family violence which labels men as the perpetrators and women as the victims and which identifies gender inequity as the principal 'cause' of family violence is problematic on a number of levels," said Professor Peter Miller principal research fellow and co-director of the violence prevention group at Deakin University.

Professor Miller was involved in a systematic review of longitudinal studies involving predictors of family violence which identified childhood experiences with abuse and violence, particularly in families with problem alcohol use, as key predictors of adult involvement in domestic violence. Miller has encountered obstruction in both conducting and publishing research into the role of drugs and alcohol in family violence.

The evidence is there about the complexities of domestic violence but on an official level no one is listening. The reason is simple. The deliberate distortion of this important social issue is all about feminists refusing to give up hard-won turf. Ogloff spelt this out to the Commission when he explained that the Victorian family violence sector feared that "recognising other potential causes of violence could cause a shift in funding away from programmes directed at gender inequity."[35]

In the mid-1970s an important feminist figure was invited to Australia to visit our newly established women's refuges. Erin Pizzey was the founder of Britain's first refuge, a woman praised around the world for her pioneering work helping women escape from violence. On the way to Australia Pizzey travelled to New Zealand where she spoke out about her changing views. She'd learnt through dealing with violent women in her own refuge that violence was not a gender issue and that it was important to tackle the complexities of violence to properly address the issue.

Pizzey quickly attracted the wrath of the women's movement in Britain, attracting death threats which forced her for a time to leave the country. "The feminists seized upon domestic violence as the cause they needed to attract more money and supporters at a time when the first flush of enthusiasm for their movement was starting to wane. Domestic violence was perfect for them — the just cause that no one dared challenge. It led to a worldwide million-dollar industry, a huge cash cow supporting legions of bureaucrats and policy makers," said Pizzey.

In Pizzey's New Zealand press interviews she challenged the gender inequality view of violence, suggesting tackling violence in the home required dealing with the real roots of violence, like intergeneration exposure to both male and female aggression. News travelled fast. By the time Pizzey was set to leave for the Australian leg of the trip she was persona non grata with the feminists running our refuges. Her visit to this country was cancelled.

That was 1976. Since then the party-line gendered view of domestic violence has totally held sway, dissenters are silenced, evidence about the true issues underlying this complex issue are ignored. And the huge cash cow supporting our blinkered domestic violence industry becomes ever more bloated.

CHAPTER 8

The fox now guards the hen house – betraying male victims

First published 2016

What a welcome surprise. In June 2016 the NSW government announced a pilot programme for male victims of domestic violence. Finally, politicians were acknowledging that women aren't the only victims of family violence. A third of victims are male, said Pru Goward, the NSW Minister for Domestic Violence and Sexual Assault, as she promised $13 million over four years for the pilot.

That's chickenfeed compared to the hundreds of millions that Prime Minister Malcolm Turnbull boasts are being spent on domestic violence across the country, all promoting an ideologically-driven agenda which pretends the problem is all about men and ignores 40 years of international research showing most family violence is two-way, involving women as well as men.

What a blow to discover in November that year that the NSW government had awarded the contract for this vital programme to Men's Referral Service, an organisation driven by feminist ideology and long known for shunning male victims. In the past, MRS was on the record for refusing to acknowledge the existence of male victims. The organisation's position then shifted to arguing male victims don't experience abuse in the same way as women and hence don't deserve support.

MRS has only ever worked with male perpetrators and is notorious for "red flagging" men who claim to be victims, attempting to prove they are in fact perpetrators.

What was really astonishing was that the NSW government boasted that this was the reason MRS was chosen for the job. In response to my questions, the Attorney General's department proudly proclaimed MRS was selected because of the organisation's expertise in "how to identify a genuine victim."

"Victims will be referred to local support services in NSW while aggressors will be encouraged to take part in Men's Behaviour Change programmes."

There are currently no local services for male victims but the government claimed to be sleuthing out "holistic support" as "referral points" in 46 locations — heaven knows from where, given that almost all DV services currently refuse to help men.

So the fox was put in charge of the hen house. Male victims, who are notoriously reluctant to seek help, are to be put through a dubious screening process run by an organisation with a long history of decrying their very existence.

The AG's department claimed the decision to use MRS is based on an evidence-based approach successfully trialled in the UK by Respect, a domestic violence organisation. Yet there has been huge controversy in Britain over the Respect approach which many see as placing unnecessary barriers in the way of men who need help. Louise Dixon, a psychology professor formerly at the University of Birmingham but now in New Zealand, sums up the criticism of Respect's work: "the ethos that informs their practice... is unsupported by the evidence, and is ideologically-based." Many alternate domestic violence programmes have been established, particularly in Scotland, which are male-friendly and genuinely dedicated to helping victims in need.

Imagine the outcry if domestic violence services for women assumed most alleged victims were in fact perpetrators. The whole domestic violence movement is based on the premise that "we believe women" yet our first government-funded programme for male victims now operates on the assumption that we shouldn't believe men.

It's hardly surprising that men working with victims around the country are up in arms. Yet this move by the NSW government is entirely in keeping with national domestic violence policy.

At a suicide prevention seminar some years back one of the speakers was manager of a male telephone helpline. He spoke about men who ring up saying they are suicidal as a result of being abused, physically and emotionally by their partners.

To the astonishment of the audience, the manager then revealed that when they receive a call from such a male victim they contact the police who track down the man's personal details by tracing the call. Assuming the male may be a perpetrator the police then contact the man's partner to check out her side of the story.

Many in the audience were incredulous at this breach of confidentiality and failure of the duty of care to the potentially suicidal client. During questioning the manager revealed government policy determined his organisation would lose government funding if they didn't assume all male victims were most likely perpetrators.

He's right. The official document spelling out Victorian government policy on DV (*Family Violence — Risk Assessment and Risk Management Framework*) assumes men who present as victims of violence will often falsely blame their partners for their own aggression and advises such men *plus* their partners must be referred for comprehensive assessment.

So, it is official government policy — not just in Victoria but under the national DV framework — to breach a male victim's privacy, contact the perpetrator of the violence and believe her side of the story at the expense of his. This could never happen in reverse, with our government hunting down the partners of female victims and choosing only to believe their version of events. The fact that our authorities are getting away with treating men this way shows the grip the anti-male DV lobby group has over this country.

And it is not just the male victims but also their children who are suffering. I listened recently to a radio interview with a man talking about his wife's mental health problems and the fears he had for his children when she had one of her regular violent outbursts. She often attacked him physically, but he didn't dare leave because he felt he was his children's only protection. There was nowhere for this family to go and he rightly feared the authorities might not believe him if he reached out for help.

There are people everywhere who grew up in such families. The men living with violent women often have relatives, brothers, parents, friends, who know all too well what is going on. These people need to have the courage to start speaking out. Change is not going to happen if governments continue to hear only one side of the story.

Now for the post-script, written twenty months after this story was first published. It appears the male-specific service have been lumped in with a revamped general service and "automated referral system" for both genders. The NSW Government's funding for support services for male victims was initially administered by the NSW Office For Women, with services provided by the Men's Referral Service. In a major shift, that role and funding was then re-directed and placed under the Attorney General's Department, which now administers the funding through its Department of Victims Services.

Requests for information from the Office for Women as to whether any men had been processed under their system showed only that around 14,000 inquiries had been fielded to the Men's Referral Service. No information was given on the outcomes for any men referred or processed by them.

NSW Victims Services now says referrals for support are being done under an automated system called *Safer Pathway,* whereby if NSW Police attend any domestic or family violence incident, "the victim is automatically referred through the Safer Pathway process and supports provided". The Safer Pathway program is fully outlined on the NSW Office For Women's website but the only reference to men's services is a line stating: "Men having problems with violent behaviour can call the Men's Referral Service." Clearly the assumption is the only men having such problems are perpetrators.

How male victims are to access support remains quite vague. NSW Victims Services claims it is conducting "Victims Services roadshows" around the state together with local services responsible for assisting "both male and female" domestic violence victims in 27 locations. But there has been no advertising of who the specific support providers are, although apparently these include organisations such as Relationships Australia, Interrelate, Catholic Care and the Family Centre Australia.

In the meantime, there remains no specific support services for male victims in Australia. Pru Goward used the funding announcement to have her moment in the sun and got away with doing nothing to help the men concerned.

CHAPTER 9

Tilting rape laws to favour women

First published 2016

Profound changes to manslaughter and rape laws in Victoria have resulted in the state now featuring one of the world's most gender-biased and anti-male jurisdictions. That's the view of Kenneth Arenson, a retired Associate Professor of Law at Deakin University and a very brave man.

In a speech delivered at the International Conference on Men's Issues, (ICMI) held on the Gold Coast in June 2017, Arenson noted that whilst sexual assault victims have not always received fair treatment before the courts, the pendulum has now swung the other way in Victoria over the last ten years. Sexual assault cases are now governed by a special set of rules that are not applicable to any other types of crimes. He says that reform in this area has been driven by a "strident feminist agenda".

Arenson identified three unique rules that Victorian sexual assault cases are now subject to, which do not apply to other serious criminal offences such as kidnapping, murder and armed robbery. Firstly, a "truncated window of opportunity to file indictments and commence legal proceedings", implying that sexual assault cases are given higher priority than other types of criminal cases.

Secondly, the exemption of complainants' testimonies in committal hearings — a "critical stage of the criminal process" — if the complainant is a child or a mentally impaired person. This exemption for children and mentally impaired persons does not apply to other types of criminal cases, which negates the claim that this exemption exists merely to "protect the victims". It does, however, put the defence at a severe disadvantage in that it precludes opportunities for full discovery of the prosecution's case, and cross examination of testimonies. According to Arenson, the exemption indulges the presumption that the complainant is telling the truth, thereby "making a mockery" of the presumption of innocence for the accused.

Finally, Arenson discussed the recent enactment of "rape shield" provisions which mandate that the accused cannot adduce the complainant's sexual history outside of encounters with the accused, unless it can be proven that the evidence is both exculpatory and "substantially relevant". The term "substantially relevant" is ill-defined, and therefore cannot be applied fairly and consistently. Prior to "rape shield" laws, the accused would have had the right to adduce *any* otherwise admissible exculpatory evidence that was deemed "relevant", which in legal parlance is a far easier standard to meet than "substantially relevant".

Arenson also produced a 68-page, meticulously referenced, scholarly paper outlining the impact of the changed laws which was published in the *Western Australian Jurist* — "The Demise of Equality Before the Law: The Pernicious Effects of Political Correctness in the Criminal Law in Victoria".[36]

As one example, Arenson asked if it is logical, fair or

compassionate to treat people who kill for reasons of revenge or thrill, for example, in the same manner as those who kill in response to severe provocation or in the belief that deadly force is required to defend themselves or others? For centuries, most western countries have chosen to make a legal distinction between the two. As Arenson explained, this no longer applies in Victoria which has chosen to abolish provocation and excessive force manslaughter as partial defences in murder prosecutions.

The major reason given at the time by Rob Hulls, then the Attorney General of Victoria, was that the provocation defence is "often relied upon by men who kill their sexual partners out of jealousy or anger." Arenson argued that this represents an example of "unprincipled and gross unfairness" in that the basis for the change in the law was spawned because "one gender appears to have invoked the defence with greater frequency than the other."

Similar changes to manslaughter have been made in Tasmania, Western Australia and New Zealand, but Victoria leads the charge when it comes to changes in rape law. The Victorian Parliament in 2014 enacted laws that changed the requirements to prove intent, changes advocated in an article by Melbourne Law School Associate Professor Wendy Larcombe in an article revealingly titled, "Falling Rape Conviction Rates: (Some) Feminist Aims and Measures for Rape Law." Larcombe's recommendations regarding proving intent were adopted verbatim in the new laws introduced in Parliament.

The consequences of the changes are difficult to describe without the detailed analysis provided in Arenson's article but in essence he argued that Victorian rape laws now contain both a subjective and objective mental element, requiring a prosecutor to prove than an accused "does not reasonably believe that [the alleged victim] consents to the penetration". In light of fairly recent decisions by the High Court and Victorian Court of Appeal, Arenson contended that this amounts to requiring the Crown to prove that an accused did not act with reasonable recklessness regarding the question of consent which, in legal parlance, is self-contradictory and "all but certain to spawn a new generation of unnecessary and costly litigation".

He pointed out that the legislation contains the same flaw in relation to a legal standard that was found wanting by both the High Court and Victorian Court of Appeal. By ignoring these decisions, Arenson suggested the Victorian parliament has probably brought in laws that will turn out to be unworkable and create a veritable nightmare for the Victorian courts.

What is particularly alarming is that Parliament would have been influenced by an academic who makes no attempt to disguise her ideological position. Arenson contended that Lacombe's writings expose "an unfettered hostility towards the notion that all persons are equal before the law, a willingness to embellish the language of key appellate decisions or an unwitting propensity to misstate well-established legal principles, an attitude towards the male gender that is predicated on overly broad, erroneous and pernicious assumptions and recommendations that are parochial, unrealistic and ill-advised."

The consent laws are only the latest volley in a series of what Arenson called "pernicious reforms ... based on upon gender bias in rape and sexual assault cases as evidenced by the fact they are applicable only in cases involving rape and other forms of sexual assault." He named other changes including: the creation of the "Victorian offence of infanticide which allows women but not men to commit what would otherwise be murder," and rape shield laws limiting a defendant's long entrenched common law right to put before a court all legally admissible evidence that helps to show they are not guilty of the alleged crime[37].

What's fascinating is that in the face of these increasingly draconian laws, conviction rates continue to fall. Both men and women on juries persist in making their own decisions about the guilt or innocence of men accused of rape or sexual assault, despite these strenuous efforts to tilt the law against them: a small mercy indeed in the face of this onslaught of gender bias.

CHAPTER 10

The growing power of left-wing women

First published 2017

As an accomplished provocateur, Milo Yiannopolous manages to rub any number of people up the wrong way. But what was most striking about the leftist crowd demonstrating against his Sydney talks in 2017 were the large numbers of earnest fresh-faced young women holding up posters that made their sentiments very clear. Like: "F--k off Nazi Scum".

Indeed, most of the protests were driven by left-wing female students, such as Sydney University's Lily Campbell, education officer for its Student Representative Council, who orchestrated the Sydney demonstrations. "If Yiannopoulos wants to visit this country and spread his filth, then we are going to be here waiting to challenge him," she promised on her Facebook page.

Well, Campbell has good reason to be concerned because Milo has women like her well and truly in his sights. In a YouTube interview with me given during his tour, he said he'd love to return to Australia for campus events similar to his Dangerous Faggot tour in the US. The purpose is to bring attention to the stifling of free speech in universities.

"For far too long the American campus has been the preserve of leftists who channel funding into crackpot gender studies courses and radicalise students against political tolerance, openness to opposing ideas and ultimately against reason itself," Milo wrote in his best-selling book *Dangerous*.

And who is taking gender studies courses and other humanities subjects preaching this intolerance? It's mainly women, of course. The hearts and minds being captured in our universities belong mainly to young women, who now comprise more than 60 per cent of graduates.

The result is successive generations of female graduates who are left wing. Leftist university education is one of many factors leading to a dramatic change in voting patterns in many Western countries — a trend that spells real trouble for conservative parties here and elsewhere.

Look at recent voting patterns in Australia. The latest 2016 results from the Australian Election Study, a collaboration between several universities but based at ANU, show women more likely to support Labor than men by seven per cent and also more likely to vote for the Greens than men, by four per cent. Fewer women than men have voted Liberal in five of the six elections since 2001. Labor has enjoyed greater support from women in all six.

That's a real shift from the Menzies era when conservatives had a decisive lead among female voters. That continued through the early 1980s when Hawke pushed the women's vote up to 50/50. Keating was less popular with women, Howard more so, but it was the 2001 election that saw the women's vote start to really shift left, with the Gillard election in 2010 the high point. So, having a Gillard or Howard in charge shifts women's choices but there's a far more critical underlying issue. "Irrespective of the political leaders and policies there's an important constant: women are now consistently more left wing in terms of their policy preferences," says ANU lecturer in government and politics Dr Jillian Sheppard, who works on the AES team.

It shows up in AES data on issue after issue: asylum-seekers; government spending on indigenous affairs; stiffer criminal penalties; positive discrimination for women; same-sex marriage. In the recent postal survey on same sex marriage more women voted yes in every age group from 18 through to 75.

The gender gap is stark. For instance, asked in 2016 whether they favour tax cuts over more social spending, 38 per cent of men think this is a good idea compared with 32 per cent of women.

And the gap is growing. A decade ago, men and women usually agreed on whether trade unions had too much power. Now there is a 16-point gender gap, with 55 per cent of men agreeing and only 39 per cent of women.

Sheppard provided me with unpublished data showing that it's actually young female graduates who are pushing the drift left. "Male graduates are not particularly more left-leaning than men without a university education, whereas female graduates are notably more left-leaning than other women without degrees," says Sheppard.

It's easy to see female graduates are a major factor explaining the overall shift to the left. Back in 2007 only 27 per cent of Australians described themselves as having left-leaning views. By 2016 that had leapt up to 37 per cent, 44 per cent for graduates and 48 per cent for those with postgraduate degrees.

Academics writing on the issue usually cite university education as a key factor in influencing the growth of left-wing female voters without asking any of the hard questions about the type of education these women are receiving. For instance, there's a pivotal article by political scientists Ronald Inglehart and Pippa Norris, who used World Values Surveys from more than 60 countries to show that by the 1990s women voters were significantly more left-wing than men. They attribute the change to a range of factors including: increased female participation in jobs as service providers in education, health care and welfare services or as public-sector professionals; transformation of gender roles; decreased religiosity and break-up of traditional family units. They note increased participation in higher education "may have encouraged more liberal values".

"Academics are unlikely to want to discuss this issue because there's abundant evidence that most are left-wing themselves. They are hardly going to be concerned that universities are churning out women who share their beliefs," says Dr Bella d'Abrera, who has just completed an audit of history teaching at Australian universities for the conservative think tank, The Institute for Public Affairs. The audit found the subject is being taught from a narrow ideological perspective that focuses almost exclusively on class, race and gender, hardly a word on democracy, liberalism, capitalism, the essential tenets of Western civilisation.

"Students are being shamelessly indoctrinated into Neo-Marxist beliefs and their education is failing to provide them with the broad knowledge of history which would encourage critical thinking, an openness to conversation rather than conscription to a fixed set of ideas," says d'Abrera.

It's not just history — "the humanities and teaching faculties which attract most female students are now tarred with the same postmodern, feminist and neo-Marxist brush," she says. An astonishing 98 per cent of our 43 universities now offer gender studies, which show a similar bias. A recent analysis of 165 university policies by the Institute of Public Affairs revealed 81 per cent of Australia's 42 universities have policies that are hostile to free speech, while a further 17 per cent threaten free speech.

"Universities are schooling women in the language of identity politics and by the time they graduate, they are fully fledged social justice warriors," d'Abrera concludes. The result is an ever-growing female voting block with blinkered leftist views.

Views that even determine which men they are prepared to date. My interest in this subject was piqued by my online dating clients, mainly professional women, most of whom are left-wing and scathing about conservative men. Like the woman who refused to meet a man who mentioned he enjoyed watching Andrew Bolt's show. Another confessed to a pact with her female friends that there'll be "no sex with anyone who likes Tony Abbott".

One client broke off a two-year relationship with a man who leapt to Trump's defence in a conversation with her friends. Another man told me his girlfriend dropped him because she was embarrassed when her friends found out he occasionally writes for *The Spectator Australia*.

Incidentally, male clients are rarely so concerned about a date's political beliefs, although some grumble about women's intolerance of diverse views. As one man put it: "They need to grow out of their childish, second-year uni views. Jesus, Girls, leave it OUT."

But they don't grow out of it. Unlike many men, who become more conservative as they age, the work/life patterns in most women's lives simply reinforce their beliefs.

Just look at the single mothers. Single parent families, more than 80 per cent of which are headed by women, are increasing in Australia — from 13 per cent of families in 1991 to 16 per cent in 2016. Although most of these families are a result of family breakup, the group includes growing numbers of women who have children on their own or in unstable de facto relationships. About 42 per cent of sole-parent households live primarily on government benefits, according to statistics in the ABS 2015-16 Household Income and Wealth, Australia report.

In 2015 American writer Kay Hymowitz was a visiting scholar at the Australian think tank, The Centre for Independent Studies in Sydney. Hymowitz has written extensively on the growth of single-mother families and says the Democratic Party in the US has long been aware of the advantage it has with this group. "They know that demographics — including declining rates of marriage — are their friend. Single mothers, who are particularly dependent on government support, are unlikely to bite the hand that helps them feed their kids. In the US that means they vote Democrat. It's a huge problem for Republicans and anyone else who wants to limit the growth of government."

An Obama campaign dubbed "Life of Julia" featured a slide show following a fictional character, Julia, from age three to 67, explaining how the Democrats' policies would provide her with a better life. Conservative commentators had great fun speculating on what else Uncle Sam could possibly do to subsidise, as one tweet described her, "the chick who depends on everyone else for everything".

Julia starts off on Head Start, uses free maternity care to become a single mother with her son going to a publicly-funded selective school, then receives a government loan to start her business and finally retires on social security benefits so she can plant zucchinis in a community garden. The conservative website Human Events ran a column asking, "Who the hell is Julia and why am I paying for her life?"

Ok, so that was blatant over-reach but the point is that the politics work for the Democrats. Pew Research Centre surveys show that during the past nine presidential elections women have consistently voted for Democrat presidential candidates at higher rates than men. On average women have been eight percentage points more likely than men to back the Democratic candidate in elections. The party holds a 16-point edge among women, the highest it has been since 2008 when Obama pushed it up to a 21-point advantage.

Australian Opposition Leader Bill Shorten, too, seems to be banking on single mothers as a key support group for his party. Associated lobby groups have long been pulling Labor's strings and the party has responded with any number of policies that benefit the group, including, for instance, winding back John Howard's reforms to family law, which introduced the presumption of shared parental responsibility, and introducing legal changes making it easy for women, in the absence of any proof, to allege domestic violence and use it to gain advantage in family law battles.

But that's only part of this story. Shorten is making a pitch for the women's vote abundantly obvious. "No more budgets for blokes," he pledged last year, outlining a slew of policies favouring women.

Look at his extraordinary statement last year on International Women's Day: "I firmly believe that if this Parliament did nothing else in the next number of years but advance the march of women through the institutions of power: in workplaces, in unpaid work, in family law and economic equality, if we did nothing else in this country as a whole in the next 15 years but install women to a place of equal treatment in our society, we will be a richer, more prosperous country with a far better prospect of a brighter future."

There's much more adding to the smiles on faces of pollsters on the left. Last year the Australian Institute of Family Studies published a study about teenagers' career aspirations that showed most girls are firmly locked into traditional female career paths. Both sexes were attracted to being doctors, dentists, architects and designers, but while the boys favoured jobs in engineering or transport, IT, construction, trades, technical jobs and sports, the top list for girls featured law, education and social professions such as counselling, plus personal services like hairdressing and beauty therapy.

This suggests we are unlikely to see significant change in the job paths of women, no real shift to the predominance of women ending up in education, health care and welfare services or as public-sector professionals — one of the key factors political scientists Ronald Ingelhart and Pippa Norris argued was contributing to the growth of leftist female voters. Women now make up 58 per cent of public service jobs and they are more likely to be in unionised jobs — 12 per cent of employed men and 15 per cent of women were trade union members in 2016, according to the ABS.

"Working in the public sector is known to be associated with voting left, support for government intervention, collective action, social welfare and so on," says ANU emeritus professor of political science professor John Warhurst, pointing to the ACT's high public-sector employment and consistent support for left-wing parties.

Then there's the motherhood issue, with mothers particularly receptive to the left's big-spending promises — and scare campaigns — on education and health. An Essential Media poll conducted during last year's election campaign found Labor's Medicare beat-up resulted in 86 per cent of women agreeing they were concerned about the privatisation of Medicare compared with 75 per cent of men. Similarly, a large gender gap emerged in an Essential Media poll asking about cut-backs in Gonski education funding — with 59 per cent of women and 50 per cent of men objecting to proposed changes.

It's hard to imagine what conservative parties can do about many factors working against them with women, like the growth in single mothers or women's job preferences. But some conservative leaders seem poised to tackle the role of publicly-funded universities in promoting ideology that so clearly favours their opponents.

Earlier this year, when violent protestors at UC Berkeley shut down a speech by Milo, US President Trump weighed in with a disapproving tweet including the threat: "NO FEDERAL FUNDS?"

When the newly elected Canadian Conservative Party leader Andrew Scheer made his acceptance speech, the loudest applause was for his commitment to punish universities that stifle free speech. "I believe the foundation of our democracy is to have a debate on any subject," he said, promising to withhold federal grants from universities that don't allow expression of differing points of view.

Similar issues are occupying the mind of our former Prime Minister John Howard. He's chairman of the board of the Paul Ramsay Foundation, which is administering a bequest left by Ramsay, the healthcare entrepreneur, designed to set up new degree programs on Western civilisation in Australian universities — courses set up to fill the gap in humanities education now dominated by identity politics. But predictably, the Left-wing activists objected and shamefully the ANU pulled out of their deal with Ramsay to establish the course, despite being given ultimate control over the choice of curriculum, staff and all other key academic issues. (The ANU, once a world-leading university, has shown itself to be morally bankrupt on a range of issues under the current administration — a source of great sadness to me, given that my father was one of the founding professors at the university and I spent almost two decades on the governing board.)

The most serious conversations about this issue are taking place on social media led by various activists campaigning to take back university campuses. The hugely popular Canadian psychology professor Jordan Peterson calls traditional universities "indoctrination cults" for abandoning the humanities and heads up one of many groups, including the IPA here in Australia, working to provide students with an analysis of university courses so they can choose between what he calls "neo-Marxist indoctrination" and "proper education". At one stage Peterson was toying with establishing an online university that set itself a lofty goal: "To cut the enrolment in postmodern neo-Marxist courses of indoctrination in universities across the Western world by 75 per cent over the next five years." That ambitious plan is currently on the backburner.

But it was a lofty goal, and certainly more obtainable if powerful conservative parties came to their senses and realised their very survival lies in coming on board.

CHAPTER 11

Cassie Jaye and the rise of Honey Badgers

First published 2017

In 2016 I wrote about the young Californian filmmaker Cassie Jaye and her movie The Red Pill, *a documentary about feminism's success in closing down debate on men's issues. The irony was feminist activists across the world demonstrated that point by attempting to stop the documentary being made and then trying to prevent it from being shown. Australia became the first country in the world to cave to pressure from these women — who hadn't even seen the movie — when cinema owners cancelled the opening night screenings of the movie in Melbourne, in November that year.*

Determined not to allow these bullies to determine what Australians should be allowed to see, I became involved and ultimately organised screenings across the country through an organisation called FanForce, which allows people to host screenings of movies of their choice. We sold out packed cinemas in all major cities, despite constant pressure from feminists who succeeded in having some viewings cancelled. It was a huge battle, with brave men and women taking on the task of promoting the movie in their local communities, surprisingly including a group of policemen in Mount Isa, in central Queensland.

Here's the whole sorry tale in three parts: Firstly, a small article I wrote in 2016 introducing Cassie Jaye and The Red Pill. *Then the story of the Honey Badgers, the female Men's Rights activists who visited Australia the following year for an international conference on men's issues. Finally, a post-script: a blog I wrote about the disgraceful treatment of Cassie Jaye by the Australian media during her visit here. That inspired my first YouTube video[38].*

Cassie Jaye and The Red Pill

"The Red Pill: The movie about men that feminists didn't want you to see." This was the provocative headline that ran in *The Telegraph* in the UK in late 2015, a teaser for a documentary made by a leading feminist filmmaker who planned to take on Men's Rights activists but was won over and crossed to the dark side to take up their cause.

Despite a ferocious campaign to stop the movie being made it was finally released and the first Australian screening was due to take place in late 2016. However, the gender warriors intervened and used a change.com petition to persuade Palace Cinemas to cancel the Melbourne cinema booking. Despite over twice as many signing a petition against the ban, organisers were forced to find another venue.

Clearly this documentary had the feminists very worried — with good reason. Cassie Jaye is an articulate, 29-year-old blonde whose previous movies on gay marriage and abstinence education won multiple awards. But then she decided to interview leaders of the Men's Rights Movement (MRM) for a documentary she was planning about rape culture on American campuses. As a committed feminist Jaye expected to be unimpressed by these renowned hate-filled misogynists but to her surprise she was exposed to a whole range of issues she came to see as unfairly stacked against men and boys.

As news of this very public conversion started to leak out, Jaye came under attack. She was smeared, told she was committing "career suicide" and saw her funding dry up to the point where it looked as if the movie would never be made. Prominent feminists she'd planned to interview refused to participate, none of the "human rights" funding she'd hoped to attract proved available for a documentary looking at men's rights.

Then a Kickstarter fund raised a staggering $211,260, ensuring the movie's cinematic release. American audiences had their first screenings, to predictably mixed reviews. Many in the mainstream media were extremely hostile to the revelations in this powerful movie. The title *The Red Pill* refers to a scene in *The Matrix*, when Keanu Reeves' character takes the red pill to expose "the truth" which challenges his closely-held beliefs. Cassie Jaye's Red Pill reveals a world where the cultural dialogue is dominated by feminists still complaining that men have all the power yet the "truth" in most Western Countries is that many of our laws, attitudes and social conventions make life tough for men.

Her fly-on-the-wall technique included interviews with MRM leaders like Paul Elam and feminists who oppose the movement, graphics and animations revealing facts about family law and child custody, male suicide rates and the not-so-privileged side of traditional manhood, such as the 90 per cent of workplace fatalities that are male. There was a powerful interview with Erin Pizzey, who is no longer allowed near the

UK women's refuge she started back in the 1970s, the first in the world. Pizzey ran afoul of the sisterhood by campaigning to expose the truth about women's equal role in domestic violence.

Jaye showed feminist protesters shutting down a talk at a Toronto campus by men's activist Warren Farrell, screeching at a young man who tried to attend and berating him as "fucking scum," and on another occasion setting off a fire alarm causing a building to be evacuated where a men's rights lecture was to have been held.

There's discussion of men's lack of reproductive rights which includes a clip from a television chat show where the audience cheers when a woman whose husband is resisting a second child announces she's considering going off birth control and not telling him.

The flamboyant anti-feminist Milo Yiannopoulos described *The Red Pill* as "a powerful film on a complicated, important, yet woefully unaddressed issue." Yiannopoulos applauded Jaye for "having the intestinal fortitude to not only tackle this subject, but to do so fairly."

But the movie was panned by left-wing *The Village Voice* which called Jaye an "MRA-bankrolled propagandist" and the *Los Angeles Times* whose reviewer claimed she failed to understand "patriarchal systems." Stephen Marche in *The Guardian* admitted that "men do sometimes suffer mistreatment from the courts or from the women in their lives" but suggested the film failed to demonstrate any kind of systemic cause. "Instead, the author of men's troubles here is always that vague bugaboo feminism, which we're told is designed to silence its opponents," sniffed Marche.

That's pretty ironic considering this "vague bugaboo

feminism" worked so hard to try to silence Cassie Jaye's attempts to tell this story. As she pointed out in her movie, the issues she examined came as a revelation not only to her but also to many others exposed to the material she put together. That damned bugaboo carries a lot of clout.

The Honey Badgers are coming

As a fresh-faced eighteen-year-old Daisy Cousens left school firmly on board the feminism bandwagon. Like many millennium women she'd been seduced by what she now sees as an "entrenched victim mentality," convinced the scales were tipped against her because of her gender. "I assumed I'd have to work twice has hard as men for half the recognition and that violent predators lurk around every street corner," she says.

It took her years to discover she'd been duped. "I realised the feminist view did not reflect my life experiences. I grew suspicious. I couldn't believe that somehow in Western society women were paid less than men or had fewer rights than men. And given my experience of men, I refused to believe there was an undercurrent of misogyny amongst all the wonderful men in my life," says the now 28-year-old who's now part of a growing international band of female activists speaking out about the demonisation of men. Some of the leading lights in this group arrived in Australia in June 2017 to speak at the International Conference on Men's Issues (ICMI-17) on the Gold Coast.

Cousen's turnaround happened when she was working as a research assistant at the Menzies Research Centre which led her to start asking the right questions. She found, for instance, that the much heralded "wage gap" could be largely explained by differences in men and women's work/lifestyle choices.

That was the beginning. Cousens discovered a thriving online world questioning the feminist narrative and revealing the silencing of critical issues impacting on men and boys. Cousens was then mainly writing for *The Spectator Australia* and *Quadrant* magazine — about what she now sees as a "silent war on men," expressing her outrage that "any discussion of male suicide, military and workplace deaths, sexual assault, and domestic violence are smothered by raging feminist mobs screaming about 'male privilege'."[39]

Cousens is one of many women who hosted screenings of Cassie Jaye's documentary *The Red Pill*. Her Sydney screening took place soon after Jaye's visit to Australia and the media coverage of her visit ensured a packed crowd, despite strenuous efforts by activists to try to bully cinemas into closing it down. It was an exciting time for Daisy Cousens because as a wannabee Honey Badger she also got to meet Karen Straughan at the Gold Coast conference and that's as good as it gets.

Karen Straughan is one of the founders of the Honey Badger brigade, a band of brash, witty female activists who've taken up the fight for a better deal for men and boys. Seven years ago, Karen was a Canadian waitress and divorced mother of three who started blogging about how easy it would have been to use the family law system to destroy her ex-husband. She was in the process of obtaining a divorce but had no interest in making her husband's life any more difficult. Her lawyer was appalled by her attitude and worked hard to try to persuade her to take him to the cleaners.

Straughan grew increasingly astonished at how the law and social institutions are now stacked against men. She posted a blog (girlwriteswhat) which included this pithy summary of marriage today: "For women, marriage is all benefit and zero risk, and that's why women are whining about men's reluctance to tie the knot. But for men, it's the other way around — no guaranteed benefit, and the kind of risk an adrenaline junkie would eschew". Next came a Youtube video — *Feminism and the Disposable Male* — which has raked up over 1.5 million views[40].

Through her social media activities, Straughan got to know other women interested in men's issues — like Alison Tieman who, with Straughan, started Honey Badger Radio Show. Then there's blogger Janet Bloomfield whose take-no-prisoners writing style soon attracted a big audience for her JudgyBitch blog promoting "the radical notion that women are adults".

When protestors threatened to shut down a Men's Rights conference in Detroit in 2011 the Honey Badger brigade flew in to act as "human shields". It helps to have females involved because women activists can't be dismissed as sad losers who can't get laid, suggests Straughan. "Men run the risk of being perceived as dangerous or threatening when speaking up," she says, adding that male activists tend to be "mocked as whiny man-babies or dismissed as dangerous extremist reactionaries who want to make it legal to beat your wife."

And the name Honey Badgers? That actually came from a funny video — *The Crazy Nastyass Honey Badger* — which shows the vicious animal sticking its nose into bee-filled holes, gnawing on mice, tearing the heads off snakes, and shaking off venomous cobra bites[41].

It's pretty silly, admits Straughan but watch her shrug off the constant abuse she receives from feminists or reducing Naomi

Wolf into a quivering heap on a television panel and you'll see there's something in it. The Honey Badger movement is swelling fast as more women, like myself, decide they have had enough of the constant denigration of men.

Cassie Jaye under attack by the Australian Media

It was a great story. Here was this lovely young woman who'd renounced her feminism after looking carefully at the way feminists were silencing discussion about men's issues. And then Australia became the first country in the world to try to ban her movie. Surely our media would line up to give her a chance to explain what it was all about?

Well, no. Within days of Cassie Jaye's arrival in Australia our media had disgraced itself by putting the young filmmaker through the most hostile, unfair interviews she had ever experienced.

There was the appearance on Channel 10's *The Project* which introduced her segment with an aggressive introduction video, which repeated many of the lies feminists have been spreading about the movie and included quotes from one of our most notorious man-haters, Van Badham, slamming the movie. Completely false information was included such as the claim the movie was funded by men's rights group. Cassie Jaye explained in her interview that she funded the movie with her mother and fiancé and only chose to launch a Kickstarter campaign in order to raise post-production funds needed. The Kickstarter backers had no stake or influence over the movie — as the producers had been told beforehand — but *The Project* chose to ignore the truth in an attempt to taint Cassie's credibility.

Then she was ferociously attacked by the entire panel with

only about a third of her interview even being shown, denying any opportunity for this calm, intelligent woman to properly explain what the movie is all about.

Next came her appearance on *Weekend Sunrise* and I sought assurance from the producers that she would not be given similar treatment and specifically that she was not to be interviewed by Andrew O'Keefe, one of the presenters well-known for his feral attacks on anyone who challenges the feminist narrative. I was assured Jaye would not be interviewed by him.

Surprise, surprise, there he was with his female co-host, tearing into her, not giving her any opportunity to answer his rude, ill-informed questions. The pair claimed they hadn't been able to view the movie prior to the interview — I published the email proof that they were given the link a month in advance. This is trite, tabloid journalism at its worst. Rather than look at the big story as to why Australia is proving itself to be one of world's most repressive countries when it comes to debates over men's issues, these mainstream TV shows chose to buy into the distorted feminist narrative and attack the filmmaker rather than allowing her to explain the issues.

That blog was written just after Cassie Jaye left the country shattered by the treatment she had received here. I ended up moving her into my home during her Sydney visit, giving the poor girl some motherlove and cancelling many of other interviews I had arranged for her. But the result was an outpouring of public sympathy and rightful condemnation of our biased media. And The Red Pill *became the highest selling movie on Amazon in Australia at that time.*

The documentary went on to become the highest trending documentary on Amazon, third on iTunes and first on Google Play and won a string of prizes, including the Women in Film award.

SECTION THREE

Universities unsafe for male students

CHAPTER 12

The campus rape frenzy – manufactured crisis

First published 2016

The *Washington Post*'s headline was grim: "Hundreds of colleges had zero rape reports and that could be worrisome."

That was in 2014 when the hysteria over "the rape culture" in American colleges was just starting to take hold. Madness ensued. College and university presidents, embarrassed by zero rape reports, scrambled to explain why their campuses made the newspaper's list. "We always operate under the assumption that zero does not really mean zero," said a California State University spokesman defensively. "Under-reporting will happen."

Years later this is the new norm on American campuses where hysteria over sex risks grows ever more strident. What's frightening is just how little time it took for one of the world's leading education systems to be captured by a gender-based culture war.

It is instructive to see how this all happened, particularly since Australia looks set to head in the same direction. In the US it started with a 2007 Campus Sexual Assault Study commissioned by the US Department of Justice. The study claimed one in five female college students were sexual assault victims. Although the respondents to the web-based study were self-selected and the definitions of sexual assault that were used were dubious, most media sources dutifully reported this astonishing claim.

Within a few years, universities across America were introducing "yes means yes" regulations that require students to give "enthusiastic" consent every step of the way in sexual activity. Campus disciplinary tribunals were set up to adjudicate accusations of sexual misconduct based on these regulations which effectively shift the burden of proof to the (usually male) student accused of such charges. The changes, in some cases tied to federal funding, have led to a spate of allegations.

"The list of falsely accused young men subjected to kangaroo court justice is growing apace," wrote Christina Hoff Sommers, a former philosophy professor and American Institute scholar in *Time* magazine in 2014. She mentioned one young male, Caleb Warner who was found guilty of sexually assaulting a fellow student by a campus tribunal and expelled from college, only to have the local police determine he was innocent and that the alleged victim had deliberately falsified her charges. "Presumed guilty is the new legal principle where sex is concerned," Hoff Sommers concluded.

In Australia we are slipping and sliding down the same slope. Similarly, unconvincing research has been published — here it was a National Union of Students survey that found 73 per cent of students had experienced sexual harassment or unwelcome sexual behaviour.

Most of these experiences involved staring or unwelcome comments or jokes. When the unwanted behaviour included assault (which could be an undesired touch) or attempted rape, most of the experiences didn't involve fellow students and the majority appear to have taken place off campus.

Of course, it is extremely important that such attacks receive proper investigation and every effort should be made to encourage victims to report rape or assault. But there's no good evidence to suggest there is a rape culture in Australian universities. In spite of this, our Human Rights and Equal Opportunities Commission leapt into action. "This is an issue that needs focus and attention," said then sex discrimination commissioner Elizabeth Broderick, announcing 39 universities would collect data on this alarming problem. Universities Australia then committed $1 million to support the project.

Meanwhile, so-called documentary *The Hunting Ground*, which had toured American universities ramping up anxiety with false claims of a rape epidemic on campus, started to be shown at Australian universities. It's strong stuff showing frightened young American female college students apparently being preyed upon by serial rapists. But the film has been thoroughly discredited. Investigative producer for the project, Amy Herdy, has admitted publicly that makers of the movie "do not operate in the same way as journalists — this is a film project that is very much in the corner of advocacy for victims, so there would be no insensitive questions or need to get the perpetrator's side".

Nineteen Harvard Law professors have denounced the film for misrepresenting key issues in the case of a law student who was ultimately cleared of sexual assault charges by a grand jury.

And the central thesis regarding the plague of serial rapists on campus stems from flawed research by psychologist David Lisak. The alleged serial rapists turned out not to be college students, nor were the rapes committed on campuses.

The statistics used in the film resulted from highly unusual research methods used in a Center for Disease Control and Prevention survey. As one example, respondents were told, "Please remember that even if someone uses alcohol or drugs what happens to them is not their fault." Then they were asked the question, "When you were drunk, high, drugged or passed out and unable to consent, how many people ever had vaginal sex with you?" The CDC counted all such incidents as rape — hence the inflated statistics.

What's crazy about all this alarmist talk about rape on campus is these privileged young women are far less likely to experience unpleasant sexual experiences than their less educated contemporaries. "Young women who don't go to college are more likely to be raped," wrote Callie Marie Rennison in *The New York Times* that year. Rennison, co-director of the Criminology and Criminal Justice Research Initiative at the University of Colorado, cited research showing young women who don't attend college are victims of sexual violence at a rate of about 30 per cent greater than their more-educated counterparts.

Other EU research suggests universities are a safer place to be than many of the home environments of these women — most incidents of serious violence involving students took place outside the university.

Similar demographics no doubt apply in Australia yet the scene is now set for exaggerated claims of sexual violence on our campuses. What's next? "Trigger warnings" protecting victims of violence from being exposed to traumatic content in university courses, limitations on what can be taught in university syllabuses?

We saw the seeds of this alarmist culture in 1992 when a

group of students at the ANU objected to rape cases used in a tutorial by former PNG Crown Prosecutor Peter Waight. Among other concerns, the students took issue with a legal example, based on known cases, that Waight had used in his teaching for more than a decade. It involved a young woman who claimed to be the victim of a sexual assault committed by her uncle, but who changed her story in court and said no assault had taken place.

The irony was the students claimed the question was objectionable because it "promoted the offensive myth that women and girls often make up allegations of rape for the fun of it". But the students had it totally wrong — the essence of the case was that the niece had really been raped and family pressure had been brought to bear on her to change her story so her uncle did not go to jail.

Under the threat of a law suit by Waight, some of the students apologised, but the legal process took years to resolve and Waight chose to retire from the university despite receiving support from nearly all of his students, many local lawyers and colleagues.

There's a growing push for trigger warnings across Australia, with the National Union of students suggesting warnings for university courses mentioning rape or sexual assault. The call for trigger warnings also applies to abuse, suicide, eating disorders, slurs, shaming, and racism. The most bizarre list comes from La Trobe where their student union suggests warnings for an astonishing 68 items including blood, vomit, fat shaming, gore, snakes, spiders, Islamophobia, corpses, needles, slimy things, insects, scarification, pregnancy, queerphobia, transphobia and Nazi paraphernalia.

It is logical to assume activity on Australian campuses
is setting the scene for further changes in our legal system.
What's the bet the Human Rights Commission's survey will
produce sufficiently alarming statistics[42] to justify a push
for "yes means yes" regulations on Australian campuses[43]?
Loraine Finlay, a former DPP prosecutor and a lecturer in
law at Murdoch University, points out the so-called "random
sampling" being used actually invites students to self-select
to do the survey. "This seems highly likely to skew the results
towards students who have experienced some form of assault
or harassment who will be more motivated to take the survey,"
she says[44].

"We should be extremely cautious about moving down the
path of changing our laws to adopt an 'enthusiastic consent'
standard," Finlay says. Her time as a prosecutor showed her
that while sexual assault offences are extremely difficult to
prosecute because victim and alleged offender often provide
different versions of events, she believes that "the current
approach to consent is fair and reasonable".

The reality is that enthusiastic consent laws can undermine
the right to a fair trial for students accused of sexual offences.
In 2015, a Tennessee judge, Carol McCoy, ruled in a case
involving a student who claimed she hadn't consented to
the drunken sex with a fellow student called "Corey Mock".
McCoy's judgment stated that the university regulations
"improperly shifted the burden of proof and imposed an
untenable standard upon Mr Mock to disprove the accusation."
She suggested it runs afoul of "the fundamental requirement of
due process".

Recently, Australian gender warrior and journalist Jane

Gilmore appeared on the ABC's *The Drum* discussing sexual assaults on campus and promoting the need for enthusiastic consent laws. She made it clear regulations on campus are just the beginning. The broader aim is strengthened rape and sexual assault laws, increasing sentences for such crimes and further eroding traditional legal protections against false allegations.

California has just expanded its definition of rape and added new mandatory-minimum sentences for sexual assaults, five months after a judge's lenient sentence for former Stanford University swimmer Brock Turner sparked outrage on social media. When Turner was released from prison, his family home was surrounded by armed protestors waving signs like "Shoot the local rapist".

New draconian laws, armed vigilante groups — arguably an inflamed reaction inspired, at least in part, by the frenzy over the rape culture on American campuses. So what's next for Australia?

CHAPTER 13

The Columbia Mattress Girl — American colleges in crisis

First published 2017

Last week the long saga over the Columbia University mattress girl came to an end. It was a costly lesson for the New York university and a sign that buying into the notion of a "campus rape culture" can prove a big mistake for esteemed centres of higher learning. Australian universities take note.

In 2015 the mattress girl, Emma Sulkowicz, became a global celebrity by turning what was found to be a false rape allegation into performance art by carrying her mattress with her everywhere on campus. She was protesting against Columbia's decision not to take action against a young German student, Paul Nungesser, whom she'd accused of choking and anally raping her.

Columbia has now reached a confidential settlement with Nungesser following his lawsuit claiming the university supported "an outrageous display of harassment and defamation" by allowing Sulkowicz for three years to use her mattress to hold campus protests where people openly called him a rapist. Sulkowicz was given academic credit for the performance as part of her visual arts major and was allowed to carry the mattress in her graduation ceremony.

It's most unlikely any jury would have convicted Nungesser given the facts of the case. There's a Facebook message from Sulkowicz to Nungesser two days after the alleged rape saying she was keen to join in a party in his room. A month later she sought more contact: "I want to see youyouyouyou". The following month she messaged: "I love you Paul. Where are you?" Hardly surprising that the university's investigation found Nungesser not guilty of assault.

Similarly murky facts emerged in accusations made by two other women about Nungesser. Investigations were held. The man was found not guilty. Yet the university chose to pander to extremists who believed the accuser was always right by allowing the mattress pantomime to continue for three whole years. Columbia is rightly out of pocket and forced to grovel, promising to update its policies to ensure "every student — accuser and accused, including those like Paul who are found not responsible — is treated respectfully".

Universities across the US are being sued for their failure to offer basic legal protections for the many young men who are being accused of such crimes on college campuses. False accusations in the quasi-judicial campus tribunals, forced on the universities by the Obama administration, have led to endless Federal Court lawsuits against the universities, which have lost most cases involving students, 53 cases to 37, according to Brooklyn College history professor KC Johnson, co-author of *The Campus Rape Frenzy: The Attack on Due Process at America's Universities*. Many colleges pay out six-figure settlements, says Johnson, who is monitoring the 170 similar cases working their way through the court system.

Many in the US university system are having second

thoughts about their adoption of the rape culture narrative that even may have encouraged false accusations. Suddenly they find themselves on the wrong side of the political debate as US President Donald Trump has promised to wind back the tribunal system because it lacks due process.

With women already comprising almost 60 per cent of student graduates, many are concerned males will be discouraged even further from entering university. "American universities have allowed feminist ideologues to set up such a strong anti-male environment that it is hardly surprising that many young men are now reluctant to put themselves at risk," says Janice Fiamengo, a University of Ottawa English professor who has long been speaking out about the feminist takeover of the US university system.

She's just published a book, *Sons of Feminism*, documenting the nightmare of false allegations, covert aggression and hostility young men face on campuses, particularly males who don't fit readily into the prevailing culture. "Men seen as outsiders, nerdy, shy young men who don't relate easily to women are quickly branded 'creepy' and are particularly at risk of false allegations," says Fiamengo.

In March 2016 a federal judge in Massachusetts ruled against Amherst College following legal action against the university by a young Chinese student, Michael Cheng, who was wrongly accused of sexual assault by a young woman who had performed oral sex on him when he was passed out drunk.

That's just one of many cases involving international students. In 2014 Colgate University in New York reported half of all students expelled for sexual misconduct were international students, yet these young men comprised only six per cent of the student body.

The vulnerability of young men who may be culturally less familiar with the prevailing social language should have Australian university administrations worried. Our cash-strapped university system is dependent on full fees paid by overseas students so it is natural that administrators quake at the knees at any threat to that lucrative market.

Remember all those vice-chancellors who went scurrying over to India to reassure potential students when racist attacks on Indian students in Melbourne hit the headlines? Pandering to feminist ideologues propagating scare stories will risk the reputation of Australian universities as a safe place for international students. Why would affluent families in India, China or Malaysia consider sending their daughters to study at such campuses, let alone their sons?

Soon we'll see the release of a million-dollar Australian Human Rights Commission survey, funded mainly by the University Commission, an exercise in advocacy research where stories of "survivors" will be used to illustrate the survey results.

Statistics pertaining to rape on campus will include behaviours such as staring and sexy comments, which will artificially inflate the statistics. Survey responders were self-selected and include those who were not students at the time of the alleged event. Universities are falling over each other already in responding to the anticipated frightening statistics, setting up a 24-hour hotline for rape survivors, sexual assault counsellors and compulsory sexual consent training for staff and students.

We are also seeing the first moves towards on-campus adjudication of such cases.

The US campus "rape frenzy" started with a survey showing one in four female students were sexually assaulted. Numerous books and articles have since shown the survey in question was totally flawed. A 2014 Bureau of Justice Statistics survey revealed about one in 40 US college students had been victims of rape or sexual assault and the rate had dropped by more than 50 per cent since 1997.

We've had our own dubious survey, from the National Union of Students, claiming 73 per cent of female students in Australia say they have experienced some form of sexual assault, harassment or unwanted sexual experience.

And as in America, the so-called documentary *The Hunting Ground* has been shown on campuses across the country as well as on the ABC. Hunting Ground Australia, the local organisation promoting the movie, provided $150,000 in seed funding for the HRCA survey. It boasts on its website that University of Sydney vice-chancellor Michael Spence was part of a group that included former sex discrimination commissioner Elizabeth Broderick and worked to orchestrate university screenings.

Australian universities seem to be engaged in a virtue-signalling contest to show they are all on board and have announced they expect a flood of "victims" to come forth following the AHRC findings. Next, we'll see pressure for the universities to deal with these cases themselves rather than rely on the criminal justice system to handle them. That's the whole point: feminists don't believe the police and the courts can handle these cases because not enough men are convicted.

Some time ago an editorial was published in *The Chicago Tribune* entitled "Campus Rape? Call the police" made the simple point that criminal law systems — civil authorities with no agenda to protect a university's reputation or to short-change an alleged victim or perpetrator — are best suited to mete out justice.

That's obviously true. Yet we find that in these "he says, she says" sexual consent cases involving alcohol-fuelled young men and women it is rare that juries convict young men, especially if there's a stream of text messages showing she was still keen on him after the alleged rape.

Margaret Cunneen SC is one of NSW's most senior crown prosecutors, best known for securing convictions in the Bilal Skaf-led gang rape cases in Sydney. She believes juries usually make sound decisions when they convict or decline to convict in date rape cases. "Juries won't find an accused man guilty in situations where the evidence discloses substantial gaps in a complainant's memory during which consent may well have been conveyed," she says. "It is a fundamental human right that a person accused of a crime, especially one as serious as sexual assault, can only be found guilty upon proof beyond reasonable doubt."

Cunneen takes issue with the view being promoted by the campus rape campaigners that sexual activity between two intoxicated young people must invariably be regarded as assault on the woman and totally the man's responsibility, as is apparently being taught in compulsory sexual consent courses being established on most Australian campuses.

A 2015 study published in *The New England Journal of Medicine* found teaching women to recognise dangerous situations and resist sexual coercion reduces the incidence of date rapes by almost 50 per cent. The study's author, University of Windsor psychologist Charlene Senn, said her program "increased women's ability to detect and interrupt men's behaviour at an early stage", hence avoiding the prolonged pressure that can result in sexual assault.

Yet naturally any notion of female agency is totally lacking from our campuses' feminist-driven consent courses.

According to the police reports collected by the NSW Bureau of Crime Statistics, university campuses are about 100 times safer than the rest of the community. There were 14 campus sexual assault reports to police between 2012 and last year compared with 24,498 across the state. So, comparing NSW university populations (students and staff) with total numbers in the state, this means people are 108 times likelier to be sexually assaulted across NSW than on one of the state's university campuses. National data is not available but there seems no reason that states would show much variation.

Cunneen says this data is readily available yet the campus rape campaigners are determined to play down official statistics by claiming students are reluctant to report sexual assault to the police. "While it is certainly true that prosecuting authorities and the courts, in the past, have not always dealt with these cases properly, now the entire criminal justice system is geared towards giving young complainants a compassionate and complete hearing," she says. "Why would highly educated, confident and privileged young women be less inclined to report sexual assault than women elsewhere? It doesn't make sense."

She's concerned that the AHRC and our universities are

participating in a deliberate effort to beat up the risk to young women on campuses by conflating the real incidence of rape or sexual assault with issues such as harassment, an unwanted stare, or a sexual joke.

"These things may in certain circumstances be confronting to a young woman, but they do not constitute the serious crime of sexual assault," she says.

Cunneen believes it is not in our universities' interest to take on the burden of adjudicating such cases, as happened in the US with such damaging results to the colleges' reputations and budgets. "Even worse, it risks stripping citizens of the fundamental protections to which we are all entitled under the rule of law," she says.

Yet already we see moves in that direction. RMIT University has proudly announced a system of "restorative justice" for rape victims that is expected to come forth in the following weeks. Normally, restorative justice programs bring together victims with perpetrators who have acknowledged their guilt but RMIT is not intending to involve the accused in the conciliation process but, rather, will make "some assessment of whether the allegation was plausible" before allowing victims to give voice to their experience of abuse and its impacts, according to Rob Hulls, director of the program.

And what of the accused young men? Says Fiamengo: "Even if these events are held in private, people talk. Imagine what it's like for a young man to discover his name is being blackened. Many young men emerge deeply scarred from being accused of such serious crimes without being given the opportunity to defend themselves."

But that's exactly what the campaigners are seeking. Nina

Funnell, a key figure in End Rape on Campus Australia, a lobby group promoting the campus rape campaign, makes it clear the goal is a "formal compliance mechanism" for sexual assault victims. She wrote on the news.com.au website of the need for universities to "discipline offenders (including staff who have raped students)".

Some of Fiamengo's powerful video blogs, The Fiamengo Files, document the risks to due process: "The resulting system of kangaroo courts is outrageously tilted in the accuser's favour with a far lower standard of proof than in the criminal system, the accused often not given details of accusations or allowed a lawyer or permitted to cross-examine his accuser, or able to provide evidence from email and text messages sent before or after the alleged encounter. It's a shocking abuse of power."

George Washington University law school professor John Banzhaf estimates the tribunal system is costing US universities more than $US700 million ($880m) a year, plus substantial costs from legal cases. Office of Civil Rights data shows across a five-year period the number of sex-related complaints increased sixfold, from 391 in 2010 to 2354 in 2014. This month campus administrators have been meeting Trump officials complaining they cannot afford to maintain this costly exercise.

And still the feminist campaigners are not satisfied. Although accused students are likeliest to sue universities, almost a quarter of the most recent cases were alleged victims who felt they weren't given a fair hearing, according to Stop Abusive and Violent Environments, which monitors all such cases.

This month feminists have been meeting with Trump's people complaining the system doesn't go far enough in supporting victims.

Just after Columbia University received its costly rap over the knuckles for pandering to the mattress girl, in Australia we saw campus "rape survivors" demonstrating outside federal parliament, claiming there was an epidemic of rape on Australian campuses and carrying mattresses to make their point.

It shows the risks our university system is taking in playing to the hands of insatiable extremists.

CHAPTER 14

Celebrating our safe universities — bad news for feminists

First published 2017

The first week in August 2017 was a very big week for Australian Universities. Across the country they had been preparing for a flood of sexual assault victims to come forward following the release of the Human Rights Commission's trumped-up survey into the rape crisis on our campuses.

Universities embarked on endless virtue-signalling in anticipation of bad tidings. Vice Chancellors boasted of spending millions on a 24-hour national hot line, sexual assault counsellors and compulsory sexual consent courses for staff and students.

Then, hilariously, came the release of the survey results and the emperor was revealed quite naked. The survey found only 1.6 per cent of students reported being sexually assaulted on campus over a two-year period from 2015-2016 — the yearly figures were too small to report. This was using a broad definition which included being "tricked into sexual acts against their will". Most of the students didn't report the sexual assaults either because they didn't feel it was serious enough (40 per cent), or because they did not need any help (another 40 per cent).

All the million-dollar survey came up with was a high incidence of low-level harassment — mainly staring and sexual jokes or comments. And a greater proportion of males than females said they'd experienced the more serious forms of harassment like unwelcome touching or inappropriate physical contact.

So, it turned out there was no rape crisis at all, although clearly it's a good idea for this harassment to be discouraged. Writing prior to the release, I predicted this good news would be totally buried in the massive media blitz, particularly on Fairfax and the ABC who have bought into the rape crisis narrative. And that's just what happened. Current affairs programmes, radio shows and journalists everywhere trotted out horrific stories from submissions from alleged rape "victims" describing their experiences — all solicited by the Commission. The problem is they are not rape "victims". They are accusers whose stories have never been tested in court. Mainly date rape cases — he-said, she-said stories revolving around sexual consent. Such cases often don't result in convictions because juries won't convict young men of these very serious crimes unless there is clear evidence of their guilt.

That's what led to the whole concocted campaign. Feminists want these young men convicted and are brow-beating universities to side-step the criminal justice system and ensure more males are punished.

In the week preceding the release of the survey results I sent out a series of questions to Vice Chancellors across the country asking why they are risking the reputation of Australian universities as a safe place for international students? Universities had been given the survey results well in advance of the release, so they were all fully aware that there was no real cause for concern, yet still they chose to pander to the feminist lobby rather than celebrate our safe universities.

Privately university officials will acknowledge they are concerned that this scare campaign may bite the hand that feeds them. Australia's proportion of full-fee paying foreign students is triple the international average. Yet publicly they run for cover. It was hilarious reading the weasel words concocted by university media units to try to avoid addressing the issue in their responses to me. Not one responded directly to my questions about the risk to the overseas student market.

"Our strong safety record is cited by 93 per cent of our international students as a key reason why they chose Australia," admitted Belinda Robinson, CEO of Universities Australia but then artfully suggested this was the reason to "address unacceptable behaviours head on." I'm told Robinson has acknowledged to campus officials that they tread a difficult line in sustaining this argument.

Many watching what's happening are bewildered by our intellectual elite's capitulation to this feminist propaganda campaign. In this globalised world it is impossible to believe that our university administrators are not aware of the troubles facing American universities battling large numbers of Federal Court law suits over young men who were unfairly treated by campus tribunals following accusations of sexual assault. Yet still our universities lack the gumption to stand up to the small numbers of feminist activists and resist following down the same path.

The real concern is not only frightening off the families of potential full-fee paying young women who might choose to study here. There's also the risk we will deter young men nervous they could be falsely accused of such crimes. I have written before that nerdy young outsiders are particularly likely to find themselves in this situation — American universities have made large payouts to wrongly accused young Asian men.

Deepika Narayan Bhardwaj, an Indian journalist and documentary filmmaker based in Gururgram, believes that the current rape culture campaign will push Australia further down the preferred list of countries for higher education for Indian parents considering our country for either daughters or sons.

Bhardwaj describes what happened in an Indian city called Rohtak in Haryana which attracted huge publicity a few years ago over alleged sexual attacks on women which ultimately turned out to be false. "The media hysteria had a huge impact on psyche of parents considering choosing the prestigious institute IIM Rohtak for their daughters." In 2013 equal numbers of males and females were studying at the Institute but by 2015, there were just 14 women and 150 men.

"Indian parents will be extremely hesitant of sending their daughters to Australia for higher education if universities claim such high rates of sexual assault," says Bhardwaj, adding that "parents will also be concerned about sons being at risk of false allegations." Her most recent documentary, *Martyrs of Marriage*, concerns the misuse of dowry laws to persecute men and their families. "I know all about how easy it is for men to have their lives ruined by this type of feminist campaign," she says.

CHAPTER 15

Yes, no, maybe – teaching the truth about sexual consent

First published 2017

Candice Jackson, a top Trump Education official, hit the headlines last year by claiming 90 per cent of sexual assault claims on campuses involve couples who are both drunk. Judging from recent media reporting of our own campus rape crisis the same might be true here.

"I didn't think I could even walk by myself. I think I knew what was going to happen but I was so drunk that I just like went along with it," said Tasmanian University student Lorna Nilssen appearing on the ABC's *7.30 Report* the night the Human Rights Commission survey was released, which the programme claimed showed alarming levels of assault and harassment.

The same programme featured ANU law student Freya Willis alleging she was raped by a fellow student at a campus event. "We were both quite intoxicated. I was much more intoxicated than he was and he separated me from my friends and we went back to a room where we were both staying and that's where it happened."

So many stories of drunken young women being taken advantage of — often by equally drunk young men. There were horrific tales of women falling victim to groups of men, having their drinks spiked or falling into the hands of serial predators. These are the cases highlighted by media promoting the feminist position that all sexual activity involving an intoxicated woman is sexual assault as she cannot give consent. And that discouraging female students from drinking risks blaming the victim and shaming such women into not seeking help.

Yet that's only part of the story as shown in an *Insight* television programme made by SBS focussing on sexual consent. The then President of the Law Society of NSW, Pauline Wright, talked about a boyfriend and girlfriend out on a date. They've had a few drinks, they regularly have sex. "They both get drunk, they go home and the usual thing for them would be to have sex. The girl might be saying yes but perhaps the next day thinks that was wrong." Maybe they split up the next day, maybe there was reason for the girl to redefine her experience, suggested Wright. "It bothers me that because she was drunk the law might say that she didn't have the capacity to say yes. That becomes really difficult for a young man."

Very difficult, because as Candice Jackson pointed out, these regret-sex incidents can easily end up with a young man being charged with sexual assault, even many months later.

Wright also described a hypothetical first date where the girl thinks she doesn't want to have sex but then they have too much to drink and do have sex. "The next morning, he doesn't call, he doesn't ring, she feels humiliated. Is that then a sexual assault?" she asked.

Certainly most juries wouldn't think so. They rarely convict in the date rape cases involving contradictory he-says, she-says evidence which constitute the bulk of campus rape allegations. That's why the activists are pressuring universities to getting involved in such cases, promoting their simple narrative of men as perpetrators and women victims.

Last year the University of Canberra website included a Party Safe page advising students to "pace yourself if you are drinking and stay alert. When you are drunk or using drugs, you are more likely to do things you normally wouldn't do when you are sober." This advice was attacked by activist Nina Funnell on abc.net.au who denounced universities for still teaching "don't get raped" rather than "don't rape". The advice was promptly removed from the Party Safe page.

"Don't get raped" was conspicuous by its absence in the universities' virtue-signalling activity following the 2017 release of the HRC data. Our universities strenuously ignored the fact that the HRC data showed mainly good news — thankfully small figures for sexual assault, 1.6 per cent over two years, and the harassment was mainly unwanted staring, which most of the women dismissed as not serious or not requiring help.

Yet most of our media choose to misrepresent the figures and promote the fake news rape narrative and all our universities fell into line and funded measures including online sexual consent courses which put the onus for preventing sexual assault squarely on the shoulders of young men.

These online consent courses are intriguing. Most are adapted from an Epigeum course constructed by proud feminists including Californian consultant Alan Berkowitz — a man who boasts of his ongoing battle against "unconscious sexism and male privilege". The programme pretends to be gender-neutral and includes case histories involving some gay couples and a few female perpetrators such as a woman who ponders going down on her sleeping partner and is later congratulated for restraining herself. But the programme is mainly pitched at teaching young men to decipher women's messages regarding consent:

"Verbal consent can be given directly in loads of different ways. Your partner may say things like: 'That feels good. Do it this way. Fuck me. YES! More! Keep going. Don't stop!'

"Always stop if you hear your partner say: 'No. I don't know. I'm not sure. Not now. I'm worried. Stop. Get off! Fuck off! Don't do that. Ouch. Not again. Do I have to?'"

What's really odd is the person sending these messages is so rarely directly addressed in the programme. It's assumed the women are inert. They are like pot plants on a gardening show teaching people how do determine if the plant has dried out. Are the leaves wilting? Flowers dropping off? Insert fingers into the soil to test for dampness.

RMIT social justice professor Nicola Henry, an expert adviser to Epigeum, boasts on video that their courses focus on perpetrators and bystanders rather than victims. These "don't rape" courses have no interest in teaching women to take proper ownership of the decision-making process that leads to a yes or no, let alone encouraging them to express those wishes clearly rather than keep men guessing.

Back in the 1990s I made a programme on sexual consent — *Yes, No, Maybe* — as a guest reporter on *Four Corners*. I had no trouble finding women who acknowledged they deliberately drink to avoid making decisions around consent. Women who admitted to playing games where they said no but wanted men to push through that resistance — a popular themes in hugely popular bodice ripper novels.

None of these complexities are addressed in the sexual consent programmes. The gender-neutral course contains only small nuggets of advice which even arguably target women: "You always have the right to change your mind about any kind of sexual activity — even right before or during sex." And "If someone forces (or tries to force) you to do something sexual that you don't want to do, remember that it's never your fault and it's not okay."

No one would deny the importance of the "don't rape" message — sexual assault is rightly a very serious criminal offence. And it makes sense to change the male culture so bystanders are empowered to intervene when women are being harassed or attacked. Yet it's shocking that feminists have persuaded our universities to absolve women of all responsibility for behaving sensibly and not putting themselves in harm's way.

Camille Paglia, speaking in 2016 at a London-based Battle of Ideas, pointed out that back in the 1960s women fought against women being locked up at night in single sex dormitories. "We are the ones who said, 'Get out of our private lives.' The colleges said, 'No, the world is dangerous. We must protect you against rape.'"

And the response to from Paglia's generation of women? "Give us the freedom to risk rape. That is true adulthood," said Paglia.

Evidence suggests that the current revival of paternalistic attitudes towards women won't protect them. An article, *Efficacy of a Sexual Assault Resistance Program for University*

Women, published in the *New England Journal of Medicine* two years ago showed the passive-woman sexual consent programmes aren't working. "Most campuses use programmes that have never been formally evaluated or have not proved to be effective in reducing the incidence of sexual assault," said the leading author, Canadian sociology professor Charlene Senn spelling out disappointing results for programmes similar to those being introduced in Australia.

As mentioned in chapter 13, Senn's resistance program teaches women to recognise dangerous situations and resist sexual coercion, reportedly reducing the incidence of date rapes by almost 50 per cent. According to Senn, rape resistance is about teaching women how to say "no earlier and more effectively", helping them to be "more confident and sure of their own desires" and "get past emotional roadblocks to resist unwanted sexual behaviour."

It sounds promising, although Senn, who describes herself as a "feminist activist", defines sexual assault to including having sex because "you feared you'd lose your relationship if you didn't." And the professor is dead against telling women to let fear restrict their lives: "If you are drinking 12 drinks, there's no risk of rape unless there's someone around who's willing to rape. The risk is not in the alcohol."

This argument is insulting to women and unfair to men suggests Canadian men's rights activist and YouTube vlogger, Karen Straughan: "In the feminist narrative regarding drunkenness and sex only men retain agency. Women are reduced to infantilised objects without the capacity for volition. She was drunk. Enough said. She bears no responsibility. Yet the drunken man's identical decision is subject to heightened scrutiny. He's seen as instigating the entire thing, and his drunkenness does not absolve him of responsibility, but in effect, makes him more morally culpable."

Isn't it odd that we encourage female responsibility in other aspects of life such as persuading young women not to drink and drive? They know they'll face the consequences if they get plastered, drive and kill a pedestrian. Being drunk isn't an excuse if they stab a homeless man to death, or molest a child. Where's the logic in women not being in any way accountable if they get drunk and make stupid decisions exposing themselves to sexual harm?

This is a hot button issue for our drug and alcohol organisations who readily supply international data showing the clear link between intoxication and risk of sexual assault. "It's well known that both victims and perpetrators of assaults and sexual assault have often been drinking prior to the event but this is largely ignored in the public debate," says Michael Thorn, CEO of the Foundation for Alcohol Research and Education. Thorn is frustrated that data on drinking by both victims and perpetrators of violence is not being systematically collected or reported and he suggests the issue may well be "being downplayed for ideological reasons".

The issue is critical to properly tackling sexual assault on campuses, according to Peter Miller, professor of Violence Prevention and Addiction Studies at Deakin University: "One of the key issues to address is the high levels of drug and alcohol consumption among university students, both male and female. We need to teach male and female students to stay sober enough to make good decisions around sexual consent."

Advice to young women on how not to get raped? Given the

grip the feminists have on our university that's just not going to happen.

CHAPTER 16

Lily-livered universities – targeting young men

First published 2016

What a marvellously McCarthyesque moment. The ABC's *The 7.30 Report* featured a shame-faced former collaborator admitted to his inquisitors that he now saw the error of his ways. James Dunn, a big burly country boy who was then treasurer of Baxter College at the University of NSW, acknowledged that the previous year he had been involved in the College's annual Boys Night Out activities where they chanted "appalling" songs.

Now that furious students are protesting about these "disgusting songs which glorify rape", he claimed he had seen the light. "I'm condemning my own actions at this time," he blushingly disclosed.

And the lyrics of the song *The 7.30 Report* described as "hideous"?

"I wish that all the ladies were buns in the oven
And if I was a baker
I'd cream them by the dozen"

Crude? Yes, bawdy and lusty but also a typical drinking song, the type of vulgar sexual ditty that has been part of our culture since well before Chaucer's time. I vividly remember the girls at my daughter's school romping through a performance of *The Canterbury Tales* which include the memorable lines:

> *And prively he caughte hire by the queynte,*
> *And seyde, 'Y-wis, but if ich have my wille,*
> *For derne love of thee, lemman, I spille.'*

Not so very different. But then, these female fascists would probably like to ban Chaucer too. The Baxter drinking song speaks not of rape but of men's desire for sex — an urge which some feminist lobby groups appear to regard as thoroughly reprehensible. Here's Jocelyn Dradakis, Student Rep on the UNSW Council: "It shows lyrics that glorify acts of rape … It's completely revolting that this kind of behaviour has been allowed to take place in the college."

Amazingly, amongst the lyrics sung by students and replayed on *The 7.30 Report* was this little gem: "I'd like to tickle their clitoris."

Rape culture? On the contrary. Isn't this exactly what we women have long been asking for?

How it is possible that this nonsense was the leading story on our ABC's top current affairs program?

The most depressing aspect of this whole affair was that the lobbyists persuaded the university administration to cave in to their strident demands that such songs be verboten. The University released a statement saying it was "appalled by the sexist and demeaning attitudes and behaviours" and had "taken steps to ensure that incidents of this kind do not occur again."

Surely our intellectual elite should have the guts to stand up to these crazy grievance-mongers. Ok, young men's right to sing a dirty ditty isn't actually a noble cause. But there are important issues at stake in the inability of university authorities to withstand such silly, vexatious campaigns.

We've also seen the University of Sydney Union give into protests and decide that the 88-year-old Catholic Society at the university should face deregistration on the grounds that it is discriminatory to require senior members to be Catholic — that's despite the Union funding a "women's room" and a Koori Centre for indigenous students.

Luckily overseas we do see some universities standing up to this type of bullying. Late 2015 British columnist James Delingpole wrote a marvelous column in response to controversy at Oriel College at Oxford regarding student demands to remove a statue of Cecil Rhodes, British imperial hero and founder of the Rhodes scholarship. Delingspole penned the letter he wished Oriel College had sent to the black South African student demonstrator. It included some memorable statements:

"Of course, you are perfectly within your rights to squander your time at Oxford on silly, vexatious, single-issue political campaigns ... We are well used to seeing undergraduates — or, in your case — postgraduates, making idiots of themselves. Just don't expect us to indulge your idiocy, let alone genuflect before it. You may be black — "BME[45]" as the grisly modern terminology has it — but we are colour-blind.

"We do not discriminate over sex, race, colour or creed. We do, however, discriminate according to intellect. That means, inter alia, that when our undergrads or postgrads come up with fatuous ideas, we don't pat them on the back, give them a red rosette and say: 'Ooh, you're black and you come from

South Africa. What a clever chap you are!'

"No. We prefer to see the quality of those ideas tested in the crucible of public debate. That's another key part of the Oxford intellectual tradition, you see: you can argue any damn thing you like but you need to be able to justify it with facts and logic — otherwise your idea is worthless."

Oxford stuck to their guns, the statues remain at Oriel College. How wonderful it would be if Australian universities showed this sort of gumption.

Where's the logic in claiming a song about tickling the clitoris contributes to the rape culture? A trivial issue, perhaps, but symptomatic of a wider malaise.

CHAPTER 17

Feminist capture of key institutions

First published 2017

Now Australian universities have caved to feminist pressure and are getting involved in the messy business of determining which story to believe in a date rape case involving two students. One Sydney university, UTS, has introduced special committees to judge other students accused of sexual assault or harassment. These extra-judicial panels comprising students and some staff members will examine evidence, conduct interrogations and recommend punishments — expulsion from the universities or withholding of degrees. How extraordinary that the university is foolishly blundering into legal territory potentially undermining proper process in what could be serious criminal matters.

Many of our universities have sensibly resisted this course, choosing instead to provide support and advice for students claiming to be rape victims but, where possible, referring such cases on to the police. But there are exceptions — like the University of Adelaide, for instance, which now has a Student Behaviour and Conduct Committee, comprised of university staff, charged with investigating sexual harassment and assault cases, making decisions ("on the balance of probabilities") as to whether the misconduct occurred and even determining appropriate outcomes.

The rashness of the university's decision to take this approach has been amply demonstrated over the past eight months by a case involving a PhD student accused of sexual assault by a fellow student which was investigated by the committee. The student — I'll call him "David" — received a series of emails trying to persuade him to attend meetings with the committee, despite being given no details of the accusation, nor any advice as to his own legal standing. Acting upon advice from a criminal lawyer, for months David resisted interrogation by the committee and demanded full details of the accusation. The committee apparently had the power to stop David being awarded his degree, which added considerably to his stress.

Then suddenly the University's general counsel stepped in and immediately back-peddled, assuring David that he too should be afforded procedural fairness and offering him support services. The lawyer finally presented David with a full statement from the accuser but also gave proper legal advice that he was under no obligation to respond. His version of events differed substantially from hers, as he explained in correspondence with the university lawyer, supplying social media messages to support some of his assertions.

The whole business came to an end when the university declared they were dropping the case. David was awarded his PhD and with great relief left the university. I've interviewed him about his ordeal for a YouTube video[46].

None of this should come as a surprise, even though you may have thought the campus feminists would have given up after their fake rape crisis proved such a fizzer. We've seen

where this leads in the US where Trump is winding back
the college tribunal system with universities facing massive
legal costs from falsely accused students and their families.
Recently 130 leading American law professors and legal experts
signed an open letter[47] condemning the use of investigative
"victim-centred" practices subverting the objective collection
and presentation of evidence in such sexual assault cases,
particularly on campuses.

Shocking evidence emerged of a report, funded by the US
Department of Justice and produced by a group called "End
Violence Against Women" which calls on police investigations
and personnel conducting investigations to "work for a
successful prosecution" — meaning, obtain a conviction by
using a number of unethical strategies. These include: making
the complainant "appear more innocent"; "not writing a
detailed report" to minimise the possibility of inconsistent
or conflicting accounts; and writing the report in such a
way that the incident does "not look like a consensual sexual
experience." The influence of this group's "Start by Believing"
campaign underpins many of the miscarriages of justice cases
now rebounding on the universities[48].

Meanwhile Britain has been rocked by the collapse of
a series of rape trials due to deliberate withholding of key
evidence by prosecutors. Alison Saunders, the former Director
of Public Prosecutions has recently stepped down, all current
rape and serious sexual assault cases are currently being
reviewed, and, according to *The Times*, Metropolitan Police
were now ditching the practice of "believing all victims."

The BBC reported that over the past two years there's been
a 70 per cent in the number of prosecutions in England and

Wales that had collapsed because of a failure by police or prosecutors to disclose evidence. Last year, 916 people had charges dropped over a failure to disclose evidence — up from 537 in 2014-15.

One notorious example involved the trial of Liam Allan, who faced 12 counts of rape and sexual assault. Allan's trial was halted, and charges dropped when it emerged evidence on a computer disc — which police had looked through — showed messages from the alleged victim pestering him for "casual sex". Feminists have long argued that such social media messages should be withheld from rape trials — evidence which often helps the accused. Clearly Britain's public prosecutors have been doing just that.

But tilting of the law in rape cases is only part of the story. As I mentioned in the introduction to this book, Rob Tiller, an experienced relationship counsellor was recently forced out of Relationships Australia in Western Australia for posting on his Facebook page an article I'd written giving the true facts about domestic violence — see chapter 7. Here is a government-funded counselling body which proudly proclaims their domestic violence policies are based on a "feminist analysis of gender power relations" — an analysis which denies women's role in family violence and paints men as the only real perpetrators. Somehow the managers of this notoriously male-hostile organisation felt entitled to summarily dismiss this respected counsellor for exposing his own experience counselling both violent men and women.

Tiller's unfair dismissal highlighted the efforts being made by key organisations in Australia to silence those who publicly challenge the feminist dogma they are promoting. It attracted widespread publicity, over $11,000 was raised through crowd-funding to support Tiller's legal and re-establishment costs. We heard stories from across the country of other people who had been forced out of organisations for challenging the distorted feminist line on domestic violence.

It is quite scandalous that such government-funded bodies feel entitled to promote dangerous ideology rather than properly address the real causes of domestic violence and provide help to all its victims. Relationships Australia WA overplayed its hand in assuming Tiller would go quietly but hopefully the whole sorry episode will serve to inspire more people to speak out about the feminist capture of so many of our organisations and professional bodies.

There are other signs of a break-through. Recently there was a successful protest against feminist journalist Clementine Ford's hateful attacks on men. The Fairfax columnist, who regularly tweets hateful comments like, "Kill all men," and "All men are scum and must die", was asked by the charity Lifeline to speak at a domestic violence forum.

This ill-considered move by the organisation led to a protest campaign which pointed out that Lifeline claims to support both men and women experiencing emotional distress and it is hardly appropriate to include such a biased person in their programme. Nearly 15,000 signed a protest petition[49] and the event was cancelled.[50] "Lifeline does not want to do anything that could create division in the community," said the charity's spokesperson.

Another charity organisation, Mission Australia, launched a homeless campaign featuring a terrified woman and her child escaping a violent man. I organised a change.com petition[51] protesting this one-sided campaign, pointing out that while everyone would acknowledge the importance of providing shelter for women and their children in such frightening circumstances that is only part of the story.

The petition included data showing children are more likely to be killed by their mothers — in Australia women account for 52 per cent of child homicides according to the Australian Institute of Criminology. It must be acknowledged that this is, at least in part, due to women spending more time with children. But the fact remains that many mothers do abuse their children and that is never mentioned in domestic violence debates.

As I explained, it is very difficult to obtain proper data about who abuses children. In 2009, Professor Woods at the University of Western Sydney published a fascinating graph[52] which very clearly showed disproportionate abuse by mothers of their children, compared to fathers. The information for this graph had been obtained using a Freedom of Information request from the West Australian Department for Child Protection. Since then no equivalent state departments have been willing to release this type of gender breakdown.

Mission Australia knows all too well that domestic violence involves violent women as well as men. Their own website points out that "research has been around for 20 years showing that men are affected by domestic violence." So here we have a major charity cynically exploiting our natural sympathy for women and children — and ignoring the vital fact that most homeless people are actually men not women. The 2016 Census showed men are 66 per cent of homeless people sleeping rough in Australia.

Thousands signed the petition, and many wrote letters of protest to Mission Australia senior executives and board members. It led to a series of meetings between Paul Toomey, CEO of the organisation and men's group leaders, including male victims of domestic violence. After talking to Toomey I was hopeful that he'd understood how offensive their campaign was to male victims of violence. He gave me to understand he would be taking measures to rectify the situation. I offered to circulate a statement to this effect and this is what he sent through:

"We know that all members of households can be victims of DFV, and that in complex violent situations family members can be both victims and perpetrators. As a result DFV drives homelessness as men, women and children seek to escape violence, frequently with nowhere to go. Our appeals seek to reflect this, and continue to be informed by our experience at the front line of homelessness services."

What appalling weasel words. Further evidence that organisations like Mission Australia are so captured by the feminist narrative that they wilfully refuse to see the wood for the trees.

SECTION FOUR

Men and sex

CHAPTER 18

The politics of desire – sexual obligation in marriage

First published 2003

On 20 July 1969, Neil Armstrong, the commander of Apollo 11, became the first person to set foot on the moon. His first words — "That's one small step for man, one giant leap for mankind" — became part of history, televised to earth and heard by millions. But just before he re-entered the lunar module, he added an enigmatic comment: "Good Luck, Mr Gorsky".

Many people at NASA thought it was a casual remark concerning some rival Soviet cosmonaut, but a check revealed there was no Gorsky in either the Russian or American space programs. Over the years, many people questioned Armstrong about what he meant, but he always just smiled. Then, on 5 July 1995 in Tampa, Florida, a reporter again raised the question and this time Armstrong responded; it seemed that Mr Gorsky had died and so Armstrong felt he could finally answer. He explained that, in 1938, when he was a kid in a small Midwest town, he was playing baseball with a friend in his backyard. The ball was hit over the fence and landed in the yard of the neighbours, the Gorskys, by their bedroom windows. As Armstrong bent down to pick up the ball, he heard Mrs Gorsky shouting at Mr Gorsky. "Sex! You want sex?! You'll get sex when the kid next door walks on the moon!"

It's a great story but, sadly, only an urban legend — one which regularly does the rounds on the Internet. Yet the world is now full of Mrs Gorskys — women who aren't interested in sex but feel absolutely entitled to shut up shop, denying their partners any sexual contact. And yes, there are also men who behave similarly. The older man who is concerned about erections may prefer to avoid sex rather than risk failure, leaving his partner feeling equally rejected and unwanted. But the Mrs Gorsky problem is the one filling the waiting rooms of sex therapists everywhere.

I've always known this. From the time I started working as a sex therapist back in the early 1970s, people have been talking to me about their sex lives. What I have heard most about most is the business of negotiating the sex supply. How do couples deal with the strain of the man wishing and hoping while all she longs for is the bliss of uninterrupted sleep? It's a night-time drama being played out in bedrooms across the nation, the source of great tension and unhappiness.

But this drama is usually a silent movie, with couples rarely talking about the subtle negotiation that goes on between them. His calculations: "What if I …? Will she then …?" Her tactics: dropping her book as he appears at the bedroom door and feigning sleep; staying up late in the hope that he'll doze off. Tensions. Resentment. Guilt.

That's what my 2009 book, *The Sex Diaries*, was all about. Through radio interviews and magazine articles, I recruited ninety-eight couples to spend six to nine months keeping diaries for me, writing about their daily negotiations over sex.

They were couples of all ages, from 20-year-old students to people in their seventies who have been married over forty years — young couples at the start of their relationships; pregnant women; couples caught up in the exhaustion of young families; women who want more sex than their husbands and women who'd live happily without it; older couples dealing with health issues like prostate surgery and arthritis. Some wrote every day for months — one man ended up providing over seventy pages of details of his love-life — while others provided only brief weekly summaries.

The diaries revealed some intriguing stories. There was the man who reported making a statement he really regrets. Fed up with always having to initiate sex, he turned to his wife and said, "I'll make no more advances until you ask me." He contacted me eight years later and they hadn't had sex since. Another couple had kept a sex diary for 23 years, tracking not only their sexual frequency but number of orgasms. Yes, there were lusty couples amongst my diaries, who wrote at length about how they maintain their passion over thirty or forty years. But there was also the Canberra man whose wife has an obsessive-compulsive disorder and who likes everything to have its time and place. They make love every Sunday morning at 9.15am.

But, as I expected the burning issue which emerged was the sex-starved men. Every day I received page after page of eloquent, often immensely sad diary material, as men grasped the opportunity to talk about what quickly emerged as being a mighty emotional issue for them. Many men feel duped, disappointed, in despair at finding themselves spending their lives begging for sex from their loved partners. They are stunned to find their needs so totally ignored. It often poured out in a howl of rage and disappointment. Here's Andrew from Queanbeyan, 41:

"I am totally at a loss as to what to do, I do love her and I think she loves me but I cannot live like a monk. I have deliberately tried not to mention sex much at all but now I am so frustrated I don't know what to do. I am at breaking point. I cannot and will not continue on like this. I refuse to go through life begging."

Lack of sexual desire is the number one sexual problem plaguing women today. Over half (55 per cent) of all women experience lack of desire according to The Sex in Australia Survey[53], a research project involving nearly 20,000 participants, which makes it one of the largest sex studies ever completed.

I've combed all available research to attempt to discover why it is that women's libido should be so much less robust than that of men. There's every reason to believe the problem is hard-wired. Many believe that women's low drive is linked to their low level of testosterone; women have ten to twenty times less of this vital hormone than men.

Evolutionary psychologists argue mothers aren't meant to be bonking all the time so their distractible libidos ensure they care for their young. And the reason so many women start off with strong drives and then appear to lose interest seems to be due to the brain chemistry associated with the early "in-love" phase of relationships, which, for a few years at best, pours firelighters on what I call the "damp wood" that is normal female libido — easily distracted, hard to light and easily wrapped up in all the garbage of the day. The testosterone-driven male is far more likely to be blessed with an eternal flame.

None of this is particularly controversial but where I knew I would run into trouble with this book was my proposed solutions — which included the notion that the low desire partner should sometimes "just do it." Now my book made it clear this is an equal opportunity measure — men too should just do it if they are the ones constantly rejecting their partners. Yes, yes, I realise there are sometimes anatomical constraints in the case of men with failing equipment but they still have hands, for heaven's sake. And lips and the capacity to make love to a woman in all manner of ways that still leave her feeling desired and desirable. These days there are also the miracle cures for failing erections, provided a man is willing to face the issue.

I should point out I didn't invent the "just do it" idea. The use of the Nike slogan comes from a well-known American sex therapist, Michele Weiner Davis, who wrote very sensibly about the problem of mismatched desire. She argues desire is a decision — you can't just wait for it to come, you have to make it happen. So Weiner Davis posed the revolutionary idea that there's no point worrying about the reasons why women aren't interested in sex — there'll always be plenty of them: squalling infants, stress, tiredness, irritation that he won't help with the housework. "Knowing why you are not so interested in sex won't boost your desire one bit. Doing something about it will," she wrote.

Critical to this argument is research by Professor Rosemary Basson from British Columbia which has shown that many women do experience arousal and orgasm if they have sex without any prior desire. Basson found that women in long-term relationships may rarely think of sex or experience a spontaneous hunger for sexual activity. So, when they do have sex, they are seeking emotional closeness or intimacy with their partners or responding to his overtures, rather than being prompted by their own desire. But even though they may not be "in the mood" to start off with, once they start making love, these women often feel sexual sensations building, desire may start to click in and then they'll want to continue. The result is that they experience sexual pleasure and perhaps orgasm. Provided there's a "willingness to be receptive", the rest follows, advised Basson.

The suggestion that women — and men too — should sometimes have sex when they are not in the mood runs into a massive ideological roadblock. Women's right to say "no" has been enshrined in our cultural history for nearly fifty years. It was one of the outstanding achievements of the women's movement to outlaw rape in marriage and teach women to resist unwanted advances. Neil Armstrong stepped onto the moon just at the time when women's sexual rights were becoming a rallying cry. Women must no longer act as spittoons for men, preached Germaine Greer, calling for an end to women's sexual subjugation. After all those years of thinking of England, now women could reclaim their bodies for their own pleasure, and that meant only having sex when they felt like it.

The work of sex researchers added force to the argument. Female desire must come first, pronounced New York sex therapist Helen Kaplan, as she adapted sex researchers Masters and Johnson's famous 1966 model of sexual pleasure to make desire the prerequisite for all that followed. Without desire there was no arousal, no pleasure, the experts pronounced, and feminists applauded. It became a total no-no to ever suggest that women should be pressured into sex. The belief was that sex must wait until women are well and truly in the mood.

But that was where we went wrong. I'm arguing that the assumption that women need to want sex to enjoy it has proved a really damaging sexual idea, one that has wrought havoc in relationships for the past forty years. The sex diaries showed that so very clearly, revealing that many women firmly believe that unless they feel like having sex, they can't possibly make love. And the men know that all too well. Many work hard to try to kindle the flame of desire in their partners, knowing that without this they will run into a brick wall of rejection. But it rarely works and the couple's sexual frequency falls hostage to women's weak libido. The result is that sex becomes a battleground as sad, rejected men rightly complain when physical intimacy and the consequent emotional connection fall by the wayside.

It was obvious that challenging these ideological assumptions about sex was bound to raise hackles. "Fuck you Bettina Arndt!" was the charming beginning to a blog responding to my writing about the "just do it" idea. The blog writer, "blue milk", felt I was suggesting that we shouldn't worry about why women aren't interested in sex anymore, but "just pressure them into it by threatening the future happiness of their families and pretty soon their libido will be bouncing right back". This chat site quickly filled with the comments of equally angry women. "It sickens me that after so many YEARS of feminism we are still arguing [for] the most basic of rights — the right for a woman to make decisions about her own body," one hissed.

There's been plenty of hissing since my book was published. Angry blogs are still appearing. My favourite is entitled "Bettina Arndt — Rape Cheerleader!" Many of my critics clearly haven't read the book and chose to interpret the "just do it" idea as a return to the bad old days of women suffering through unwanted sex.

Virginia Haussegger in *The Canberra Times* was determined to see my argument as simply lie back and think of England. "The notion of women passively submitting to uninspiring sex is an archaic and unforgivable suggestion that takes us back to some very dark old days indeed … For Arndt to suggest that women should simply put out, in order to keep a marriage alive, is a frightening, but timely, reminder of why we clearly need a sexual revolution," she wrote.

But while newspaper columnists and bloggists bleat, I've been swamped with mail from men and women who understand what I am trying to say and agree with it.

"Thank you for lifting the lid on this unspoken, sad fact of life that diminishes many of our marriages. I am a 30-year-old wife and mother … It is with great sadness that my husband and I have watched as a trench has grown between us on account of the lack of sex in our relationship…We have finally got to a point where we realise we have been leading parallel lives and that things have to change. In my own bumbling way, I have come to understand that the onus is on me to instigate change in our relationship. My husband will never demand sex from me yet I have the choice to just do it and to take the steps that I know will reap huge benefits for our relationship and our marriage."

*"I just want to thank you for your new book about men
and women's differing libidos! My husband and I have had
mismatched libidos for years and it was a relief to know that
we are not alone with this. Funnily enough, just before reading
about your book in the paper I had come to the agreement with
my husband (completely voluntarily) that I was going to make a
greater effort, to break the horrible dynamic of pursuit/resistance
we had got stuck in. After reading about your book, I really knew
that we were on the right track. Our relationship has improved
by a great quantum leap and our home is now a much more
relaxed environment."*

I was never suggesting women should suffer through
unwanted sex — simply that in a loving relationship it is
important not to leave one's partner feeling constantly unwanted
and undesirable. "Just do it" doesn't always mean bonking. It is
possible to sometimes just give pleasure. And Basson's research
is important in raising the possibility of pleasure in sex without
prior desire, a notion well worth exploring.

Clearly this is a complex issue — as the "just do it" chapter
shows. Many of my diarists explored this as a "solution" to the
problem of mismatched desire, with varying degrees of success
— some found it helped, others hated the idea. The whole idea
of my diaries was to explore this complexity and encourage
couples struggling with these issues to see they are not alone.
It was heartening to learn many people who actually read the
book got that message, despite the flack I received.

I received this intriguing letter from a man responding to
the "just do it" section in the book. *"The flow of the first part of
the book led me down an orderly path to a solution, Just Do It.
Emotionally I was starting to get my bold highlighters out and*

start making very large placards 'Bettina for Nobel Peace Prize'
and then you waded in the middle road of understanding both
sides — all sides actually. The murky world of reality sunk in as I
read on. It is said we — guys — seek to problem solve, 'fix things,'
so the simple JUST DO IT is such a beautiful solution. But then
you bugger it up with other points of view, other experiences,
considerations, failures. Why couldn't it remain a nice fresh
crisp answer, without doubt and not open to re-interpretation?
Ho-hum. Clear as mud."

The business of sex is as clear as mud — which is why
many of the other attacks on my book are so simplistic.
Virginia Haussegger wonders "why Arndt isn't turning her
spotlight instead on the reason some women may have lost
interest in sex. In addition to being worn out and over-tired,
the real reason might have a lot to do with their uninspiring,
unstimulating partners. Where is the focus on how unsexy it is
to try snogging a dull, lazy, tenderless man?"

It is true that some of my female diarists complained about
their lover's failure to make any effort to light their fire let
alone to provide real pleasure when they did end up in the cot.
I put together a little collection of truly appalling stories from
the women about their crude, fumbling lovers. Yet many other
women admit their partners make strenuous efforts to get
things right and are superb sexual craftsmen — yet the women
still don't want sex.

Adding to the complexity is the fact that many women
simply aren't easy to please in bed — as they readily admit. My
chapter on love making techniques was entitled, "Blind man
in the dark searching for a black cat that isn't there" — from a
frustrated male diarist describing his efforts to stimulate his

wife's clitoris in just the way she likes it. He never got it right.

There's a wonderful skit on the subject by British comic Jenny Lecoat: *"He, labouring away, pauses to ask, 'Are you nearly there?' 'It's hard to say,' says she. He plunges on. 'If you imagine it as a journey from here to China, where would you be?' She considers. 'The kitchen.'"*

The other extremely predictable reaction to my book has been women arguing that if men did more housework they would get more sex. "Don't men realise that the most erotic call they can make is "Cupcake, don't walk on the floor, I've just washed it", suggests Helen Elliot, writing in *The Age*. Of course, there is some truth in this argument. In my chapter, "Laundry Gets you laid?" many of my female diarists talk about resentment eroding their desire. It is pretty obvious that men who don't contribute to household chores will incur female ire.

But I had a great diarist I called "Mary" (all names were disguised) — who complained bitterly that her husband does so little to help her. *"I'm working a full five-day week, 6.00am to 6.30pm days. I come home, usually have to cook (because he cannot and will not cook, at least, not reliably) … Yes, he does 'do the washing'— which consists of putting the washing into our 10kg washer/dryer, and putting the finished dried washing onto a pile on the lounge floor, where the dog promptly lies all over it. Now if he took the clothes out straight away and hung them up or folded them, life would be sweet. BUT he piles them load on top of load on top of load — so by the time I get to them, I've got steam-dried, cardboard lumps covered in dog-hair and he wonders why I'm so bloody ungrateful and why that night I'll knock his block off when he wants 'it'."*

Mary was absolutely bewildered as to why her man was

allowing this issue to sabotage what she saw as an otherwise beautiful marriage. But Peter felt that it is incredibly unfair of her to use sex as a weapon. Mary explained:

"He argues that even if I were a lady of leisure with a maid and housekeeper and no need to work with a million dollars in the bank, I still wouldn't be interested in sex. I deny, deny and deny that but deep inside I have to admit there is a chance he is right."

That's the crux of the sex–housework issue. Yes, women are understandably resentful when they feel their partners aren't sharing their second shift. Why should they put out, "just do it", if their partners aren't prepared to consider their needs and pull their own weight when it comes to the relentless burden of housework and child care? The resentment these women feel is often a sure-fire passion killer.

But even in the best of circumstances, even with the most considerate, helpful partners, the fact remains that many women still try to avoid sex. Listen to Fran. This 53-year-old Sydney woman is married to a saint, and she knows it: "Julian runs the house, apart from cooking. He does all the washing but I won't let him do the ironing because he doesn't do a good enough job." She knows he works very hard to try to make sure everything is running smoothly, in the hope she may want sex — but he still rarely gets the green light. "Sometimes I think I'm such a bitch," she confessed with a laugh.

It's fascinating that the household issue so often gets a run whenever there is any criticism of women's behaviour. And even here the "truth" regarding men's participation in household work rarely gets an airing. Just after I published *The Sex Diaries*, it was widely reported that the latest social trends survey found that women do almost twice as much housework as men — 33 hours and 45 minutes a week. What the media failed to mention was men spend a lot more time in paid jobs — an average of 31 hours and 50 minutes a week, compared with women's 16 hours and 25 minutes. In other words, men and women do about the same amount of work in total — about 50 hours a week each. How is it that we never hear this side of the story?

There are no easy answers to tensions over mismatched desire. Despite the misleading publicity, my book did not promote any quick fixes but the diary idea proved a marvellous means of illustrating the complexities of the issue. Yes, there were women reluctantly doling out sexual favours but there were also lusty, sexually-deprived women who craved more sex, just as there were men indifferent to its delights. There were couples who both preferred to eat chocolate. And there were also passionate couples married for forty years writing about the sexual joy they share together. That was the real fascination — this rich tapestry of experience laid bare through the revelations of the his-and-hers diaries. It was quite a journey.

CHAPTER 19

Growing sex drought for men – sex-starved husbands

First published 2015

In the midst of the salacious reporting following the 2015 Ashley Maddison sex website hack there was one particularly startling revelation. Contrary to the site's claims about plenty of female as well as male users, it turned out there were about 28 million men and five million women in the account list. Only 14 per cent of the users of the site were women.

"The Ashley Madison hack proves men are dogs. But the Ashley Madison service itself proves men are suckers," gloated Naomi Schaefer Riley in the *New York Post*.

Perhaps it proves something very different. For all the male blaming that went on over the hacking scandal, the malicious delight at male cheaters and scumbags getting their comeuppance, there was remarkably little attention paid to what drives these huge numbers of men to seek sexual relief outside their marriages.

The missing part of the puzzle is strong evidence that many men are facing an increasing problem in achieving sexually fulfilling marriages or long-term relationships. With swelling numbers of sexually-disinterested women determining the sexual frequency in their relationships, men face a male sex deficit which shows every sign of growing stronger.

Surveys from across the world are now reporting dropping sexual frequencies, more celibate marriages and an increasing gap between male and female sexual desire with even young women reporting loss of sexual interest.

British sociologist Catherine Hakim produced a report that same year, *Supply and Desire: Sexuality and the Sex Industry in the 21st Century,* which argued for decriminalisation of prostitution. In the paper, published by the Institute of Economic Affairs, Hakim summed up a series of international sex surveys which show male sexual desire is manifested as least twice as often as female desire. "The gap is growing over time so the sexual deficit among men is growing steadily," she wrote, spelling out the many reasons why this situation is likely to get worse for men.

"Male demand for sexual entertainments of all kinds is thus growing and ineradicable," Hakim concluded. Her most recent book, *The New Rules,* examined Internet sex sites and found a sexless or low-sex marriage to be the most common cause for people choosing to use such sites.

Around the same time another sex news story was making a splash — approval by the US Food and Drug Administration of Flibanserin, the libido-enhancing drug for women. It's not particularly effective — only 8-13 per cent of users have increased libido — and it had already been rejected twice due to possible side effects like fainting and dizziness but many were applauding this first cab off the rank in the pharmaceutical race to find some means of helping women with low desire. Yet the drug attracted critics who argue the manufacturers are exploiting a "natural mismatch" between female and male expectations of sex by creating a creepy "on" switch for female lust. The answer, according to these critics, is for men to curb their unreasonable, unseemly desires.

Whilst arguments rage over solutions to the male sex deficit, the more important question is why is it growing? It's over fifty years since the arrival of the contraceptive pill was celebrated by the women's movement as launching the liberation of female sexuality. Women's sexuality began to blossom: less guilt, more desire, more pleasure, more orgasms. The gap between men and women decreased with more women openly enjoying their sexuality. So why has this progress now derailed? Why the sudden drop in female desire and response?

These questions have long been shaping the work of one of the leading lights in the current world of sexology. In 2015 I spoke to the head of The Society for the Scientific Study of Sexuality (SSSS) Finish sociologist, Osmo Kontula, who was preparing his presidential address to be delivered at their November conference. Kontula was pondering the results of sex surveys he'd been conducting since 1971 which revealed some startling results:

- A big drop in female orgasms. More women, particularly young women having trouble climaxing.

- More arousal and lubrication problems, especially in younger and much older women.

- An increasing desire gap between men and women, with more women going off sex.

- Even young women experience loss of desire, with one in four losing interest even less than two years into a relationship.

- A big drop in sexual frequency, with more and more couples celibate.

"There are some real mysteries here," said Kontula, speaking from his office at the Population Research Institute in Helsinki. "Why was there such a decline in intercourse frequency in the 2000s? There's been a 10 to 15 per cent drop in people of all ages who say they've had sex in the last week. People are now having less sex than the early 1970s and the greatest decline has been for young people, those aged 25-40."

Kontula's 2009 book *Between Sexual Desire and Reality* was based on surveys conducted regularly between 1971 and 2007. When we spoke, he was analysing the results of a brand-new survey from 2015, finding a further small drop in sexual frequency in the previous eight years, with the gap between male and female desire continuing to widen. Plus couples were reporting increasing difficulty discussing sex in their relationships, which is hardly surprising when mismatched desire is so often the source of marital tension.

"I thought of it as the gulf war," wrote a male participant my own research on mismatched desire. "She felt pressures and I felt frustrated. Mostly she went along with sex, albeit unenthusiastically. I remember one time she said, 'Forget the foreplay, let's get the thing over with.' Now that's how to make a bloke feel wanted. I didn't know whether to laugh or leave."

Kontula said he didn't know why the gulf war is increasing. "The desires of men and women seem at times to be on different planets," he said, noting that women were able to fulfil their lower desires for sexual intercourse more successfully than men and many ended up having the frequency of sex they wanted. "It seems women are more frequently gatekeepers, deciding on when and how often the couple had sex."

Interestingly in living-apart relationships women were least likely to show loss of desire — regular absences seem to make lust easier to maintain. But the huge leap in lost libido in cohabiting women remains a mystery although it may link to happiness research showing a big drop in happiness in women who remain for long periods in defacto relationship without marrying.

The dropping sexual frequency reflects a recent shift in the balance of sexual power in relationships, suggest the authors of the latest Sex in Australia survey[54]. "These changes in attitudes and behaviour may reflect a shift away from a model of sexuality in which women's sexual behaviour is shaped by men's needs towards a feminist model of female sexuality in which women have the right to refuse or initiate sex," concluded University of Sussex psychologist, Richard de Visser and his Australian colleagues who co-authored the study.

Their latest findings found a small but significant decline over the last decade in the average weekly frequency of sex — from 1.9 to 1.5 times per week among men and from 1.8 to 1.5 times per week among women. Most men (85 per cent) and women (69 per cent) wanted to have sex more often than they actually did.

Kontula's data showed many women who indicated that they would prefer a higher frequency of sex also experienced a fairly frequent lack of sexual desire. (We don't have the most recent survey data covering sexual desire available in Australia as yet, although back in 2005 a majority of women in all age groups over 20 reported lack of sexual interest.)

Kontula speculates that women's preference for a higher frequency relates to a desire to please their partners. Yet leading Melbourne sex therapist, Lynda Carlyle, believes it also may be about women wanting to want sex. "Although there are many women who aren't bothered by their lack of desire there *are* women who are miserable about their lost libido. They want to feel sexy again and know their disinterest is causing enormous strain in relationships, which is what's driving the demand for libido-enhancing drugs. There are women who would love to pop a little pink pill to make them feel like sex again."

In my research there was a lovely young mother of twins who reported she had apparently mastered saying, "Get that thing away from me" in her sleep. But she didn't want to be like that. She hated rejecting her husband and longed for the early days in their marriage when she couldn't get enough of him.

So why is this problem of mismatched desire getting worse? It's not just Finland where this is showing up. Hakim reported international surveys also reveal a decline in sexual frequency in Britain, the United States, Germany and Japan. A review of research on female desire by psychologist Marta Meana from the University of Nevada found that discrepancies in desire within relationships are now the norm rather than the exception but that very few women are distressed by their lack of desire per se. They are more likely to worry about the impact on their relationships.

What we are now seeing is many more women who don't want sex and can't be bothered trying to get aroused — it's just all become too hard. One of Australia's experts on desire, sex therapist Dr Sanda Pertot believes it's partly a reaction to the new demand for women to climax during sexual activity — it's not good enough for them to just enjoy giving pleasure to their partners. "Women say no to sex if they are uncertain whether they will climax or worry it will take forever. The women know they take longer to come if they are tired, stressed or anxious and direct sexual touch can sometimes be annoying when they aren't in the mood. The man, with the best of intentions, often puts pressure on her to keep trying."

The author of *When Your Sex Drives Don't Match* and other books on desire, Sandra Pertot talks openly about her own experience with loss of libido during years when her second child was a bad sleeper. She was happy to have sex knowing it was ok if she didn't climax or even if she fell asleep — which she did on various occasions. "It was still great sex in the circumstances, which suited us both. It was about feeling loved and accepted," says Pertot.

These days suggesting women are sometimes happy to have one for the team attracts howls of derision. Yet there's ample evidence from the work done by Canadian psychiatry professor Rosemary Basson that women with no spontaneous desire will often seek sex to achieve intimacy in their relationships and that sometimes, in the process, desire kicks in and they become aroused and reach orgasm.

It's not just libido that is waning but also women's capacity to reach orgasm, according to Osmo Kontula's research. That's the other puzzle: "There's been a large drop since 1999 — over ten percentage points — in the proportion of young women reporting they always have an orgasm during sexual activity. And we find this is linked to women's perception of sexual enjoyment. One in two women who usually reach orgasm during lovemaking continue to view sex as enjoyable but only 15 per cent of women who rarely had orgasm saw sex as highly enjoyable," Konula reported.

The latest ASRH2 survey also showed an orgasm drop for women — the percentage of Australian women climaxing at their last sexual encounter dropped from 69 to 66 per cent, a far smaller change. Lynda Carlyle, who's been working as a sex therapist for over a decade, said she was seeing increasing numbers of younger women struggling with orgasms.

She reeled off a string of reasons why this could be happening. Busyness, for a start. Women's crazy pressured working lives are coupled with the excessive zeal shown by helicopter parents always hovering over their children. Unlike some lucky men who can use sex as stress relief, most tired cranky women find nothing lights their fire.

Then there's the distraction issue. Carlyle speculated that our younger generations of women, having grown up multi-tasking and flitting from one form of social media to another, may have far more difficulty concentrating on the task in hand. "Arousal and orgasm are all about learning to switch off and tune into sensations," she said. Distraction is the enemy of female arousal.

There's a great video clip from upriseworldwise.com featuring a smiling woman in bed. All that's visible is her face and the occasional movement beneath the sheets. She starts off blissfully happy … "Hmm, that feels good … Wait, wait, oh yes, that's so good."

But then thoughts start to intrude: "Shit, he's getting bored." And then, "Oh no, don't go down there. I didn't get waxed this week." So it goes on, all her worries start crowding in — about her weight, how she's got to work out more, all sorts of crazy thoughts.

Her ramblings are interrupted by a stern message from her cranky vagina — "Will you shut the hell up and let me enjoy myself?"

Then there's our obesity epidemic. Just as overweight men have problems with erections — blood has too far to travel to get through to the areas where it is needed — so too overweight women may have issues with arousal. Even if there's no physical impediment, body image can stop women relaxing enough to enjoy a lover's attention. The earth is unlikely to move if you're busy keeping clutched sheets hiding an unsightly body. The crazy thing is that so many women with nothing to hide are still crippled with self-consciousness during lovemaking. "Many women lack confidence if they put on a kilo or two," said Carlyle.

What else? Well, there's porn which many, like Carlyle, believe to be encouraging men to only offer "genitally focussed, hard and fast stimulation" which doesn't give women the opportunity to build up arousal. It leads women into feeling they should come quickly and worrying when they don't.

There *is* an upside to all that hot and heavy male viewing — Sydney University researcher Kath Albury found the promotion of cunnilingus on the Internet meant many young men now see this activity as highly desirable. But a major stumbling block is female discomfort with their bodies — the second Sex in Australia survey[55], showed most young women don't masturbate. Only 30 per cent of 16-19-year-olds do so, up about seven per cent from a decade ago. There's much else suggesting many young women are simply not comfortable with their nether regions — including the new demand for cosmetic surgery. When it comes to oral sex the yuk factor means girls are far more likely to give than receive.

ASRH2 found only 24 per cent of women in all age groups

said they'd received oral sex last time there'd been sexual activity — shagging remains the steady diet featuring on most couples' sex life. The researchers noted their previous survey revealed women are more likely to climax if there is a variety of delights on offer — intercourse, plus manual and oral — rather than simply this white bread solution.

That's no doubt true but in these rushed and busy times, it certainly makes matters simpler if bonking does the trick. One very interesting issue is whether women might be losing the art of responding to this most basic form of lovemaking. Over the last few decades there's been much debate over the proportion of women reach vaginal orgasm rather than requiring direct clitoral stimulation. We often still hear American sex researcher Shere Hite's claim — made in 1976 — that only a third of women respond without that direct clitoral contact. Yet there's plenty of more recent research suggesting the numbers are far higher, including European studies showing a majority of older women respond vaginally most of the time.

It's a confusing picture with research highlighting the extensive hidden anatomy of the clitoris which suggests clitoral stimulation may always be part of the story but also work by US professors Beverly Whipple and Barry Komisaruk showing a distinct, separate nerve pathway for vaginally-induced orgasm.

Catherine Blackledge, the author of an excellent book on the vagina, *The Story of V*, argued many women today never learn to tune in to the subtler delight a vagina may offer because they are growing up in a culture which promotes the clitoris as the gold standard of female pleasure. She also believes porn movies don't help matters — "all that quick thrusting. To experience vaginal orgasm you need to slow down so you can think and feel deep into these vaginal sensations."

These days many young women also spend years in casual relationships where they may learn very little about their own response. The decade of dating which proceeds first marriage for most women today will often include hook-ups and other short-term relationships where women never have the trust and confidence to really express their needs.

Back in the 1970s, all the talk was about new research showing the incredible capacity of women for sexual enjoyment and multiple orgasms. A psychoanalyst called Mary Jane Sherfey published a provocative article predicting men would struggle to deal with women's sexual appetites. "The sexual hunger of the female and her capacity for copulation completely exceeds that of any male," she wrote.

Who would have predicted that fifty years later the story behind the sex scandals dominating our news would be the male sex deficit, with sex-hungry men risking so much to cope with their mounting frustrations?

CHAPTER 20

Hard dogs to keep on the porch – sexually restless men

First published 2015

How did Australian men end up on such a short leash? It was a question that emerged in a fascinating conversation I had with an Argentinian journalist after my book *The Sex Diaries* was published in her country. She couldn't believe the sexual restraint shown by sex-starved Australian husbands. "Here if the wife doesn't offer any sex the husbands will be off finding other women, a mistress, a whore. There's no way they'd put up with getting no sex."

As my diaries demonstrated, in this country there are plenty of men were dealing with just that situation and still they remained faithful. Listen to this 50-year-old man who spent 19 years of his long marriage without any physical intimacy: "Try sleeping next to your wife night after night and not being able to touch her. Try watching her shower, dress and undress and not be able to have her ... God only knows I tried to love her, care for her, understand her and appreciate her. I never had an affair, never went to brothels or even bought a dirty magazine."

Many Australian men not only put up with it but seem to have bought the idea that restraint is their only real option.

The Sex in Australia survey[56] of almost 20,000 people, revealed an ever-growing commitment to monogamy — from both men and women. Most (85 per cent) of men and women (83 per cent) now believe having an affair is always wrong in a committed relationship — up from a decade ago when 78 per cent of both men and women believed this to be true. Almost 96 per cent of men believe their relationships will always be sexually exclusive with 98 per cent of women showing similar optimism.

It's quite a shift from the sexual licence historically available to men who once were entitled to demand sex in their marriages, given legal support for conjugal rights over their economically-dependent wives. Many women in this situation had no choice but to turn a blind eye to whatever extramarital activity the man chose to enjoy.

This subjugation of women has ended, thank goodness, but men's essential sexual nature hasn't changed. "Men want sex more often than women at the start of a relationship, in the middle of it, and after many years of it," reports Roy F Baumeister, a psychology professor at Florida State University who has written extensively on gender differences in sexual drive. His team's research concludes that men not only think about sex more often, they have more frequent and varied fantasies, desire sex more often, desire more partners, are less able or willing to live without sexual gratification, expend more resources and make more sacrifices for sex, desire and enjoy a broader variety of sexual practices, and have more favourable and permissive attitudes toward more sexual activities.

This is not to say that women don't like sex nor that there aren't some women with far stronger drives than most men, but research clearly shows that on average men are more interested. Yet most married men remain faithful for most of their marriages. Yes, there are philanderers, men who just can't keep their trousers zipped. As Hillary Clinton quipped about her husband, "He's a hard dog to keep on the porch."

But they are rare. The first Sex in Australia survey[57] found only five per cent of men (and three per cent of women) in a regular relationship had strayed in the previous year. Of course over a long relationship these tiny percentages add up and significant numbers of men in long-term relationships have had some extramarital experience — a one-night stand perhaps, or an affair lasting a few weeks, months or even a year or more. But these are tiny lapses compared to the commitment they show to staying on the straight and narrow.

The problem is the extraordinary value we now place on sexual fidelity in a marriage means that the discovery of an affair often leads to irretrievable breakdown. Twenty per cent of people surveyed in the Australian Divorce Transitions project conducted by the Australian Institute of Family Studies cited an affair as the reason for the marriage breakdown. Over the years I've counselled so many couples who are dealing with the aftermath of the discovery of an affair and I'm always struck by how many wives come under pressure from friends to turf the husband out, to give up on the marriage rather than allow the bad dog back on the porch.

Of course sometimes it's a husband who's unwilling to forgive but more about female infidelity later.

It's crazy to give up on a marriage simply because a spouse has been naked with someone else, says America's leading sex advice columnists Dan Savage, who's running what is pretty much a one-man campaign to persuade his countrymen to rethink their views on monogamy. Savage, who presented his views at the 2013 Sydney Festival of Dangerous Ideas, is better known for the *It Gets Better* project, an archive of hopeful videos aimed at troubled gay youth. But his determination to persuade society to adjust expectations about marriage was one of the highlights of his 2014 book *American Savage*.

It's a strange position for a gay advocate. As Savage explains it's often assumed he'll take a very liberal position on sexual freedom in marriage but he's actually quite conservative. He's not promoting "wide open relationships, not swinger's conventions nor fucking in the streets." He believes we should value monogamy and if we make vows to be sexually exclusive in a marriage, we should work hard to stick to that promise. All that he's suggesting is "perhaps a little licence, a little latitude. An understanding that two people can't be all things to each other sexually all of their adult lives. An understanding that life is long and circumstances change and some things — love, devotion, loyalty — are more important than sex and that lifelong, perfectly executed sexual exclusivity is not the only measure of love, devotion and loyalty."

The chapter in his essay collection on this topic — *It's never Okay to Cheat (Except When It Is)* — spells out his considered position, reached after fourteen years of dealing with a deluge of daily emails from people trapped in sexless marriages. He concludes that it's sometimes ok to cheat, for instance, when a man has "a wife who mysteriously loses her libido or has never had much of a libido to begin with and decides she's finished with sex and then engages in emotional blackmail in an effort to get her duped husband to drop the subject." And that "it's ok for men and women who are married to people who don't like sex and do their best to make sure sex is so lousy that their spouses will stop pestering them for it."

But it's not ok to cheat when "you've made a monogamous commitment and your partner is doing his or her best to meet your sexual needs." It's also not ok to seek sex elsewhere "because you're horny *right now* and she happens to have the flu *right now*." Nor simply because you are bored or she recently had a baby.

The Savage view is that even if it's sometimes ok to get sex elsewhere that's provided you have only safe sex, provided you are discrete and don't humiliate your spouse and provided you don't tell your spouse — unless you are sure the deal is they want to be told. Of course very few couples ever properly discuss in advance how they wish to handle this issue. The first Sex in Australia survey[58] found 48 per cent of men and 66 per cent of women in committed relationships believed that they had discussed and reached agreement about sexual fidelity — a very revealing gap in perception[59].

In fact most affairs remain undetected — two in three are never discovered, according to US research. They usually come to light when the unfaithful spouse blurts out the truth, as revealed by Annette Lawson in her book *Adultery — An Analysis of Love and Betrayal*. Lawson showed how "this telling business", prompted by the current obsession with total honesty, takes such a toll on marriage. Confessions are often made in the name of honest disclosure when people don't have the backbone to live with their guilt.

Yes, this whole business is mighty complicated. But Dan Savage's essential argument is the current head-in-the-sand approach is a disaster waiting to happen. Treating monogamy as the main indicator of a successful marriage gives people unrealistic expectations of themselves and their partners and destroys more marriages than it saves. For total numbers having affairs he cites figures of 50–60 per cent of men and 40-50 of women. (There's no good Australian data on lifetime totals — one Australian Women's Weekly survey of almost 15,000 people found 14 per cent had had affairs but one of the few experts in this area, Juliet Richters from the University of NSW believes this is probably a little low.)

There's no question many married women also struggle with fidelity issues — although far fewer than men. Savage's book showed that the American marriage advice industry, dominated mainly by women, tends to always blame the husband. So even when it is the wife who strays, the man is at fault for not keeping her happy. Savage finds it astonishing that the feminist revolution, instead of extending to women "the same latitude and licence and pressure-release valve that men always enjoyed," has chosen instead to impose on men "the confines women had always endured." It's an interesting point.

How rare it is that we hear these arguments publicly voiced. Another challenging American orthodoxy on the subject is New York therapist Esther Perel, whose hugely successful book *Mating in Captivity* argued the stifling intimacy of modern marriage is leading to marital bed death. Her 2017 book *The State of Affairs* looked at happily married people who have affairs — her experience is plenty of people in loving, committed relationships do sometime stray.

For decades I've been hearing from people wrestling with this dilemma. People who believe in monogamy, who would prefer to remain faithful but find themselves going outside the marriage for sex because they aren't prepared to end a marriage nor kiss goodbye to any future hope of physical intimacy in their lives.

People like Robert who is in a loving relationship, married 12 years. "Somewhere along the way we have lost that passion and intimacy. Never thought in my mind I would ever consider cheating but I guess that lack of intimacy has got the better of me. We do not have a sexual relationship at all at the moment and it has been like that for a while now. It's the usual reasons you have heard before such as kids have come along, too tired, too busy, lack of desire. It's strange I have taken this route I never thought I would ever become un-loyal. I consider marriage vows very important."

Robert has had a number of sexual encounters through the online sex site Ashley Madison — intense, passionate experiences but he still thinks he's "an asshole for cheating."

But Sally is sure she's doing the right thing. She's 55, in a very happy seven-year relationship but also using Ashley Madison. "I love my partner very much and he loves me unfortunately for me he doesn't love sex and finds my enthusiasm for sex and all the wonderful things associated with a happy sexual relationship embarrassing. After many discussions about this, seeing doctors and going to a sex therapist I decided that I was going to stop hassling him about sex. I'm old enough to know exactly what I'm doing. I love all the good things my partner brings to my life and if I have to have this side of my life satisfied in a way society deems as unconventional, well so be it."

Unsurprisingly women using these sites are hugely

outnumbered by males. Men pay to contact women on the sites but women's activity is free. Most women get swamped with attention, some of it most unsavoury. "I was floored, gobsmacked, overwhelmed and actually filled with anxiety from the experience. On the mobile you can't exclude graphic imagery so it was wall-to-wall local and international cock," says Claire, 42-year-old mother of a pre-schooler who joined the site after endless fighting with her sexually-disinterested husband. "I was going nuts, we were fighting a lot and I was ready to walk out even though it's absolutely not what I want," she explains, adding she's now learnt to avoid the sleazy males and had some good experiences.

I've talked to people using these sites with the full-knowledge of their spouses, others who participate together, seeking threesomes and other exotic sexual combinations. There are men and women seeking love affairs, others just passing encounters. Sometimes they find what they are looking for, others are disappointed, with many men angry about wasting money trying to sort out the far fewer legitimate female participants from the scammers.

But just as the online dating sites have proved a game-changer for singles seeking a partner, the new sex sites offer married people the best possible chance of a discreet dalliance. As British sociologist Catherine Hakim pointed out in her book on these sex sites, *The New Rules*, the Internet enables people to meet others well beyond their own social circle, own neighbourhood or workplace community, providing opportunities for carefully-handled erotic connections between like-minded people.

Hakim suggested this is promising "a different type of liaison between people who are both married, both committed to their marriages, who are discreet enough to avoid social and emotional catastrophe." Hakim's research showed that across the world this is just what is happening. Her conclusion: "In this different, special situation, the impacts can potentially be almost entirely positive."

Hakim grew up in France a country which she argues has a far more enlightened view of these matters. "It is divorce which is frowned on. There is no assumption that spouses must fulfil of all of each other's needs, all of the time — exclusively." In such countries extra-marital affairs, she writes, are generally "conducted with great discretion, with consideration for the dignity of the spouse who must never be embarrassed in any way."

It wasn't just the French who took this view. Savage quoted a *New York Times* interview with the Duchess of Devonshire, Deborah Cavendish, one of the famous Mitford sisters. Asked about her late husband's discreet dalliances, she replied "It was absolutely fixed that we shouldn't divorce or get rid of each other in any way. It is completely different to Americans, who all divorce each other the whole time. Such a bore for everyone, having to say who's going to have the dogs, who's going to have the photograph books."

In Australia there are far too many unnecessary fights over dogs and photograph books... not to mention children and houses. It's very sad that so many good marriages flounder over the discovery of some sexual infidelity. Surely Dan Savage is right in seeking better conversations about how hard monogamy is, how hard marriage is and whether we are making unrealistic demands on that institution and on ourselves.

CHAPTER 21

Doing the laundry doesn't get you laid – housework and sex

First published 2013

Certain newspaper stories are bound to bring a smile to the face of any man scanning the daily news over his cornflakes. A CCN report on research from North Carolina University came up with a ripper yarn which suggested regular fellatio could reduce women's risk of breast cancer by up to forty per cent. Sadly that one proved bogus — the report, which went viral, had been faked by a college student.

But another story also worth a wry grin was a 2013 research report suggesting doing housework means men get less sex. That was pretty funny news given the constant efforts to dragoon men into housework on the promise that doing the laundry would get them laid. Any bloke knows that rarely works — however deftly he sorts whites from coloureds. The housework/sex connection comes with no guarantees.

But that research did raise some interesting issues. That time it *was* legitimate research — from the University of Washington where sociologists studied almost 7,000 couples, relating the division of household labour to their sexual frequency. They found men reported having sex 5.2 times per month on average while women suggested the rate was more like 5.6 times. Couples where men did more traditionally female household chores reported less sex than men who did less "women's work". The real domestic gods — men who did all the household work — had a third less sex than men who did none of it.

Surprisingly it was the men who didn't lift a finger on the domestic front but made their manly presence felt through traditional chores like emptying the gutters or fixing the fence were the ones most likely to score, upping the average sex frequency by 1.6 more times per month.

What's going on here? Do hairy dishwasher hands not do it for women? It seems unlikely that helping with household chores would really work against men's chances. Indeed the study author Julie Brines warned domesticated men not to hang up their dishcloths because that's likely to trigger anger which could make things far worse — resentment is a major passion-killer.

Perhaps the real story had more to do with attitudes towards mutual caring. It could be that women in more traditional households are more likely to feel some obligation to care about their partner's sexual needs, harbouring a spirit of sexual generosity rather than embracing the modern creed that if a wife isn't interested in sex, it just ain't going to happen. There are now two very distinct camps of women. Some see sex as just another area of marital life where husbands and wives look out for each other and make efforts to please their partners. Just as a woman might cook her husband's favourite salmon rissoles even though she's not into seafood, she'll also sometimes make the effort to respond to his sexual invitation even though she'd far prefer to stay up and watch her favourite late night television show.

But others rankle at any suggestion that it's ok to have sex without initial desire — even though research shows many women cheerfully do this and find desire and arousal often kick in once they get started. Ana Carvalheira and colleagues from the University of Applied Psychology in Lisbon, Portugal, found that roughly half (42 per cent) of women in long term relationships are willing to engage in sex without desire — whilst the other half won't have a bar of it.

Maybe women in egalitarian relationships with their domestically well-trained husbands are less likely to contemplate one for the team — hence their sexual pace drops below average? But it could be that watching a husband tackle manly chores just triggers something wild and primitive in the female psyche. One woman taking part in my research on desire wrote at length about her husband's miserliness and other irritating characteristics — "all the petty little niggling things that make you resentful and you think, 'why would I bother to even be interested in sex?'" But she changed her tune the day she'd witnessed him wrestling the fridge back into place after their new kitchen renovation. "Hmm, he looks pretty good down there. Wouldn't mind if we had a go on this new black slate floor," she pondered.

Watching a man push a Hoover around the floor simply isn't on the same page.

CHAPTER 22

Doctors fail prostate cancer sufferers – penis rehabilitation

First published 2013

When Brisbane woman Jill Costello received treatment for breast cancer seven years ago, she found herself surrounded by expert care and support. Her "fairy-godmother," a breast care nurse, just made things happen. Her questions were fully answered, her doctors went out of their way to make sure she had proper advice and every possible aid to her recovery.

Four years later, when her husband Brian had surgery for prostate cancer, the couple discovered they were on their own. Questions about lasting side-effects from the surgery were fobbed off and Jill found herself googling late into the night, reading up on risks of incontinence and erection problems resulting from damage to the penile nerves. "Even when I made an appointment to see the urologist myself, he simply warned there could be difficulties but gave no advice on what to do or where to go," Jill says.

The couple muddled through themselves, asking around until they found one of the few local doctors offering specialist help with the erection recovery process and a physiotherapist for the incontinence. With her daughter Leah, Jill now runs the organisation ManUp which raises money for more prostate cancer nurses. There are only 12 specialist prostate cancer nurses in Australia (with new federal funding for an additional 13 next year) compared to 85 for breast cancer. More men are diagnosed each year with prostate cancer than women with breast cancer (18,560 compared to 14,560, according to 2012 Australian Institute of Health and Welfare figures).

ManUp hears regularly from men whose urologists have shown no interest in what happens to their patients after prostate cancer treatment. One man left impotent and incontinent after his robotic surgery was told the doctor's job was simply to deal with the cancer. "That's crazy. It's like a knee surgeon not caring whether the man can walk again. It's appalling how few urologists are making sure men have the help they need to regain erections and continence yet the impact of these problems can be just as devastating to a man as a mastectomy can be to a woman," says Jill.

A world congress on prostate cancer is soon being held in Melbourne, with up to 300 urologists amongst 1,000 delegates from Australia and overseas. Although there are sessions on sexual functioning and continence what inevitably happens at such events is urologists choose instead to attend talks on the latest cutting-edge treatments or diagnostic techniques.

"We have got better with the technical aspects of the surgery to remove the prostate and preserve function but I think we have a long way to go with all aspects of rehabilitation, including the psychology of facing a serious illness, urinary incontinence and erectile failure," says University of NSW urology associate professor Prem Rashid who's spent over 15 years involved with urology training.

Rashid points out that it's hard for busy practitioners to keep up to date with the recently developed erection treatments. "It's also a two-way street with some men finding it difficult to talk about these issues," he adds.

"We really need to be proactive in helping our patients" says Dr Darren Katz, a speaker at the conference who was just back from working with world experts in erectile dysfunction and incontinence at New York's Memorial Sloan-Kettering Cancer Center. Katz, a urologist and prosthetic surgeon, has established a specialist men's health clinic in Melbourne[60] with Dr Christopher Love, one of Australia's most experienced penile implant surgeons and experts in the erection recovery process.

As he'll explain at the conference, there's a growing international consensus that men should be treated with pro-erection medications rather than just hoping erections will return years after prostate cancer surgery. Ideally men should start treatment as soon as possible (even before the surgery) to maximise their chances of regaining natural erections. "Regular erections supply oxygen to the penis through increased blood flow. This helps to prevent scarring and keeps erectile tissues healthy until the erection nerves have a chance to recover," he says, explaining this is necessary even if surgery has spared these nerves. Treatments such as radiation can cause similar damage.

Lost erections aren't the only problem. "Some men leak urine when they orgasm and up to 70 per cent report some shortening of the penis after prostate surgery, a major concern for many men," says Katz, explaining this shrinkage can be due to scarring of erectile tissue and the casing of the erection chambers which can also cause abnormal bending of the penis.

Katz will speak at the conference about penile rehabilitation[61] aimed at preventing this shrinkage and helping restore erections. "This usually involves a combination of regular doses of one of the erection pills like Viagra, Cialis or Levitra and, if needed, injection therapy a few times a week and possible use of a vacuum erection device." Ideally the man's erectile functioning is assessed before and after prostate cancer treatment leading to an individually tailored treatment plan.

"Many men are really nervous about the idea of injecting the penis but if they are carefully taught how to use the injection medication that's right for them, they discover these treatments are really effective and quite painless," adds Katz.

But that's just the problem. Most of men receiving treatment for prostate cancer receive little or no help for their erection problems let alone receiving the careful assessment to determine the exact prescription they need. As Katz explains, the Sloan Kettering clinic finds many men respond better to injection therapy involving a combination of drugs, like Trimix or Bimix, available only from compounding chemists. There are pre-mixed injections available, like Caverject, but for many men premixed drugs are less effective and more likely to cause pain.

With only about 15 compounding pharmacies in Australia with the sterile rooms required to produce these drugs, many of these pharmacists report that these drugs are being prescribed by only a handful or so of urologists in each city. That strongly suggests most of our country's 400 urologists are not doing their job.

Some urologists do refer patients on to ED specialists, like Melbourne urologist Chris Love, or Sydney sexual health physician Michael Lowy but experts working in this area all acknowledge most of their referrals are coming from a small group of doctors. Michael Lowy: "Most patients who find their way to me have searched for proper help themselves after prostate cancer treatment. Men often tell me their urologist gave them little or no advice whatsoever about what to do about their loss of erections."

Professor Mark Frydenberg, Vice President of the Urology Society of Australia and New Zealand, believes men deserve proper care to recover their sexual functioning. "If a patient is not getting the help they need they should seek another opinion, preferably from urologists providing the multi-disciplinary team needed for rehabilitation," he says, adding many doctors struggle to provide these services with so little funding for training of prostate cancer nurses.

Many of these men end up in the hands of shonky organisations which charge thousands of dollars often for ineffective treatments. One of the key offenders, Advanced Medical Institute, makes over $70 million a year ripping off Australian men. Our media, particularly the Fairfax newspapers, have published many reports about this company's practices: lies about the effectiveness of their treatments; sales people illegally withdrawing money from a patient's credit cards; dubious tactics to avoid money-back guarantees; failure to properly check medical histories or warn of dangerous side-effects. The clinics offer compound injection treatments but charge up to 10 times the cost of legitimate compounding pharmacies with no proper medical examinations or education.

"Vulnerable men end up paying big money for ineffective treatments because they aren't getting the help they need from their own doctors," says David Sandoe, then the National Chairman of Prostate Cancer Foundation of Australia.

It's an issue close to Sandoe's heart. With his wife Pam, he's spent years talking publicly about his own experiences with various erection treatments following his prostate cancer surgery. This remarkable couple regularly entertains conference rooms full of doctors and consumers with stories of the first time they used the injection therapy. David rushed home from the doctor's surgery with a full erection only to discover their house was full of painters — they were in the middle of a renovation. That didn't stop them. "With a couple of lame excuses we made it to the bedroom and put 'it' to good use," says Pam.

The couple are regular travellers and found the vacuum pump led to funny moments at airports as they explained to embarrassed customs officers exactly what it was. David is now the proud owner of an inflatable penile prosthesis which works wonderfully well, even though the noise of the pump as it pushes liquid into the penis still gives Pam the giggles.

The Sandoes were lucky in their choice of urologist, as Sydney-based Philip Katalaris provides a comprehensive service which includes a psychologist and nurse educator to explain the erection treatments and teach the pelvic floor exercises essential for incontinence.

Many men are forced to suffer the humiliation of spending years wearing nappies or pads due to incontinence after prostate cancer treatments. Research from Cancer Council NSW found five years after a radical prostatectomy, three-quarters of the men have erectile dysfunction and 12 per cent are still incontinent. Associate professor David Smith, one of the authors of the study, suggests the erectile dysfunction numbers are twice what you'd expect through the ageing process and the incontinence figures are also too high.

"Most men aren't aware that they needn't live with long-lasting embarrassing continence problems. A physiotherapy pelvic floor rehabilitation program usually results in continence within 6-12 weeks of prostate cancer surgery," says Shan Morrison, Director of Women's and Men's Health Physiotherapy in Malvern, which specialises in treating men with this problem.

Sydney psychologist Patrick Lumbroso, who is undertaking doctoral research into erection problems after prostate cancer surgery, is frustrated at how poorly these issues are handled:

"Problems such as incontinence and erectile dysfunction can have a devastating impact on a man's confidence and masculine self-image, leading to depression, relationship problems and sexual difficulties for the partner."

His research reveals why so many men in this circumstance fail to receive proper advice on erection treatments, finding most men are given little or no information by their urologists and what they received was often inaccurate and poorly handled. "One doctor asked his patient 'Have you ever considered jabbing a needle into your penis to get an erection?' That was hardly a sensitive approach given the squeamishness of most men to using injections," says Lumbroso.

Patrick Lumbroso also provides counselling to couples, helping them adjust to the impact of prostate cancer treatments on their sex lives (www.sexafterprostatecancer.com.au). Like most experts in the field, he'd like to see much more being done to reach people in this situation. "It's tragic how many couples are left floundering on their own when so much could be done to help them resume sexual intimacy."

SECTION FIVE

Work and family life

CHAPTER 23

Marriage dud deal for men – the power shift

First published 2012

"There's got to be something more than this!" This howl of discontent comes from Alex, a thirtysomething married executive, one of four Aussie males romping their way through *Certified Male*, a blokey Australian comedy.

Alex rarely questions the 65-plus working hours he puts in each week. He's always agreed with his wife, Sam, that he has to work long hours, so she can be there for the kids. Besides, she's got her charity work and, as she says, there's no point in her taking up a job just for the sake of earning money, is there? All her friends at book club totally agree.

But during the days Alex spends with his mates on a work retreat, his alienation in his marriage starts to surface. "I get into bed next to my wife and it's the loneliest place on earth." He determines he's going to have it out with her.

This conversation starts well. "It's just that I'd like some time with the kids, too. Perhaps you could take up some part-time work?"

The response is a solid jab to the head. His long list of concerns doesn't get a look in. "What do you mean I don't appreciate you?" He wails as her punches hit home. He's reduced to pitiful bleating: "Of course, you're a good mum."

(THUMP.) "I love it when your parents stay the weekend." (WALLOP.) "I was not looking at your cellulite." (BASH — and he's knocked out.)

Welcome to the world of modern marriage — a world where men's needs, wants and desires don't always feature highly on the agenda. Marriage has changed dramatically over the past 50 years since the sociologist Jessie Bernard wrote her influential book *The Future of Marriage*. There was his marriage, which offered power and satisfaction, while her marriage brought stress, dissatisfaction and loss of self. Bernard's depiction of women suffering through marriage as a kind of psychological torture drew on feminist Betty Friedan's discovery, a decade earlier, of "the problem that had no name" — wives' unvoiced frustrations with their confined, housewifely role.

Marriage was good for men and bad for women, Bernard concluded.

But has that all changed? Women's lives and marriages have been transformed, but now many men are wondering if they may be the ones being offered a dud deal. It's rare that they complain openly about their lot but, beneath the surface, there's an undercurrent of discontent, suggests the men's health expert Steve Carroll.

Carroll has spent more than 30 years travelling around rural Australia talking to groups of men about their health — conversations that often end up focusing on relationships. He reports of men bewildered to find themselves in marriages where they never get it right or get any thanks for what they do. A typical lament to Carroll: "Why in the f--- am I doing all this when I don't get given the time of day?"

Carroll mentions a 35-year-old agricultural worker in Hay, who felt after he married "the noose got tightened" and he was no longer given support or respect. Rather, he was just there to "do the heavy lifting". A 42-year-old miner from Broken Hill said his wife had "all the important stuff and my stuff is just not important". Carroll's conversations reveal a mood of resignation and despondency in many married men: "They can't understand why they are always in trouble with their wives."

Others are noticing that men's stuff doesn't make it on to the marital agenda. Spend any Saturday at the Deus Ex Machina in Camperdown, Sydney and there'll be a bunch of men wandering around, gazing at the ultimate male excitement machine — a custom-made motorcycle. The shop's owner Dare Jennings — a co-founder of Mambo — regularly talks to men who yearn to lash out on one of his dream bikes. They are mainly married men, he says, many clearly well-heeled. Yet as much as they are tempted to indulge themselves, they rarely take that step without checking with the wife. Flushed with enthusiasm, they rush home — and rarely come back.

Jennings argues that men's dreams are clearly not a high priority in modern marriage. "The wives play the safety card, arguing the bikes are just too dangerous." But he adds: "I've had women joke to me that they've got the men under control and don't want trouble. These days married men are on an incredibly short leash."

Think about men's leisure time — or what's left of it. If men ever dare to reflect wistfully on past glory days of patriarchy, high on the list would be the freedom enjoyed by the man of the house to come and go as he pleased. Gone are the days when married men were free to drop off at the pub for a beer or three on the way home from work. Or spend most weekends playing golf, or at the dogs, or tinkering under a car. Men's discretionary leisure time has been shrinking for years, says New England University sociology professor, Michael Bittman. He discovered it fell by more than two hours a week between 1974 and 1987. Bureau of Statistics time-use data showed a further drop between 1992 and 2006 of about 45 minutes, with the more recent figures showing men average 37 minutes free time a day compared with 30 minutes for women.

Men rarely talk about their leisure, or lack of it. But is that because they spend their lives on the back-foot cowering from constant complaints about their failure to share the domestic load, the burden of childcare and housework carried largely by women? Women's dual shift — doing most of the domestic work while many also have paid jobs — is very real. But it is odd that public discussion of this issue, including regular reports from the ABS, somehow fails to mention that there is no difference in the total work load of men and women, if you add paid and unpaid work.

Men are doing more hours of paid work than ever — two to three hours a week more than in 1985, according to a National Centre for Social and Economic Modelling report. Housework hours for men in dual full-time-earner families increased from 14 hours in 1986 to 17 hours in 2005, according to research by Belinda Hewitt and colleagues from the University of Queensland.

"Men notice they don't get much kudos for all that they do," says Steve Carroll, pointing out many men are doing it tough, spending years doing jobs they don't like, facing job uncertainty, seeing little of their children. "When they were growing up, dad's contribution was acknowledged and respected. You know, 'Dad's home! Come on, kids, don't bother your dad. He needs some peace'."

Comedy is one of the few outlets for men's disappointment about their changing deal in marriage. Witness the ABC's comedy series *Agony Uncles,* with constant jokes about men in trouble with their partners for missing the target in late-night trips to the loo, for not cutting their nose hair, for not doing enough housework, and so on.

And the risks of getting it wrong, ending up divorced and losing a house. There are endless jokes about men's post-divorce finances, like the one about the man who goes to buy a Barbie doll for his daughter. He's offered a range of different dolls, all selling for $19.95, except for Divorced Barbie. This one comes with the hefty price tag of $265. He asks why? "Well, it's like this: Divorced Barbie comes with Ken's house, Ken's car, Ken's boat, Ken's furniture …"

The truth, of course, is more complex. Well-heeled men often recover financially from divorce more easily than their ex-wives and some evade all responsibilities. But an Australian Institute of Family Studies report found a quarter of older divorced men who remain single experience financial hardship.

Men are also aware of the legacy of decades of legal decisions favouring mothers in custody battles. They've witnessed the public agony of men denied a proper role in their children's lives. Singer-activist Sir Bob Geldof — in an essay in Andrew Bainham's book *Children and Their Families* — wrote about being offered "access" to his children: "A huge emptiness would well in my stomach, a deep loathing for those who would deign to tell me that they would ALLOW ACCESS to my children —

those I loved above all, those I created, those who give meaning to everything I did, those that were the very best of us two and the absolute physical manifestation of our once binding love. "Who the f--- are they that they should ALLOW anything? REASONABLE CONTACT! Is the law mad? Am I a criminal?"

Generations of males have watched friends, relatives and perhaps their own fathers lose contact with children through divorce. At the time this article was written almost 50,000 Australian children were being affected by their parents' divorce each year and almost a quarter of people aged 18 to 34 experienced such a break-up as children[62]. Half of all children not living with their divorced fathers see them less than once a fortnight, a quarter have contact once a year or less (ABS, Australian Social Trends March 2012). So huge numbers of young men have grown up seeing their fathers alienated from their families. These young men know what they have to lose if a marriage goes wrong. And in two-thirds of divorces it is the mother's decision to leave.

Despite new freedoms and choices available to women, their happiness — their subjective well-being — has actually declined over the past 35 years, according to research by the economics professor Betsey Stevenson and colleagues at the Wharton School in Philadelphia. Women have become less happy with their marriages over that time, perhaps due to the gap between their expectations and reality. For men this is a disaster. Think of that truism: happy wife, happy life. The reverse is even more true.

"Men have a very real fear of being turfed out or becoming redundant," says the clinical psychologist Owen Pershouse, who has spent more than 15 years helping men through separation and divorce through his Brisbane group MENDS. "Men know they often pay a huge price if a marriage ends and can be held hostage by women who are usually the ones to pull the plug." Pershouse notes that many men only question the costs of marriage after it is all over.

Many divorced men are now very publicly questioning whether the risks of marriage work mainly in women's favour, which may be why we so often hear complaints about men's reluctance to commit. There's been a huge drop in the crude marriage rate (the number of marriages per 1,000 people) over the past five decades, dropping from 9.3 in 1970 to 5.5 in 2010[63]. Yet this is mainly due to more couples in de facto relationships. There is overseas research suggesting cohabiting men are more likely to resist the shift to marriage.

They may have good reason. For a start, marriage may well mean less sex. There's no Australian research on the subject but a 1992 US national sex survey shows co-habiting men have more sex than husbands do.

That really matters to men, as evidenced by psychology professor Roy F. Baumeister's observations on significant gender differences in sex drive: "Men initiate sex often and refuse it rarely. Women initiate it much more rarely and refuse it much more often than men" (Psychologytoday.com).

There's been the most extraordinary shift from the 1950s, when sex was among a wife's marital duties, to the current situation where so many wives feel entitled to shut up shop if they are not interested. The men taking part in my research projects (published in *The Sex Diaries* and *What Men Want*) poured their hearts out about their misery at finding themselves in marriages where they had to grovel for sexual favours. One man went for 19 years with no sex in his marriage. His wife announced when his second child was born that their sex life was over.

But these murmurs of discontent are largely hidden from public view, as was the case back in the 1960s when Betty Friedan wrote in *The Feminine Mystique* about "the problem which has no name". Friedan gave voice to women's frustrations about the limitations imposed on them by the wifely role and decades of consciousness-raising followed. Now women grasp every opportunity to state their case, loud and clear.

Yet most men still lead unexamined lives. Their "problem which has no name" — marital discontent — remains unexplored. But one day that too will change.

CHAPTER 24

Single mothers – society's new heroines

First published 1998

The summer break was over and the two million regular viewers of the Seven Network's *Home and Away* were discovering the fate of one of the series' most popular characters. Chloe was a smart, studious girl who had just tackled her final school exams. But she was pregnant and her determination to keep the baby, with or without the support of her doctor boyfriend, had been the subject of much heady drama.

Her decision met with general approval from the close-knit coastal community in which she lived. The boyfriend was still on the scene and the couple seemed set on staying together. But single motherhood was always on the cards. In the world of the soaps, solo child-rearing had become all the rage.

"Single motherhood is now totally acceptable," said Susan Bower, who has spent the previous nine years working as a writer and story editor for local television dramas. "Particularly with the older women in their 20s, you may choose to have a character become a single mother because then she'll be seen as a strong role model. She's not a victim; she's taking charge of her life."

Bower explained that since the early 1980s single motherhood had emerged as an increasingly popular solution to unwanted pregnancy in local television dramas, a decision she saw as reflecting the prevailing belief in women's right to make choices about their lives.

The early evening time slot and young audience for many of these family dramas invited extra caution and also placed restrictions on discussions of contraception. The result was a real distortion of presentation of the choices available to single pregnant women, with solo parenting increasingly promoted as the most acceptable option. "There is also an extraordinary number of miscarriages," said Carol Long, another editor with long experience in local drama. "Women picking up heavy suitcases or falling down stairs. That's the easiest road we go down because that way the character comes out looking rosy because she hasn't had to make a decision."

Many writers mention the single mother scenario as having particular dramatic appeal, adding many possible twists and turns to the plot.

So here we have these enormously popular television dramas not only reflecting growing community acceptance of childrearing by unmarried mothers but perhaps adding momentum to the trend. The possibility left Bower and some colleagues feeling distinctly uneasy. "What we present is so unrealistic," she said. "Writers often get unbelievably frustrated because abortion would often be the best solution for these young women. It worries me that single motherhood is so often promoted as the right way to go."

There are good reasons to be concerned. At the time I wrote this, 27 per cent of all Australian children were being born out of wedlock. The ex-nuptial birth rate had increased by a staggering 70 per cent in the previous 10 years[64].

These figures were often dismissed as simply reflecting a shift towards non-marital child-rearing. Talking to experts around the country, I was constantly assured that these large numbers of ex-nuptial children were, in fact, being raised by parents in de facto relationships, rather than lone mothers. In the past, the only real data bearing on the true circumstances of these children came from a 1984 Australian Institute of Family Studies (AIFS) maternity leave study, which found that less than half of the women having ex-nuptial births were in de facto relationships at the time of the birth[65].

Many of these unions were found to be extremely unstable — within 18 months of the birth of the child, 19 per cent of the de facto relationships had broken up. Other research from the Institute has shown de facto partnerships are 10 times more likely to break up than a marriage[66].

But more recent evidence of the true state of affairs came from research produced for this article by Peter McDonald, then a demography professor at the Australian National University. McDonald was analysing data for a Research School of Social Sciences project, "Negotiating the Life Course", which included information about the relationship histories of women having ex-nuptial births.

The emerging picture was bleak. Yes, it was true that increasing numbers of ex-nuptial births were to couples in de facto relationships. Sixty-five per cent of the ex-nuptial births in the ANU survey were to never-married women in de facto relationships, 18 per cent to never-married solo women, 8.5 per cent to divorced but solo women, and 8.5 per cent to women divorced but in a de facto relationship.

But patterns following the birth revealed many of these

de facto relationships to be quite transitory. McDonald says: "About half of the ex-nuptial births are to women who are in and out of relationships, women with complex relationship histories. Even if the child is born in a de facto relationship, that often breaks down."

And the result is that most of these children do end up being raised by a lone mother, at least until she finds another partner. And we are often not talking just about one ex-nuptial child — almost half of the women McDonald surveyed had more than one such child, children who often accompanied their mother through any number of complex and unstable family situations. The ANU research showed a third of the de facto parents married after the birth of their child but 15 per cent of these marriages ended within a few years. Where the child's parents didn't marry, 38 per cent of the relationships broke up in less than five years.

Despite the prominence given in the media to educated, more affluent women who decide to bear children on their own, the ANU research showed that this is a tiny proportion of the swelling numbers of never-married lone mothers — 51 per cent of the women having ex-nuptial children didn't finish secondary school and 70 per cent had no post-school qualifications. AIFS research has found that couples bearing children in de facto relationships were usually from low socio-economic backgrounds. And most were young. More than half of all ex-nuptial children are born to women under 25. Even more striking is that most children of women in this age group are born outside marriage.

Most such women are incapable of supporting their children on their own and even though many do receive child support from fathers, most end up joining the ranks supported by our escalating welfare bill. More than 75 per cent of never-married lone mothers were then on the sole parent pension (Australian Bureau of Statistics Family Survey, 1992)[67], representing more than a quarter of the lone-parent population, which receives an annual $3 billion in welfare payments. Since sole parents in de facto relationships are not eligible for lone parent benefits, the substantial number of never-married lone mothers receiving pensions is proof that either most of these de facto couples are unable to sustain lasting relationships or else they are defrauding the system.

There were then two times more lone parents with dependent children than there were 20 years before. In 1975 about nine per cent of families with dependent children were lone-parent families, compared with about 19 per cent in 1996. Never-married women were emerging as an increasing proportion of the lone-parent population — in 1993, 27 per cent of female sole parent pensioners had never married, compared with 19 per cent in 1974.

In 1972 an intriguing discussion between Germaine Greer and Margaret Whitlam was published in *The National Times*. Whitlam, whose husband had just become prime minister, was outspoken in her criticism of ex-nuptial births, declaring it was irresponsible to produce children outside a family situation. When Greer confessed she was considering having a child on her own, Whitlam was forthright: "Well, I think that's just a selfish thought."

Later in the interview, she relented a little: "It may be all right for people who are well known and who have position and who can organise themselves … but it's not OK for everybody."

But it wasn't long before it was ok for everyone. The early '70s were a turning point. Up to this time single mothers and their children were stigmatised; the children were legally labelled "illegitimate" and suffered penalties concerning inheritance. There was very little welfare support — most single pregnant women were persuaded to relinquish their children. Large numbers of women entered shotgun marriages — in 1971 more than 40 per cent of births to women under 20 took place in the first eight months of the marriage.

Within months of Margaret Whitlam's confrontation with Germaine Greer, the Whitlam Government granted single mothers the same welfare payments as widows. This was the official signal that the ground was shifting; the rapid changes taking place in social and sexual attitudes were slowly reducing the shame associated with illegitimacy.

Soon Australian celebrities were proudly showing off ex-nuptial children in the women's magazines and promoting the joys of non-marital child-rearing. By January 1977, Kasey Findlay, the blonde baby daughter of a 24-year-old single primary school teacher, was crowned "Baby Australia".

"It's the year of the unmarried mother," announced the newspaper headline describing the occasion. "To the great majority of people in 1977 the unmarried mother is no longer a source of shock or shame but someone who is admired for the sacrifice she is prepared to make and the courage she often shows in a demanding role," pronounced the editorial in Sydney's *The Daily Telegraph*.

With the Family Law Act in 1975, huge numbers of divorced and separated women began to swell the ranks of lone parents — by 1986 there were three times as many lone mothers through divorce than never-married sole mothers, and large numbers of babies born to couples in de facto relationships were adding to the never-married group.

Joy Goodsell, convener of the Sole Parent Union, was quoted in the *Sydney Morning Herald* in 1991 as saying: "People having children without being married has just become part of society. I think that we have become more mature in our morality."

The most startling evidence of the dramatic shift that occurred in social attitudes came from an AIFS study on family values released in 1997. The study, conducted by David de Vaus, included a number of questions on attitudes to single motherhood and ex-nuptial children. De Vaus found most people then believed that you need two parents to bring up a child (68 per cent of males and 58 per cent of females). But when women in their 20s — the group most likely to become unmarried mothers — were asked the same question, only 39 per cent felt that two parents were important.

So a majority of young women then felt fathers were incidental to the task of raising children — just as many men were expressing a desire for more involved, hands-on fatherhood.

These trends raise interesting questions about attitudes in future generations — particularly the many young boys being brought up by the new generations of single mothers. One wonders if a boy raised in such circumstances can grow to understand and aspire to the role of family man, valued for his contribution to his children. Are we destined to mimic the tragedy of the young black American males raised by successive generations of single mothers — young men who so often grow up alienated from family life? The adverse economic and social consequences of this trend are easily documented.

Single parents are the fastest-growing demographic group in the country and among the most disadvantaged. Sole mothers are more likely to live in poverty, far less likely to be in the full-time workforce than other women.

In recent years there has been increasing evidence of the disadvantage suffered by children being raised in sole-parent families, with children in these families experiencing more mental and physical health problems and having poorer educational outcomes than children in two-parent families. Adolescent children in such families are more at risk of delinquency, early sexual activity and substance abuse.

The escalating cost to the community of the problems faced by such children are all too apparent — in our schools, in juvenile crime statistics, in over-burdened social welfare services and community welfare organisations and in increasing social welfare payments.

But equally important is the effect on the women making the decision to bear a child on their own or in unstable de facto relationships. Of course, not all women have a choice — for religious or cultural reasons, abortion or contraception may not be an option. And it is certainly true that some women have babies in what they believe are lasting relationships, only to be abandoned by their partners.

But whether or not the decision is deliberate, the results are the same. Most women who end up taking this path are already disadvantaged. By taking on the burden of raising a child or children on their own, they dramatically reduce their opportunities for further education or for achieving stable employment. Research on sole mothers by the AIFS has documented their vulnerability to poverty, their dependence on social security and the difficulties they face in working their way out of their deprived circumstances.

There is also good reason to believe these women are reducing their chances of ever achieving a stable relationship or secure marriage. All subsequent relationships are burdened by the difficulties faced by a new partner in dealing with the woman's children — a proven liability for successful re-partnering.

It all adds up to increasing numbers of Australian women embarking on a mighty risky path — risky to themselves and their children. And they are doing so in the absence of any substantial public debate about the consequences. That's what's surprising about the Australian situation — in contrast to other countries such as the United States and Britain.

Public discussion of the issue erupted in the US during the 1992 presidential election campaign when the Vice-President, Dan Quayle, criticised a TV sitcom character, Murphy Brown, for having a child outside marriage. Although Quayle's comments incited an initially hostile media reaction, within a year an influential article by Barbara Dafoe Whitehead in *Atlantic Monthly*, "Dan Quayle was right", led to widespread discussion on the damaging consequences of the trend towards lone parenthood. In 1997 Bill Clinton referred to the trend as "the single biggest social problem in our society".

Similarly, in Britain there was considerable debate over these issues, culminating in a controversy when the Prime Minister, Tony Blair, suffered a serious party rebellion over plans to reduce benefits for single parents. Blair prevailed, but politically the move proved costly, with the resignation of one minister and a big revolt on the Labour back benches. Nevertheless, in the 1990s concern about the growing numbers of sole parents remained very much on the government's agenda.

Certainly, the trend towards sole parenting was more extreme at that time in Britain and the US, with far more adverse consequences. But comment on Australia's dramatic shift in this direction during this time was largely left to a few conservative commentators and radio announcers and the tabloid press. In 1997 figures on ex-nuptial births were greeted by *The Daily Telegraph* with a thundering full-page story headlined "A nation of bastards".

Strangely silent were the many social commentators and policy analysts usually so keen to decry social trends detrimental to women's welfare. The Women's Movement had long preached to women, particularly in developing countries, the importance of controlling fertility and delaying childbearing until they are adequately educated or have acquired work skills. Why the unwillingness to speak out when so many young Australian women were choosing to derail their prospects by having babies on their own or in unstable de facto relationships?

Anne Callanan was then a policy worker for the Council of Single Mothers and their Children, a vigorous lobby group. Callanan agreed with me that there was a reluctance to face the issue. "I think we should be talking about it but I feel so nervous about what would happen in a public debate," she says. "Our concern is that the issue tends to get hijacked by people with a particular agenda. I don't know if I'd want to open that can of worms."

Yet Callanan's extensive personal experience with the struggles faced by single mothers had convinced her that society should be discouraging women from taking on such a burden. "It isn't something we want to encourage, because when you live it on a day-to-day basis, it's so bloody difficult." Having worked to try to reduce the prejudice faced by single mothers, Callanan was forthright about the dilemma she faced: "I'm not sure how you provide proper support to those who are already single mothers and still try to give the message to people who haven't yet done it that it isn't such a good idea."

Despite all the evidence, not everyone is willing to acknowledge it isn't a good idea. I spoke to numerous social policy analysts and spokespeople on women's issues who were loath to acknowledge any detriment to women in this trend. They spoke only of the need to decrease the stigma still attached to lone parenting and increase support to reduce the financial consequences for women of making this choice. Many were angry that women are invariably the ones left to face the consequences of unplanned pregnancy.

Yet of all women's choices, it is unfair to suggest single motherhood lets men off the hook. Single motherhood keeps men liable — at minimum through the payment of child support — but often facing only slender opportunities for a real paternal relationship. Kathleen Swinbourne was then a single mother and the Women's Electoral Lobby spokeswoman on family issues. She felt that if society is concerned about single mothers living in poverty and being undereducated, we should be providing them with more welfare support.

Questioned about the rising costs inherent in this support, Swinbourne argued that the two-parent family also comes at a price to the community. "There's all the costs of domestic violence. That's a very high cost." Swinbourne's view was that we have so many single-parent families because the nuclear family no longer works. "Younger women have been brought up to know they don't need to be treated like second-class citizens. They can do anything they want to do and they aren't willing to accept a relationship that says they can't."

While most women would like to have children within a good relationship, Swinbourne felt that they were no longer willing to compromise about that relationship. "Many's the time I've come across women talking about their husbands or their ex-husbands and making the comment, 'It's like having another child around'. They don't want that sort of relationship." Swinbourne was totally opposed to any attempt to discourage women from becoming single mothers. She believes motherhood is the problem when it comes to limiting women's lives, not just single motherhood. "I wouldn't make a moral judgment on the way anyone makes these decisions. I would never tell them it's not what they should do."

Yet the Women's Electoral Lobby is clearly prescriptive about other aspects of women's lives. Swinbourne explained that "WEL is in favour of getting women into the workforce, getting them financially independent and getting them in charge of their own lives." And even if the decision to bear a child as a single woman places limits on such achievements, Swinbourne believed WEL should still promote women's right to make such a choice. "If that is the choice a woman wants to make, that is a choice that should be supported. I wouldn't push two-parent families at the expense of women living fulfilled lives."

It is sadly true that many adults are failing to find fulfilment in the two-parent family. But having spent five years as a single mother, I baulk at the notion that single motherhood should be promoted as a more rewarding option. My own circumstances were immensely privileged. As a widow I had financial security, a well-paid job and wonderful support, but it was still tough going.

And that is why I shudder when, at the time I wrote this article my nine-year-old daughter beamed at the news that one of her favourite television characters was becoming a single mother. It was frightening to see her celebrating such a risky start to adult life. When I asked her whether anyone on the show had suggested the character have an abortion, she was horrified to discover I was talking about killing an unborn baby. This led to a very difficult conversation about why anyone would want to do such a thing and how Chloe was silly enough to get pregnant in the first place — a conversation I can understand many parents wishing to avoid.

But I wonder whether we have gone too far in avoiding difficult conversations about good and bad choices in dealing with unplanned pregnancy, let alone how to avoid it. In recent years we have allowed conservative politicians and lobby groups to limit many of these options — by restricting funding for sex education and family planning services and by limiting discussion of abortion, which remains one means of ensuring fewer Australian children are born into poverty and disadvantage.

Perhaps it's time we started talking long and hard about the risks of having children in de facto relationships, since such partnerships so often lack the commitment that renders marriages a more secure context for raising families. In the absence of this much-needed debate and public education about the real facts of life, child-bearing outside marriage has gained dangerous appeal. We reap the consequences.

CHAPTER 25

Some families are better than others for children

First published 2014

What a revealing tribute marking the fifth season finale of the popular television drama series *Offspring*. Comedian and actor Eddie Perfect, who plays a central role in the drama, wrote about how the show has morphed from a sexy exploration of relationships to a celebration of dysfunctional families.

As he explained on theguardian.com, *Offspring* was now a show about family, "not outdated conservative notions of family but a broader ideology of who we include in our family." It's very simple really, he suggested. All we need is to have "full enriching lives surrounded by people we love. One big dysfunctional family."

Offspring does dysfunctional families so wonderfully well. There's a rich vein of comedy in the constant relationship stuff-ups which mark the Proudman family, from the chaotic love lives of the ageing baby-boomer parents to their three neurotic adult children and their merry band of screwy friends. And yes, as they romp through these messy unions they are endlessly creating families. Offspring are born in all manner of strange circumstances, to parental relationships which usually fall apart. But the children do fine, of course, because they feel The Love.

Here's Billie, who was then toying with the idea of having a baby with her new boyfriend Lawrence. She had feelings for Lawrence, she said. "Quite strong feelings. Maybe I don't need to love him? Plenty of mismatched people have kids together. People who hate each other have kids together. And the kids survive. Most of the time. And if things don't work out romantically, he'd be a first-class co-parent."

That pretty much sums up the new relaxed approach to parenting which is gaining such a grip in Australia, particularly in our lower socio-economic communities. The casualisation of families is one of the major factors entrenching disadvantage for children in this country. Yet no one wants to talk about it.

Witness the tirade of abuse received by Senator Cory Bernardi for summarising research showing poorer outcomes for children in single parent and stepfamilies in his book *The Conservative Revolution*. Bernardi is known for sometimes making ill-considered remarks but his comments on sole parent families were sensible and evidence-based, mentioning higher rates of mental health disorders, more exposure to abuse and neglect, higher levels of criminality and promiscuity. Yet ABC journalists took these statements as further example of his "far-right" views and commentators lined up to tear him to shreds. Opposition politicians gleefully took their own pot shots, with Bill Shorten condemning Bernardi's "offensive" comments about families, claiming they were based on "out-of-date prejudices."

Kay Hymowitz has seen this all before. A renowned family

scholar with New York's Manhattan Institute in 1915 she spoke about these issues at Consilium, the Centre for Independent Studies' elite gathering of leaders from business, finance, academia, politics and community organisations.

Hymowitz reported a sense of déjà vu witnessing the struggle Australia is having in coming to terms with the essential truth about family life — namely that children do better with two parents, particularly married parents. Whilst Australian public discourse remains locked into the comforting fantasy that all families are equally good for children, America has faced up to the fact that growing up in a single parent home, or stepfamily or with unmarried parents puts children at risk. These children are less likely to do well in school, suffer more mental health and behavioural problems, and be more likely to be abused and become single parents themselves than children in stable traditional families.

In the United States it took many decades of fierce public debate before this reality sunk in. Fifty years back Patrick Moynihan came under fire for suggesting that the growth of single mothers in black communities was largely responsible for the "tangle of pathology" contributing to their disadvantage. "A national effort towards the problems of Negro Americans must be directed towards the question of family structure," concluded the Moynihan Report which was promptly charged with "blaming the victim", academics stepped in to challenge its statistics and Moynihan was attacked for "subtle racism".

Then followed what Hymowitz calls "forty-plus years of lies," systematically down-playing the importance of father absence in black families. Yet over the next three decades most social scientists, decision-makers and politicians took note of the emerging body of research providing solid evidence that children with two married parents are far more likely to flourish. By 1994 President Bill Clinton, who was raised by a single mother, was declaring in his State of the Union address: "We cannot renew our country when, within a decade more than half of our children will be born into families where there is no marriage."

Barack Obama, also the product of a single parent family, has been outspoken about the problems facing his community where 70 per cent of children are now born to unmarried mothers. "We know the statistics — that children who grow up without a father are five times more likely to live in poverty and commit crime; nine times more likely to drop out of schools and 20 times more likely to end up in prison. They are more likely to have behavioural problems or run away from home or become teenage parents themselves. And the foundations of our community are weaker because of it."

These statistics, which seem to have escaped so many of our blinkered local commentators, come from incontrovertible international evidence from European countries and Australia as well as the United States. "The non-marital birth and divorce rate started climbing from 1960s and by the '90s many countries had acquired large scale data sets like the US National Longitudinal Survey of Youth that allowed them to compare children growing up in different types of families," says Hymowitz, who presented some of this data at the 2015 Festival of Dangerous Ideas, appearing with me in a controversial session entitled "Some Families are Better than Others for Children". Interestingly, we attracted an appreciative, sold-out crowd, despite the fact that this Festival is renowned for presenting politically correct ideas that rarely challenge their trendy audiences.

In her book *Marriage and Caste in America — Separate and Unequal Families in a Post-Marital Age* Hymowitz explained the pivotal role played by ground-breaking research from Princeton sociology professor Sara McLanahan. A divorced mother herself, McLanahan was shocked to discover how little evidence underpinned the fierce debate over the Moynihan Report. Over the next decade she analysed whatever numbers she could find and discovered children in single parent homes were not doing as well as children from two parent homes on a wide variety of different measures.

Throughout the late '80s and early '90s, she presented her emerging findings over strenuous protests from feminists, academics and the mainstream media. In 1994 she published, with Gary Sandfur, her book *Growing Up with a Single Parent*, which proved a game-changer.

"It was a turning point. One by one, leading family researchers gradually came around, concluding that McLanahan — and perhaps even Moynihan — was right," reported Hymowitz.

These results apply not only to the United States where many single parent families are black or Hispanic and include many teenage mothers but also to European countries which have more adult single mothers and better welfare support for lone parents. Although critics of this type of research often argue the difference between outcomes for children are mainly due to poverty, sophisticated statistical analysis has shown that's only part of the story.

Hymowitz: "Researchers have tried to figure out whether it was poverty rather than family structure that was causing kids' problems. That's not what they found. Even when kids were growing up in comfortable circumstances, their outcomes were worse than their peers with married parents. Two hands are better than one — a single parent just can't bring the same time or energy to the complicated enterprise that is contemporary parenting. But that's not the whole story. A young single parent generally wants a new partner and perhaps more children. That's understandable, but new boyfriends, husbands, half-siblings require children to re-adjust over and over and they may well be losing contact with their own fathers. All of it adds up to a childhood of instability and loss with life-long consequences."

The real surprise that emerged from all this research was that children of separated mothers who remarry don't fare any better, even though these families are less likely to be in poverty. Children in stepfamilies are just as much at risk of a range of adverse outcomes as children in single parent homes. "That was unexpected, since it was assumed that the improved financial circumstances of these families would make a difference. Yet these children were just as much at risk as those in sole parent families of problems such as emotional and behavioural difficulties, poor academic performance, leaving home early and dropping out of school," says Bryan Rodgers, Professor of Family Health and Wellbeing at the ANU, then one of our key researcher in this area. His 2009 book *Children in Changing Families* (co-authored by Jan Pryor) contained over 30 pages reviewing over 400 studies comparing outcomes for children in different family structures.

The final piece of the puzzle came with work — in the US, Britain, Europe and Australia — comparing children with cohabiting and married parents. It turns out that marriage matters. The instability of defacto relationships means many children with unmarried parents end up in lone parent families. Using data from the Longitudinal Study of Australian children, Lixia Qu and Ruth Weston from the Australian Institute of Family Studies found young families with cohabiting parents are nearly three times more likely to break up than married families — 19 per cent of the cohabiting-parent families compared to seven per cent of the marrieds separated within four years. The same researchers showed children in cohabiting families lag behind children with married parents in overall socio-emotional and general development, show poorer learning, more conduct problems and experience poorer parenting.

Of course, there are huge numbers of children thriving in families with unmarried parents, just as many single mothers do a splendid job, against the odds, providing an excellent, stable upbringing for their children. Whenever this issue is raised in Australia there's an outcry from people who have been brought up by wonderful single mothers outraged at any suggestion that children in single parent families don't do so well.

What we are talking about here is simply an increased *risk* that children will have mental health problems, or not do as well at school, or be subjected to more abuse. The chance is usually small that children in these families suffer these problems yet when increasing numbers of children end up being raised in such families, the cost to society is huge.

"What is a matter of private concern when it is on a small scale becomes a matter of public concern when it reaches epidemic proportions," argued UK family law judge Paul Coleridge prior to his recent retirement, speaking out about the "misery" of family breakdown. He challenged the common notion that it makes no difference whether parents cohabit or marry. "One [arrangement] tends to last and the other doesn't," he said, quoting British research suggesting children with unmarried parents were twice as likely to suffer a family break-up as those with married parents.

He makes an important point — it should be a matter of public concern when one in four Australian children are now born to single or unmarried parents. Divorce is no longer the major reason kids are being brought up in single parent homes — most end up that way because women have children on their own or in unstable defacto relationships. And these are mainly women who can't afford to raise these children — hence they end up growing up in poverty. That was the fascinating twist to Bob Hawke's famous election pledge that no child would live in poverty by 1990. Hawke's promise fell in a heap because that was the decade when the shift towards the current family patterns really started to kick in — the 1990s saw a staggering 70 per cent increase in the ex-nuptial birth rate.

While most well-educated women are now delaying marriage but still tying the knot before they have children, it's mainly less educated women who do not get married and instead have children on their own or in de facto relationships, a choice that greatly disadvantages their children. Degree-qualified women are now the group most likely to be married in all age groups from 30-44 according to research from Genevieve Heard, from the Centre of Population and Urban Research at Monash University[68].

"It is women from higher socioeconomic backgrounds who are tending to delay marriage and child-rearing. The less educated women are less likely to marry at all but are having more children and having them earlier. They are much more likely to end up as lone parents," comments Heard.

Her best known work has focussed on this "marriage gap" which she argues is increasing the divide between the haves and the have nots. "The marriage gap greatly exacerbates income inequality and reduces the chances these families will make it out of poverty. Educated parents bring all sorts of advantages to their childrearing: money, skills, stable Kay Hymowitz's neighbourhoods and better schools. Add to that the enormous advantage of a second parent and the stability that marriage tends to bring and with few exceptions these kids have it made. The child from a more disadvantaged background has a far greater chance of overcoming challenges when she has two parents in a stable relationship. Instead, these days, she's usually hit with a double whammy of low income and a single overstressed parent."

Of course, there are well-educated people who buck these trends — professional women having children on their own, or affluent couples who raise happy children in stable relationships — and *their* children are likely to do just fine. But the choices they make don't pan out nearly as well for sole families who can't afford these children nor for the society which ends up supporting them.

It is all very well for the good folk on *Offspring*, these

families filled with doctors and other professionals, to make fun of marriage. But consider the impact on the many thousands of viewers who can ill-afford to follow their cheerful embrace of dysfunctional families. In a recent episode, Jimmy Proudman was trying to persuade his partner Zara, who is pregnant with his second child, to marry him. She fobbed him off saying she doesn't believe in that "inherited garbage" and joked they were already bound together by children and real estate.

Debra Oswald, creator and head writer of *Offspring* is the partner of Sydney ABC radio personality Richard Glover whose newspaper columns often proudly boast of their thirty-two-year unmarried union which has raised two sons. When I wrote about this topic some time ago he took me on. "Do our children miss out on anything?" he wrote, "Well, yes, Bettina. Principally, I think, they miss out on vases," says the well-known, well-positioned journalist, referring to his family's lack of wedding presents. An elitist, facile response which speaks to the journalist's disconnect from real world issues leading to such instability for lower-income defacto relationships.

Every year in Australia there are conferences held on child abuse, papers published, academics and child protection officers ponder whys and wherefores of this scourge that costs our country over $2 billion a year. But never any mention of the fact that child abuse in lone parent families is about two and half times higher than would be expected given the number of children living in such families, according to the Australian Institute of Family Studies.

Turn on the ABC news and every few days there's another report on institutional child sexual abuse. Yet the chances of being felt up by a horny priest or YMCA child care worker are mighty slim compared to the numbers of children at risk from Mum's boyfriend. A report by Jeremy Sammut from the Centre for Independent Studies reviewed more than seventy research studies to provide overwhelming evidence that girls are sexually abused by "stepfathers" — partners of their single, remarried or repartnered mothers — at up to 20 times the rate of abuse by biological fathers.

For all the talk about homelessness, how rarely we hear mention of the fact that conflict in families, particularly step-families, is a major cause of the 20 to 25,000 youth not living with their families.

What about the education specialists? There's rarely any mention in education circles of the disruptive effects on education of family breakup. Australian Bureau of Statistics analysis shows that for 18-24-year-olds, 62 per cent of those who experience parental separation during their childhood completed year 12 compared with 77 per cent of those whose parents did not separate.

Family type is one of the most important factors determining mental health of children, according to our most comprehensive study in the area, the Western Australian Child Health Survey which followed 2,790 children from ages 4 to 16. When they announced this finding, the researchers told me they shuddered when they received a message saying I had called — they'd hoped this issue would slip under the media radar.

So, what's the explanation of our country's determination to keep the head firmly stuck in the sand? Don Edgar, founding director of the Australian Institute of Family Studies, says he often struck resistance to the idea that marriage as such made a difference to children's wellbeing. "The old Labor-leftie group have a residual distrust of the 'bourgeois' notion of marriage and family. They remain determined to embrace the new diversity of family forms and just don't want to hear that a committed marriage might be better for children than other structures," he says.

This blinkered promotion of family diversity remains hugely influential with any challenge to its benefits firmly buried or shouted down. "Family structure is one of the major issues diminishing the lives of many Australian children. But sadly, we have a long way to go before that truth finds its rightful place on the public agenda," concludes Edgar.

CHAPTER 26

Why men earn more – the truth about the wage gap

First published 2006

As our country held its breath awaiting the rescue of trapped Beaconsfield miners Brant Webb and Todd Russell, we received a grim reminder of why miners earn big money. The work is hard, dirty and often very dangerous. That's why miners make it into the top twenty earners in Australia.

Men do most of the dirty, dangerous work — that's one reason they end up earning more. But there are other good reasons for why, in 2006, the average woman in Australia earns only about 92 cents for every dollar paid to a man[69]. Yes, there are still glass ceilings, women don't always receive equal pay for equal work. But according to Sex Discrimination Commissioner Pru Goward[70] the most important factor is "trade-offs men and women choose to make"[71].

Most women simply aren't interested in buying into the trade-offs that earn men the big bucks. They don't want to miss out — on their children's first words, first steps, the school plays, the precious gift of time, for friends and family. Women tend to be picky, looking for jobs that offer fulfillment, convenient hours, and a good working environment. Sure, there are women competing with men in the high-paying jobs — putting in the same long hours and matching men, dollar for dollar. But most are resisting, with the result that the proportion of women working full-time in this country has barely shifted in the past thirty years[72].

Men and women with similar training generally show similar earnings until they reach their 30s[73], says Mark Wooden from the Melbourne Institute. But in the older age groups, the gap begins to widen, as motherhood undermines women's ambition, or deprives them of real choices to continue forging ahead[74]. But women also handicap themselves by not daring to take risks, not knowing their own worth, not negotiating their salaries and selling themselves short.

Mary Hasouros, 45, is a Sydney pharmacist who is happy making her trade-offs. She's currently working three days a week in a pharmacy close to home, allowing her time for her two teenage children plus some time out. Her husband has his own computer company and isn't available to help with the children so Mary's only worked part-time since they were born. But she likes it that way. "My life is pretty good now. This way I've got time for the children. When I work full-time, it's a 55-hour week, standing up all day. The pharmacy closes at six, you are running around picking up kids, trying to do everything. I don't know how people do it. I love having time to go to Pilates classes, to catch up with my friends. It's a better life."

Although she'd like the freedom of running the business in the way she would like, she's resisted the idea of owning a pharmacy — "I like to be able to walk away at the end of the day." She can't face the risk involved in buying her own pharmacy. "I don't know that I would want that level of stress. I've always chosen the safe route." While the couple borrowed a large amount of money to set up her husband's firm — "That was very risky at the time," says Mary — she couldn't cope with the worry of doing that for her own business. And she has other priorities. "Money is not the main thing for me," she adds.

Pharmacy is a career which allows women to make choices. Most men choose it as a route into self-employment, small business ownership or management jobs with large retail chain-stores. While some women do the same and earn good money as a result, most use it as a source of mother-friendly, flexible part-time jobs, with limited responsibilities that do not spill over into their family time.

Jocelyn Bussing, 37, is not averse to taking risks. She bought her second pharmacy in Sydney's beach-side Cronulla just before the suburb erupted into race riots. She admits this was a hair-raising time, particularly since she'd spent months persuading narrow-minded old-school male landlord that she was ready to run a second business. This is a woman who knew very early where she was heading. At 21 she was managing a pharmacy, at 27 she bought her first. "It was always my goal, to own my own business." Or two.

She realises she's a rare breed through contact with other women pharmacists in her professional network. "Most want to be able to go home and leave work at work." Jocelyn's not like that. "Sometimes people ask me how many hours a week I work. It is probably easier to ask me how many hours I don't work," she says with a laugh. This mother of two children (aged five and seven) hopes to be earning $120-130,000 within a year or so, when her new business settles in. That's almost double what many employed pharmacists earn. "Most women don't want to take that step of running their own businesses. I can understand why they are nervous, but I see so much scope for them. They can do the same job they are doing now but share in the profits."

Jocelyn is competing with men at their own game — and earning the rewards. But there are far more women like Mary, in pharmacy and other jobs, who prefer a better balance between work and the rest of life. So, they work shorter hours, choose jobs that offer more flexibility, less travel, less risk and responsibility.

That's why women short-change their earnings, according to Warren Farrell, the author of the provocative book *Why Men Earn More*. Dr Farrell has a long history of dealing with gender issues — he's the only man ever elected three times to the board of America's National Organization for Women. Using all available statistics on men and women's working habits, he's come up with a list of ways women can increase their pay. Here's how women can join the big earners:

1. Put in more hours.
It seems obvious but it's *the* key issue. In Australia the average hours worked by men are almost twice that of women. Men are almost twice as likely to work more than 50 hours a week, with 19 per cent of women and 35 per cent of men putting in these long hours — according to data from the Household, Income and Labour Dynamics and Australia survey (HILDA).

Even our smartest women end up working far shorter hours. Look at women doctors. To get into medicine, these young women were as ambitious and hard-working as any of their male colleagues. But a few years down the track it's a different story. Current figures show a female GPs works only 63 per cent of the hours put in by a male GP over his lifetime.

Amongst the specialist doctors, this figure ends up 75 per cent, still a large difference[75].

As with other women, the reason the female doctors end up working shorter hours is all about caring for families. Most carry the major responsibility for caring for their children (a third of female GPs are married to other doctors), most work minimal hours when their children are young and tend to retire, or cut back their hours earlier than men. "Many women GPs, who have young children, tell me of the difficulties balancing long, demanding hours of general practices with family responsibilities," says South Australian GP Leanne Rowe, an executive member of the Royal College of General Practitioners. When their own children are ill, they face a terrible choice. "Having to choose between sick patients and their own sick children, that's very tough."

2. Choose careers that pay more.

Supply and demand means you earn more by choosing a job that:

- Requires hard-to-attain skills (engineering vs arts)
- Is in an unpleasant environment (prison vs childcare)
- Requires long hours (retail manager vs shop assistant)
- Is unrewarding to most people (tax accountant vs artist)
- Demands physical risk (miner vs public servant)
- Is inconvenient (travelling salesman vs teacher)
- Is hazardous (policeman vs librarian.)

Many more men than women choose such jobs, even when women are paid more to do them. For instance, female crane operators in Australia earn twice as much as men in the same job but only four per cent of these jobs are filled by women. Only three per cent of forklift drivers are female but they earn almost a fifth more than male drivers.

3. The bigger risks you take at work, the more you earn.
In high-earning financial careers, investment bankers often earn a percentage of the profit they bring in. While many men are comfortable with that pay-for-play compensation, a much smaller percentage of women are willing to be paid for their productivity.

It's not surprising women are reluctant to borrow money to buy into a business or take on jobs involving big risks, says Professor Leonie Still, director of the Centre for Women and Business at the University of Western Australia "Women are used to being looked after. There's that legacy of never having to put their own money on the line," she says, mentioned her experience is many women are reluctant to pay out money to further their own careers — "They won't even buy a self-improvement book. They'll borrow it from the library whereas the guys will say, 'I need that, so I'd better buy it'."

And once again women's family responsibilities get in the way. Professor Still: "Women tend to worry, 'If anything goes wrong who's going to feed the kids?' whereas the man thinks, 'If this goes well it will make me wealthy and I'll be admired by everyone'. It's a different mindset that translates into bigger earnings."

4. Don't go for feel-good jobs.
A London School of Economics study of over 10,000 British graduates found the men started off earning 12 per cent more than the women. The reason? Most of the women had

majored in the social sciences and the arts, while men chose engineering, maths and computing. While over half the women said their primary interest was a socially useful job, men were almost twice as likely to stress salary.

Yet graduate women who move into traditional male professions often start off earning more than the men. The average starting salary for female geologists in Australia is $60,000 compared to $52,000 for men, female electrical engineering technicians start out $3,000 ahead of their male colleagues, mechanical engineers and computer professionals a $1,000 ahead.

5. Accept responsibility.
Women often go for jobs which carry less responsibility. "Women tend not to be in line management jobs, jobs where they are required to take responsibility for profit and loss," says Professor Still. She finds women are more likely to choose jobs they feel will be more fulfilling, people-contact jobs that, she says, are often "peripheral to the main game in an organisation". Women could be much more effective and rewarded more effectively if they were strategic about what they are doing, she adds.

Professor Still was disappointed by the result of a recent survey of her university's MBA students. "The men had headed off and many were earning in the millions. They'd used the MBA as leverage for their careers." And what had the women done? "Many had had a baby, taken time out, gone overseas or started their own business. They'd done the MBA to get career leverage and wasted it as soon as they came out."

But the reason many women make these decisions is they

realise they won't be able to take on the big jobs and still look after their families. "So many workplaces don't offer sensible flexibilities which would allow women to look up the ladder and say, 'There's a life there for me'," says Pru Goward.

6. Sell yourself.

Negotiating a salary is like a wrestling match. At least, that's how men see it but when women are asked how they view such negotiations, they see it very differently — "it's like going to the dentist." The result is women are far less likely to push for what they are worth, which makes a major difference to their earnings.

Linda Babcock and Sara Laschever, authors of *Women Don't Ask: Negotiation and the Gender Divide* have calculated that as a result not negotiating the terms of their first job, women stand to lose out on more than $500,000 by age 60.

Fiona Krautil spent some time as Director of the Equal Opportunity for Women in the Workplace Agency before moving into her current position as head of diversity at ANZ. Despite her string of big jobs, she admits she is terrible at negotiating her own salary. "I am good at negotiating for other people, but not good at negotiating my own value."

She finds most women she deals with have trouble selling themselves and things haven't changed much since she first worked in a bank ten years ago. "I'm still struggling with the low aspirations of women." While the ANZ now has more women in middle management there's still a major task pushing women through into the senior ranks. "The women think. 'I just have to work hard and do a good job and someone will notice me.' They focus so hard on doing a good job, head down, tail up, and don't realise the important of networking and managing what they are doing to do next. They are not tuned into the pecking order stuff so they don't sell themselves, don't self-nominate and therefore often get overlooked," she says.

Fiona works on supporting the diverse needs of women in her bank, split between a majority of women who are happy with part-time work with few career aspirations and those keen to move up through the ranks. She mentions a survey of part-time workers in retail banks which found about a third worked for social contact, a third simply for the money and the rest wanted careers. But she argues women often limit their ambitions because the workplace doesn't provide the flexibility they need — "A lot to the choices women make are forced choices."

Despite women's lower earnings, they may still come out ahead — in terms of fulfillment. That's one point Warren Farrell makes very clear. Yes, women can increase their earning capacity but every suggestion he has for making this happen requires "trading quality of life for money".

Women in this country may be earning less than men but they are more content. Australian women continue to show a strong preference for part-time work — particularly when they become mothers — and reap the psychological rewards. The latest HILDA survey clearly shows women working part-time are more satisfied than full-time women. The part-times are far happier with their work-life balance and just as satisfied with their jobs as the full-timers. In fact, over half the women working full-time want to work fewer hours, while just over a third of the part-timers want to work more[76][77].

There are risks with this course, says Pru Goward, warning

many women pay the price of their lower earnings when lower superannuation means they end up poor. But our Sex Discrimination Commissioner still feels most women know what they are doing: "There's no question that some of the choices women make are better choices."

CHAPTER 27

Busy women, bored men – men's retirement blues

First published 2014

Shirley is bursting with energy. The 70-year-old Sydney woman has always embraced life, cramming her days with endless activities. She has a law degree but worked part-time from when her children were at school and she became caught up in parents' committees and running the tuckshop. She has now cut her work days right back, but has plenty to keep her busy, including evening meetings planning campaigns for local environmental issues.

It was fine while her dentist husband was busy with his own career but then he retired, and the cracks started to appear. "Even if I prepare a meal for him in advance he drives me crazy ringing to see if I'll be there to join him. He's resentful that I still have so much on my plate, yet he never takes up my suggestions of things for him to do. I know he wants me home to do things with him, but I don't want my life shrinking."

For all the jokes about men and women living on different planets, it's the post-retirement period that lays bare the telling consequences of the way modern men and women live their lives.

That's when the chickens come home to roost from men's dependence on women for their social networks, the failure of many men to develop close, lasting friendships and their devotion to their careers, often at the expense of developing other interests and worthwhile activities.

The golden years burn brightly for many older women but for men they often splutter as they struggle with creating a meaningful life post-retirement. Once the lives of older women were dominated by the "empty nest" as mothers struggled to come to terms with the loss of their mothering role. But for years now, research has shown many older women are thriving. As noted feminist Betty Friedan explained in the book *The Fountain of Age*, "What the women experienced was increased activity, increased excitement, increased overall happiness, a decrease in depression and an increase in pride. No such change was found for men."

Research shows that when Australian married men give up work they tend to come home to their wives, with the bulk of their social contact shifting from time spent with work colleagues to time with their partners. But many of the women move in the opposite direction — instead of increased time with their families they are out and about, enjoying friends and other social contacts.

"Retired women recorded a big increase in time spent with family/ friends outside the household, while retired men recorded a decrease," reports Roger Patulny, a sociology lecturer at the University of Wollongong, who analysed data on social contact in old age in the journal *Family Matters*.

Most of the time retired men used to spend with work colleagues now gets spent with their wives. Patulny: "After retirement men's family time increases from 13 to 15.7 hours per day, while their daily time with friends decreases by nearly

20 minutes and with colleagues/acquaintances by over 2½ hours. By contrast, many women grasp the opportunity for more time spent away from their partners when they retire, increasing average time spent with nonfamily members from 75 to 103 minutes a day."

"Men are hit pretty hard by retirement because they haven't really had the opportunity to diversify their social networks as much and then find themselves devoid of the one network they have constantly relied upon for years," Patulny comments.

It's hard on marriages, particularly because for men this stage of life was traditionally associated with a new drive for intimacy and closeness after his big career thrust was over. But a man's new neediness is hardly welcome to the wife enjoying spreading her wings.

A longitudinal study conducted by Marjorie Fiske and colleagues from the University of California Medical School interviewed men and women before and after retirement and found retired women often made positive changes in their lives — like training, travel, more education — but many of the men were bored and isolated. Fiske: "The men got angrier and angrier as their wives over the years got more confident and began to do more things, instead of just taking care of them. The wives began to resent their husbands' demands on them. The men simply got more and more depressed."

Most men brush off the idea that they resent their wives' new enthusiasms. "Every time I turn around she's off again. Off to her choir one minute, then shopping, or a book club, then off to have coffee. It's endless," laughs Peter McNeil, 82, before hastily explaining that it's not that he's resentful of her busy life. He's also a very busy man, he tells me, explaining the various discussion groups he's involved in as well as taking a very active role in the Blackheath Men's Shed. It's just that sometimes there's a problem when she's off in their shared car, he says.

It was interesting how often older women list off a string of activities they are involved in — learning painting or pottery, attending university courses, writers festivals, book clubs, all sorts of stimulating activities, but ask their husbands what their wives are up to and they'll mention shopping or the hairdresser. And talking ... "I don't know what these women find to talk about all the time," one man grumbled to me.

Melbourne psychologist Dr Peter O'Connor sees many older men in this situation who react to their wives' desire to pursue new interests with obstruction and objections. "There's often a resentment fuelled by envy. The man finds himself with no one dependent on him and, even more frightening, he encounters his own feelings of vulnerability, loss of power and potency and increasing dependence. Sometimes these men defend against the anxiety generated by their wives' changes by deriding and denigrating their activities, denying that they are doing anything remotely important," O'Connor says.

In his book *Facing the Fifties — from denial to reflection,* O'Connor draws on important work by American geropsychologist David Gutmann, who wrote about the "crossover effect" where psychologically older men develop passive, nurturing or contemplative "feminine" qualities while older women acquire more bold, assertive, adventurous "masculine" qualities.

O'Connor says he's watched many older women acquire a new zest for life as they make these changes. "It's my turn," they tell him as they move away from the "accommodating self" they used for so long to keep the peace in their marriages. O'Connor reports great conflict in some marriages as women pursue new interests while men flounder to re-create a meaningful post-career life.

"I often see retired men who are genuinely lost. They no longer see the point of life. They have always focused on problem solving, 'doing' privileged over 'being', and are ill-prepared for the chaos and uncertainty that comes with change," says O'Connor, suggesting women tend to be more flexible, partly because women's lives include more transitions and they learn to be adaptable.

It all leaves many older men playing more and more golf or making a fetish out of the size of their super. "Superannuation is like secular heaven, a rewarding after-work life," jokes O'Connor, suggesting an obsessive preoccupation with retirement finances can reflect a deepening anxiety about dependency and older age — issues men find hard to confront.

For single men, the problem of boredom and isolation looms even larger, with research showing they are much less active than partnered men. According to the 2012 Disability, Ageing and Carers survey, over a three-month period only 31 per cent of men in this age group living alone attended a movie, concert or other live event compared to 40 per cent of men with partners. Single men were less likely than partnered men to be involved with arts or craft, go to church or restaurants or clubs, be involved with voluntary activities, visit museums, art galleries or botanical gardens, participate in physical activities or attend sporting events or education groups.

"They are so boring! Bored and boring," says one of my

dating clients, Sharon, a lively 62-year-old Melbourne woman who's spent much of the last decade looking for a mate. She's met dozens of retired men through online dating who are often shocked by her busy schedule. A former physiotherapist, Sharon has found retirement has opened up endless opportunities for expanding her horizons. She jams philosophy lessons, art shows and anti-fracking meetings in between music and writers' festivals, with her active social and family life filling in the few gaps.

She's increasingly disenchanted about her chances of meeting a simpatico companion. "What is it with these men? They expect me to entertain them, to share my busy life and enjoy my friends, yet they have so little to contribute. They are often men who had interesting careers, big lives, yet when they gave up work their lives shrank to hitting little white balls into holes. And they have no friends. How's it possible for a 65-year-old man to have no real friends?"

That's all too common, says men's health expert Steve Carroll. He's spent more than 30 years travelling around rural Australia talking to groups of men about their health — conversations that often end up focusing on men's relationships.

"For many men, the problem is their lack of real relationships. While they have a working life they have plenty of social contact, superficial banter with their workmates, although it is striking how rarely they actually see their work companions outside of work. But when they retire they lose their major source of social contact and they become increasingly dependent on their wives," he says, mentioning a gregarious elderly former businessman who hasn't left his house since his wife's death three years ago.

They just don't have the skill set to establish more meaningful relationships with other men, says Carroll. While he applauds efforts being made by the Men's Shed Association to bring older men together for shared activities, he believes very little of the interaction taking part in the sheds translates into proper friendships. "That's not addressing the problem of changing the male culture that leads to men's isolation," he says.

Peter McNeil admits this is true. He sees retirement for many men as like "turning off a tap", denying men of their major source of a social life. But he acknowledges the type of relationships that develop in most sheds seem simply to replace the "working association" that men used to share in their workplaces, centred around superficial conversation concerning their joint projects, chat about politics or the football. "Nothing too deep. We rarely get into our personal lives, apart from some skylarking or banter about our wives — 'Couldn't have the car again yesterday because the wife was off having her hair done', that sort of thing. It's pretty rare that men develop friendships that extend beyond the hours they spend together in the sheds."

Asked whether they'd ever talk about their wife leaving them or erection problems after prostate cancer, there was an audible shudder from some Men's Shed participants. "There's a few doctors in our group. We'd go to them about that sort of thing," one commented dismissively.

Most women are still thrilled that the Men's Sheds are keeping their men busy. "I was delighted when he got involved," says Peter NcNeil's wife, Bev, 77. "It meant I could go out without him saying, 'You're not going out again?'"

Privately, some of the wives admit they can't understand

how men can spend so much time together and know so little about each other. "Men are hopeless," says a partner of one of the silent men of the shed. "I'll ask him, 'What did you talk about?' Blank. Or 'What's so and so's wife doing?' Blank. We women are so different. We never shut up." She mentioned a recent cruise with her husband where she got so bored with the one-sided conversation that she spent the whole time reading books. "I'd love a deep conversation," she says wistfully.

"If you are not in touch with your feelings you can't offer proper companionship and it seems to me that's what women are now yearning for," says Peter O'Connor, who believes men's resistance to tuning in to their 'inner life' and sharing their feelings not only prevents close friendships with other men but lies at the heart of the demise of many long marriages.

While we constantly hear stories about older men dumping their wives for the younger woman it is far more common for men to find themselves turfed out of a marriage. The percentage of divorces involving men over 50 more than doubled between 1985 and 2010, from 11 to 22 per cent for men in their 50s and four to 10 per cent for men aged 60-plus.

A Family Court study by Pauline Presland and Helen Gluckstern back in 1993 showed women made the decision to leave in two-thirds of mature-aged marital separations. Australian National University professor Matthew Gray confirms this is most likely still the case: "Research from around the world shows women make the decision in most, around two-thirds, of all marital separations," he says.

Of course, there are exceptions to these patterns, gregarious older men with strong friendship networks, males totally connected with their inner lives and keen to share them. Many experts working with men also see hopeful signs that younger men are learning to break down traditional mateship barriers. But elderly men are currently one of the key risk groups for suicide, which has led to new attention being focused on the failure of these older men to develop meaningful lives and strong social connections.

Beyond Blue sponsored research that found the Men's Sheds are reducing isolation of men, particularly in rural areas, improving wellbeing, promoting friendships and providing men with a new sense of purpose.

It's a positive start, suggests David Helmers, executive officer of the Australian Men's Shed Association. It's a movement, he says, that has created an environment in which men can gather, socialise and share," he says. That's all good stuff, but in the meantime the busy women and bored men of our senior world will just keep rubbing each other up the wrong way. Harmony in the golden years seems a long way off.

CHAPTER 28

The Splintering
Rainbow Coalition

First published 2017

In March 2016, the Scottish philosopher John Haldane took part in a Sydney Ethics Centre debate challenging the notion that "Society Must Recognise Trans People's Gender Identities". Facing a hostile audience filled with Mardi Gras visitors, his reasoned arguments took issue with the coercion implied in that "must". "We need toleration, a principled response to difference but toleration is not endorsement," he said. "We need to hold back the forces of coercion," he added.

We've had decades of this compulsory politics of inclusion, a highly selective process where the elite crowd decides who is to be included in any debate or lobbying effort, whilst omitting whole sectors of communities when it suits them.

This was very much in evident at the Ethics Centre debate where the so-called "Rainbow Coalition" was out in force. What shone through the occasionally acrimonious debate was perilous state of this splintering coalition. How ironic that we have been bullied into using the crazy "LGBTIQ" terminology — "alphabet soup" as some call it — when the various factions are at each other's throats.

Take British journalist and provocateur Milo Yiannoplouos' efforts to promote a "Drop the T" campaign, lobbying to have transsexuals turfed out of the coalition. Milo, who had been campaigning on US campuses on his self-described "Dangerous Faggot" tour, argues that the lobby for gay rights and freedoms is being undermined by transsexuals' demands. "Everyone's pretty much sold on gays and lesbians as a sexual orientation now. But you can't do the same with trannies who require hormone treatments and the services of a skilled butcher." Complicating matters still further, many key medical authorities are now refusing to do sex reassignment surgery arguing transgenderism is actually a psychiatric disorder.

Lesbian feminists are up in arms about T campaigners riding roughshod over women's rights. The tension between the two groups erupted at a 2016 women's festival in Auckland which included cupcakes shaped like vulvas (to encourage women to accept their own nether regions). Transgender activists complained this created an "unsafe environment for them" and tried to shut down the event.

And so it goes on. Gay men are grumbling about lesbians commandeering the Rainbow float, muscling in to head up the alphabet soup and promoting an anti-male hate movement hell-bent on undermining the rights and welfare of boys and men. Australian blogger Andy Bob mentions Betty Friedan's 1960s warning that the lesbian feminists she called the "Lavender Menace" were bad news. "Perhaps if G had paid closer attention to this warning it may be have been better prepared to handle the moment when L told G to check its privilege and remove its limp-wristed self from the front of the queue," he writes how gay men have been brainwashed into accusing their straight brothers of being responsible for every injustice the world has ever known.

And here's Milo: "Let's not forget, the majority of LGBT people, gay men, put in all the work to make gay rights happen. So stop taking us for granted and stop crapping on us just because we're not going along with your latest fad. The G in LGBT has been a load-bearing wall for the whole alphabet soup crew for decades, and we extraordinary gays, the best gays, are tired of pulling along every single alternative sexuality when they expect us to do the heavy lifting while they do the easy grifting."

Recently in America the reputation of the coalition took a hit following battles over bathrooms, as state governments opposed Obama's decree that American kids in public schools can choose any bathroom which fits their perceived gender identity.

The Sydney Festival recently enjoyed performances from Ivan Coyote, a superb storyteller who thrilled audiences with moving tales of struggles with gender identity. Coyote takes issue with women's complaints about being afraid of men in women's washroom because of what might happen. "I'm afraid of women in the women's washroom because of what happens to me all the time … Who in the hell decides who gets to feel comfortable?" Coyote asks.

Much as I was won over by Coyote's powerful stories, I suspect compulsory unisex toilets are just not going to happen — at least not until we find some way of teaching drunken men not to pee on the floor. But more seriously, it just doesn't make sense to threaten the safety and comfort of the majority to cater to such a tiny minority group.

It all comes back to John Haldane's plea for tolerance but not coercion and the T lobby, Coyote aside, shows no sign of getting that message. In late 2016 an article was published in *Quadrant* magazine by John Whitehall[78], Professor of Paediatrics at Western Sydney University presented worrying evidence of surgical abuse of so-called "transgender" children, most of whom would have grown out of any gender confusion. Whitehall proves activists are grossly inflating figures regarding the prevalence of transgender children and describes alarming laws being introduced in Victoria which essentially prohibit professionals from sensible "wait and see" policies with children, demanding they intervene with puberty blockers, cross-sex-hormones and even surgery. "What astonishes me is the lack of evidence to support massive medical invention in the face of evidence that it is not necessary," writes Professor Whitehall [79] [80].

Coercion has defined our recent debate over gay marriage — just look at the way the ABC used endless news reports to proselytise "marriage equality" and belittle people who challenged their propaganda. There were many who predicted the success of the same sex marriage postal survey would embolden the trans lobby towards more radical social engineering and that is exactly what has happened.

But eventually people tend to rebel against this type of intimidation. It's a lesson Hillary Clinton confronted through the ballot box. Her downfall was a clear sign that mainstream communities have had a gutful of forces of coercion bullying them into accepting views which they find uncomfortable or inappropriate.

There must be a way of giving enthusiastic support for rightful claims for tolerance and understanding to minority groups without being bullied into absurd policies which subvert the needs of the general population.

SECTION SIX

Fatherhood

CHAPTER 29

"You've been McIntoshed" – toddler's overnight care

First published 2014

This article was bravely published by The Age *in 2014 after a barrage of legal threats from Melbourne psychologist Jennifer McIntosh, who wasn't keen on me exposing the fact that an international panel of experts had denounced her work — research which had been used to deny fathers across the world overnight contact with very young children. My published article had the lawyer's finger prints all over it! Typically, despite this being a big story, most of the media, including almost all the ABC, refused to touch it.*

Harold Bulman can't wait until Sunday. That's when he'll get the chance to spend four whole hours with his one-year-old daughter, Cora. Since he split from his de facto partner 12 months ago he's only been allowed two hours a week with Cora, generally spent in a park near where she lives with her mum in Sale.

After mediation at Roundtable Dispute Management in Gippsland, he's now spending a little more time with her and will soon get six hours straight, enough time to take her to his home 80 kilometres away in Narracan. "I miss her so much and think of her every day. I can't wait to have her home so I can be a proper dad to her instead of hanging around in the park or shopping centre."

Bulman's ex-partner is still breastfeeding Cora which precludes any chance of having Cora stay overnight with him, but he's hopeful that will change after the next mediation session in six months' time. Bulman, 42, was lucky to have found a mediator who worked hard to encourage Cora's mother to allow gradual increases in the amount of contact Cora could have with him.

Across Australia, fathers are being told in mediation sessions or by lawyers that there's no hope of overnight contact with children under three. At Family Relationship Centres where couples attend compulsory mediation prior to any Family Court appearance, any sharing of overnight care of infants and toddlers tends to be discouraged.

"Sharing of overnight care of infants is problematic," states a South Australian Family Law Pathways document produced for local family law organisations. The document, funded by the Commonwealth Attorney General's department, is circulated by many FPAs throughout the country.

It stresses the "importance of the primary attachment relationship" with the mother and reassures dads that with regular contact, even of a few hours, they can "readily develop close and loving relationships" with their children.

But according to an academic paper endorsed by 110 leading international experts that is not the case. The paper "Social Science and Parenting Plans for Young Children: A consensus report" was published in February 2014, in the American Psychological Association's journal *Psychology, Public Policy and Law*.

It is backed by leading Australian academics including Don Edgar, the former head of the Australian Institute of Family Studies, Judy Cashmore, Associate Professor in Socio-Legal Studies at Sydney University and Barry Nurcombe, Emeritus Professor of Child & Adolescent Psychiatry, University of Queensland.

This article analysed existing research and found that infants commonly develop attachment relationships with more than one caregiver and concluded that in normal circumstances children are likely to do better if they have overnight contact with both parents and that depriving young children of the opportunity to stay overnight with their fathers could compromise the quality of developing father-child relationships. The article makes compelling reading because it challenges current policy on the care of young children — policy which has such a firm grip on Australia's family law system.

The report also provided a review of the research underpinning that policy, specifically a study led by La Trobe university adjunct professor and clinical psychologist Jennifer McIntosh which suggested even one night a week of overnight care undertaken by the non-primary parent may increase the stress levels of children aged zero to two in certain circumstances.

The influence of this study on Australia's family law system has been so profound that barristers have a special phrase to describe the common experience of losing the battle for some overnight care of toddlers — they joke they've been "McIntoshed". But for the fathers concerned it is no joking matter.

The McIntosh era dates back to 2010 when the Labor government commissioned her to lead an investigation into the impact on pre-schoolers of overnight contact in their father's care.

The previous Coalition government had implemented a series of reforms to family law aimed at enabling children to have more contact with their fathers after a divorce, including in 2006, a presumption of shared parental responsibility for children. John Howard was an outspoken advocate of father's role in children's lives but the Rudd government showed no such inclination.

"Our government supported the right of children to contact with both their parents, provided the child is not exposed to any risk," said Phillip Ruddock, the Attorney General who implemented the 2006 reform. "Labor has sought to wind that back. They've long been captured by the female lobby determined to retain sole control over their children."

In 2007, McIntosh published a report highly critical of the Coalition's shared custody reforms. When Labor Attorney General Robert McClelland appointed a lead researcher for the new "pre-schoolers" study, McIntosh was the obvious candidate.

The results brought bad news for fathers. McIntosh's key finding was that infants under two who spent one night a week and toddlers who spend 10 days a month of overnight time in their non-primary caregiver's care are more irritable, more severely distressed and insecure in their relationships with their primary parent, less persistent at tasks, and more physically and emotionally stressed.

However, the significance of these findings was questioned in two papers published online in 2014 in *Psychology, Public*

Policy and Law. The expert report, "Social Science and
Parenting Plans for Young Children: A consensus report,"
written by Richard Warshak, psychiatry professor from the
University of Texas Southwestern Medical Center claimed that
McIntosh and her colleagues "drew unwarranted conclusions
from their data". The report found that there are issues with
the way the data in McIntosh's study was collected and
analysed and this led to problems with the way the findings
were later applied in policy making and agenda setting. The
report found that the study provided no reliable basis to
support custody policy, recommendations or decisions and
hence the findings from the data should not have been used as
a platform for developing public policy in the area[81].

Further criticisms of McIntosh's study and the way it has
been used are laid out in the second paper by Linda Nielsen:
"Woozles: Their Role in Custody Law Reform, Parenting Plans
and Family Court" which was published much the same time
in the same psychology journal. This claims the McIntosh
research has been used by policy makers, the media and
academic circles in a way that goes beyond its original findings.

McIntosh later co-authored a two-part paper published
in *The Family Court Review* — "Parental separation and
overnight care of young children: Consensus through
Theoretical and Empirical Integration" — which examined
the current research evidence and finally acknowledged that
"cautions against any overnight care during the first three
years have not been supported."

This paper is welcome, says University of Sydney Law
professor Patrick Parkinson. Parkinson applauds the emerging
consensus that it is fine for infants and toddlers to stay

overnight with their fathers provided the child is comfortable in his care.

"Blanket statements to the effect that children under three should never stay overnight with their non-resident fathers should now be treated as entirely incorrect," he says. However he says that many family law practitioners, counsellors and mediators have had the impression that the research supported such a policy.

McIntosh claims she has "never suggested that children under three should never stay overnight with the father." While acknowledging that the limitations of her study have always been on clear view, she defends the reliability of the data upon which her study was based.

McIntosh, through her lawyer, says she never published "conclusions that have found any overnight care of infants is necessarily harmful".

Yet, in a discussion paper for the Australian Association for Infant Mental Health (AAIMH) in 2011, McIntosh wrote that: "Regardless of socio-economic background, parenting warmth or cooperation between parents, the shared overnight care of children less than four years of age had a significantly negative impact on the emotional and behavioural well-being of the child. Babies under two years who lived one or more overnights a week with both parents were significantly stressed."

The same year she also wrote a guest editorial for *The Family Court Review* which included the following summary: "Repeated overnight stays away from the primary caregiver in the first year or two may strain the infant and disrupt formation of secure attachment with both parents. Overnight stays away from the primary caregiver in early infancy are generally best avoided unless of benefit to the primary caregiver."

In response to questions I asked at the time of writing this article McIntosh said the overnight studies "should not on their own dictate any kind of policy".

McIntosh's background papers were used to prepare guidelines on infant care for a number of leading organisations such the Australian Psychology Society and AAIMHI. She is listed as the lead author of the APS position paper which states "infants (under three) have biologically grounded needs for continuous reliable care from a primary caregiver".

McIntosh claimed Richard Warshak and Linda Nielsen are "impassioned advocates who have sought to discredit me … to further political agendas." Warshak is an international authority on parental alienation in child custody who has worked as a White House consultant on family law reform. Nielsen is a professor of adolescent and educational psychology who has published extensively on father-daughter relationships and shared parenting.

"The experts who signed the report are amongst the best in the world in their fields," says Barry Nurcombe, Emeritus Professor of Child & Adolescent Psychiatry at the University of Queensland, who is among the 110 academics who endorse the dissenting paper.

Nurcombe says the paper highlights the fact that current policies relating to overnight contact with these young children have been excessively affected by misplaced concern about the primary attachment to the mother.

"Since we didn't know whether any shared overnight care was harmful we fell back on the default position assuming that primary attachment was all important," he says, explaining that many experts, like him, have now been convinced that these children can form multiple attachments.

He notes that the consensus report was signed by world authorities on attachment such as Ross Thompson, Karin Grossmann and Avi Sagi-Schwartz and the editor of the leading journal in the area, Howard Steele.

The very notion of a "primary parent" or "primary attachment" has come in for a battering in the fierce public discussion that has taken place over this issue. Many academic and media articles point out this doesn't make sense given that most children under two living with single mothers are at least occasionally and sometimes frequently stay overnight with other people — grandparents or other relatives, babysitters, nannies plus spending long hours in childcare. There are also many cultures where shared care is normal in extended families.

There have been some humorous published views on this issue. "My 22-month grandson loves spending two or three nights sleeping over at his grandparent's house," writes British advocate for fathers, Robert Whiston in a recent blog. He explains that as grandparents they have the time and patience — "as do divorced fathers" — to give one-to-one attention and allow the frazzled mother time to "de-frazzle". His article highlights what many see as the absurdity of fathers being the only ones totally precluded from providing overnight care.

For the last few years thousands of Australian fathers have had their contact with their young children limited to a few hours often spent wandering in parks or fast food restaurants. They have been forced to spend huge sums on lawyers, fighting to be able to care for their children overnight.

The McIntosh study is one of the major reasons they have not been successful, says Justin Dowd, a leading family lawyer and past president of the Law Society of NSW. "It led to the belief, almost a presumption, that children under three should not spend overnight time with their non-resident parent. Faced with that research many fathers have been discouraged from even bringing applications for overnight time with very young children and the ones who have gone to court have often been disappointed to find that research being quoted against their application."

While many fathers will celebrate if that research finally loses the hold it has had on our family law system, others will be angry that it cost them years of being active fathers closely involved in the lives of their children.

There are welcome signs that the expert consensus paper may prove a game changer for many fathers trying to negotiate overnight care of young children. Diana Bryant, the Chief Justice of the Family Court, whilst stressing cases before the Court are subject to individual assessment, says it is vitally important that "family consultants and experts giving evidence in family law proceedings, as well as judges, are familiar with the current research and differing views about it." She also expects the Court's Family Consultants to keep up to date with current debates: "They have been made aware of this particular issue in relation to overnights and young children."

The Australian Association for Infant Mental Health is revising its policies as are some key organisations which run the FPAs. "Given the new positions papers that have recently been published we will be reviewing the literature that we give to parents to help them make the best decisions they can for

their children," says Matt Stubbs, the Acting Clinical Services
Director of Interrelate.

Relationships Australia which runs most of the FPAs issued
the following statement:

"If there has been a trend towards limiting shared parenting
and overnight contact with young children and fathers in
recent years, it has not been a move advocated by Relationships
Australia. We have noted an increase in shared parenting in
recent years and consider this a positive outcome for both
children and parents."

But it is the fathers themselves who have the strongest
motivation to ensure the family law system responds to these
new events. Their support groups are determined this will
happen. Barry Guidera, CEO of Dads in Distress Support
Services: "We will make sure fathers are informed about
new consensus statement so that they choose lawyers and
mediators who are up to date with the current expert opinion
on this vital issue."

*Sadly, three years later not that much has changed. Some
judges tell me that they believe Warshak's consensus paper had
a significant influence on some of the decisions being made in
the Family Court but I also hear from fathers across the country
who tell me McIntosh's research is still being used to deny them
overnight care. If you are a father facing a legal battle over care
of young children, do look at Warshak's article[82] which updates
the research proving clear benefits to children of any age when
fathers are involved in proper shared parenting, including
overnight care.*

CHAPTER 30

Donor dads – men fathering via the Internet

First published 2004

Make me a mum. That's the title of what critics were calling "the sickest ever reality show", which in 2002 was being planned for British television. *Make Me a Mum* was a sperm race. A woman would take fertility drugs to produce eggs and 1,000 men would compete to have their sperm selected for a competition to create a baby. The race would be between two finalists — a man selected for his sex appeal, personality, wealth and fitness by the mum-to-be, and a man selected by scientists for the quality of his sperm. At the end of the six-part series, viewers would have seen which sperm wriggled its way first into the egg, which would then be implanted in the woman's womb.

Crazy stuff, eh? The idea, which luckily never came to fruition, rightly brought the ethics boffins out in force, condemning the creation of children as TV fodder. British productive ethics expert Josephine Quintavalle was disgusted: "My first thoughts go to the child who will be created — what is he or she going to be told about how they were conceived?"

There are children being created in Australia today who are also destined to discover disturbing truths about how they were conceived. All over the country, hundreds of men are lining up to offer their sperm to strangers — sperm to produce children they may never know and who may never find out whose sperm won the race to the mother's egg.

These are the children conceived via the Internet, chosen by mothers who scan donors' ads for the biological father for their child. "I have a very high sperm count and motility," boasts one donor advertising on an Australian site. "Great dad quality here!" Claims another. "Sperm donor with high IQ," says a third.

At the time this article was written some 112 donors were offering their semen on a single South Australian web site. Lesbian couple Sally Ryan and Jenny Mann set up the Australian Sperm Donor Registry to help other same-sex couples but almost two-thirds of the donors and a third of the recipients were heterosexual. The men were not paid while the recipients paid $50 for access to each donor plus a $50 registration fee. Most of the men claimed to be driven by altruism: "I detest needles so donating blood is out of the question. This is a way I can do something to help," wrote one on his donor profile.

They all talked about wanting to help women have children. For some, it was an act of defiance, deliberately helping lesbian women conceive because they objected to governments at the time denying them access to IVF clinics. And it is something they could do without too much bother.

"If I have something and am able to help someone else and it's not going to cost me, then I'll do it," said 46-year-old Melbourne project manager Eric, heterosexual and divorced with no children from his marriage. His hunch was that there was something like 20 to 30 kids somewhere in Australia born as a result of his 18 years of sperm donation. He started donating in clinics after meeting infertile couples during investigations of his former wife's infertility. Then he branched out to the Internet, donating mainly to lesbian couples.

Private donation involves the delivery of semen in a specimen jar (although the sites do attract the odd crank keen on delivery "the natural way"). There's about a two-hour window for delivery of the fresh sample, organised for when the woman is ovulating.

And the turkey baster once fashionable for lesbian self-insemination has been replaced by syringes (without needles) which waste less of the precious fluid. The worry is the "fresh" semen hasn't been tested and found disease-free — as is the case with frozen semen used by clinics. Some making private arrangements organise these tests, but not all.

"Often the women just want the sperm and don't seem to care about quality or anything else at all," said Eric.

For Eric, Internet donation led to a real novelty: he became involved in the lives of some of the children. Not too involved, mind you. "There are about eight kids I do run into occasionally. Some mothers want to catch up on the child's birthdays, others don't want to know me at all." Eric happily supplied semen anonymously (his early donations via the clinics were anonymous): "Some women didn't want any of my contact details, didn't even want my surname. We did it all on just a first-name basis and I've never heard from them since."

He was fine with this but did acknowledge that not being able to trace a parent would be a problem. "I would not want to have someone live their life wondering where they came from, what dad looked like," he said, seemingly unconcerned about the inconsistencies in his position.

He realised some children may want to contact him at adulthood, but he was quite happy to leave it to their mothers to decide whether they will ever have his contact details. But those kids shouldn't expect too much from the meeting. "I don't want children landing on my doorstep. I don't want to be involved with them. I don't want to be a father. I've got no fathering instincts at all."

Eric didn't like questions about the fall-out for these children of never being able to trace their biological father or tracking him down only to be brushed off. Does he feel any responsibility for them? "No, I don't," he said curtly, adding in a peevish tone: "You're causing me a lot of bother. I don't know why I rang you."

Eric's fecundity pales next to the American donor in email correspondence with an Australian Donor Insemination (DI) support group who claims to have more than 600 children, the last 100 through the Internet. Meeting them all, he says, would be "taxing".

Of 16 Australian sperm donors interviewed for this article, many made it clear they weren't keen on these questions. They simply weren't interested in the repercussions for the children; they focused only on the rights of the mothers. The most thoughtful tend to be the gay donors who seek to create some sort of family. Many hear a clock ticking: in their late 30s or 40s, they are sad to have missed out on having children.

Noel Posus, 37, a gay Sydney life coach has just put his name down on a donor site. His motivation: "I have quite a lot of love to give." Love without strings, and while he'd prefer to have contact, it is not essential: "I'm happy to be in a father-like role. If I could support the family in any way, emotionally, financially, I would."

He'd prefer the children eventually had his contact details but he'll leave that to the lesbian couple. "They are the parents and I'd want them to make that call." He doesn't put much store in biological origins partly due to his own background. Born the 13th child in an American family, he was given up for adoption to friends. Raised in a happy family, Posus discovered his true origins at 13 and says the knowledge didn't have a huge impact on his life; he is sure that if he chooses the right couple, the children will do fine.

The belief that mothers know best was one of the most striking themes to emerge from donor interviews. Most were happy to leave decision-making in the hands of the women: "I'm a small link in the chain," said Adam, 42, a Sydney sales manager. "The upbringing is the couple's affair. I just provide the sperm and off they go." He was married at the time of our interview, trying for his own family and had just started offering his sperm on the net.

Adam was happy if his seed was spread as far is it will go: "Thirty, fifty. If the people kept coming and I can keep going, that's fine by me." Most of the women he'd met don't want involvement and he sees no reason why the children need a father: "Two mothers are just as good as a mother and father. That old traditional John Howard mother-father thing, I don't think that's important in today's society." And what should the kids be told about their origins? "They may tell them they had a one-night stand, that's up to them."

Then there was Hugh, 44, a heterosexual Sydney pharmacist. He'd sired four children in the previous eight months, all to lesbian women via the net. Two single women in their mid-40s were also trying to conceive using his sperm. He'd been willing to do it anonymously, although he'd preferred the kids one day knew who he was. He would not say "no" to anyone wanting his semen (except perhaps "druggies"): "Who am I to say who should or should not be a parent? I don't feel there needs to be a father for a happy family."

So, there they were — man after man — all convinced males are irrelevant to children's upbringing. Justin, a donor who worked in IT at a Melbourne university, already had one child and his partner was pregnant. He donated sperm to one lesbian couple, producing a daughter, and he was about to donate sperm to another, both via the Internet. So which child would he rather be: the child to be born to his partner or the one about to be conceived by the lesbian couple? He was emphatic neither child would have an advantage: "Historically, children have been brought up in all sorts of families. Diversity appeals to me."

All this was happening at a time in history when fatherhood was receiving unprecedented attention. New fatherhood books were appearing constantly; there was talk of "father hunger", of young men lamenting the lack of closer relationships with their fathers. And decades of public debate about the impact on children of losing contact with their fathers after divorce had largely concluded it was not in the children's interests. So why were so many men virtually deciding the opposite is true?

Adrienne Burgess is a fathering expert, an adviser to the British government on fatherhood policy and author of the ground-breaking *Fatherhood Reclaimed*. To someone who's been working for decades to promote positive, involved fathering, did the attitudes of these donors suggest she's fighting a losing battle?

"Yes and no. No in the sense that research shows real progress, incontrovertible evidence, that dads in intact families are increasingly close to their children," said Burgess, an Australian who has spent most of her adult life in London. "But this is undermined by this widespread notion, so clear in the responses of the men you've interviewed, that dads don't matter at all. This is complete rubbish if you look at it from the child's point of view, which hardly anyone ever does. The truth is that an absent or detached father is a serious stressor, which, when combined with other stressors, can have a massively negative impact on a child's life chances."

Burgess wasn't surprised the men who were close to their own fathers were more likely to insist on contact when offering sperm and to refuse to donate anonymously. "My relationship with my father was something I couldn't have missed ... I wouldn't be who I am today without him in my life," says Paul Cortissos, 32, a gay Melbourne nurse who had just started offering his sperm on the net. He was determined there would be contact: "The child will have a sense they've got a father or at least a male figure in their lives."

Andrew Barrett's parents were both teachers and he spent a lot of school holiday time with his dad. Barrett, a divorced 38-year-old working for a truck manufacturing company, was considering his first sperm donation via a Melbourne clinic and he said he'd want the children to know who he is. "I certainly wouldn't be rejecting a child. If they wanted me to be involved in their lives I would be."

In contrast, the donors who wished to remain anonymous or have no contact were more likely to be from family backgrounds involving an absent dad, either through divorce or simply hard work. Chris, 39, a heterosexual Melbourne-based articled clerk, was the son of a politician. "My father was very much the absent father," says Chris, who was organising to donate to a lesbian neighbour and is also advertising on the net. He said he'd be willing to meet the children but wanted no involvement. He was convinced that two lesbian parents, both coming home at night to share the parenting, would do a better job than many traditional families. "Fathers don't offer anything unique."

Richard Fletcher, director of the Engaging Fathers project at Newcastle University, suggested males who grew up with absent dads face an interesting dilemma. Confronted with the societal message that father involvement is critical, "they are forced to either conclude they must themselves be damaged or else to decide it doesn't matter". Rather than judging themselves poorly, they conclude dads simply don't rate and are happy to conceive children who may never know them.

Many of their children will face that fate since no official records are kept of donors using the Internet. (This also raises real concerns of inter-breeding, where Internet offspring unknowingly mate with half-siblings.)

Unlike donor insemination children born to heterosexual couples, those raised by lesbians or single women know there must have been a donor. How will they feel about their mothers using anonymous donors? Or a donor who was only willing to meet them provided there was no "involvement"?

Intentionality is the key issue here. Many of these children are being deliberately conceived in circumstances where they will grow up to have to deal with the harrowing truth about the irresponsible way they were conceived. Unlike 30 or 40 years ago, when infertile couples were advised to keep secret the circumstances of the child's creation, these children will know there was a donor; many, perhaps most, will want to get to know that donor. And many will be doomed to disappointment.

It is finally being recognised that DI offspring have a right to know their biological origins, many years after we enshrined that right for adopted children. In 2002, Democrat senators Andrew Murray and Aden Ridgeway pushed through an amendment to a bill on embryos, declaring DI children had right to identifying information about their biological parents.[83]

Australian Health Ethics Committee collaborated with the NHMRC to establish a series of Ethical Guidelines for Assisted Reproductive Technology. Within these guidelines is clear support for the right of DI offspring to such information, banning the use of anonymous sperm and requiring clinics to remind potential donors of "the significance of the biological connection they will have with the persons conceived"[84]. Anonymous sperm is still being used in a number of Sydney clinics and in the states that have not banned its use. Nevertheless, most DI children are unlikely to be informed about their origins because they are being raised by couples who will keep it a secret. A survey by the Royal Hospital for Women in Sydney indicated less than 10 per cent of couples using its clinic tell their offspring the truth.

Yet the push is on, led by a generation of DI young adults actively lobbying for less secrecy. Most of them were conceived using anonymous sperm and face the immense frustration of probably never tracing their biological fathers. Victoria established a voluntary register for donors who previously gave anonymously but were now willing to be contacted. However, only 58 of the hundreds of donors have come forward.[85]

At the time this article was being written, I talked to Narelle Grech, then a 21-year-old Melbourne social work student, about her terrible frustration over talking to the doctor at the clinic where she was conceived, knowing he had the information in front of him and was unable to give it to her. He had written to her anonymous donor asking if he'd meet Narelle but received no reply. "I have so much frustration and anger toward the doctor but I know he's legally bound not to tell me," she says. Having recently discovered she has four half-sisters and three half-brothers, she wanted to know them, too.

Grech was a member of TangledWebs (tangled-webs_cdc@ yahoo.com.au), an Australian group concerned about some of the hidden complexities surrounding donor insemination. Members have all been involved in DI and include donors, DI offspring and their families. TangledWebs was started by Michael Linden and his partner Lia Vandersant after Linden discovered through a newspaper story that a daughter conceived from sperm he'd donated 18 years before was looking for him. He immediately recognised Myfanwy Walker as his daughter; they met and photographs of the two — both fair-haired, blue-eyed and remarkably similar — were splashed across the media as the happy end to Myfanwy's painful search. TangledWebs is one of a growing community of online support groups for those struggling with the complexities of donor conception. An international directory of support groups that can be found via the infertility network.[86]

But for the families, this was only the beginning of years of stressful interaction as Vandersant and her son, Liam, coped with the initial infatuation between Linden and his new daughter then helped Myfanwy's brother Michael (also Linden's son) find a place in the family. "I really love Michael's kids but it was such an invasion ... the initial feelings between Michael [Linden] and Myfanwy were so intense that the rest of us felt abandoned, rejected, redundant," said Vandersant who acknowledged it was a very rocky period in their marriage. She says there are real issues in meeting the woman who has had her partner's children — it is not uncommon for such reunions to ignite sparks between donors and the mothers of the children. (In the US, a similar reunion led to the mother of the DI offspring falling in love with the donor and she subsequently moved with her daughter to live near him — not much fun for the donor's wife.)

Michael Linden became very close to his new children but donating sperm, he has decided, is "an act of stupidity". It is grossly irresponsible for men "to intentionally create a situation where a child is never going to know who their biological father is, or if they do find him, may never be able to establish a good relationship with him". TangledWebs wants a parliamentary inquiry into DI and argues the procedures may ultimately need to be outlawed, a stance that attracts great hostility. Myfanwy Walker and another young DI woman appeared on Channel 9's *60 Minutes*, then the following week were criticised by journalist Peter Harvey: "These two young women have been given life ... How dare they seek to deny it to others?"

Surely it is only those who have personal experience who are in a position to warn of the pitfalls. Linden points out that the emphasis on children being able to trace the donor won't solve the problems — in fact, it's "where many of the problems begin".

Like young people discovering their fathers don't want to meet them (even with identified sperm, the donor retains the right to refuse contact), or will meet just the once, or donors enthusiastic over meeting their first DI offspring but then the novelty wears off. In the US, 13-year-old Ryan Kramer and his mother Wendy set up a website, Donor Sibling Registry, for DI offspring connection. Ryan said he hoped that if he does find his father, he's the first rather than the 20th.

Reunions can be plain sailing or, even better, joyous events. Peter Browne, 53, met his daughter Danielle Heath, 22, at a Donor Conception Support Group. She guessed he was her father when she saw him, DNA tests confirmed it and the two lived together for a period in Brisbane. Peter, who never had children, was thrilled: "It's gone a long way towards validating my whole existence." The two were trying to trace Danielle's brother, another product of Browne's sperm.

Given that decades of research have underlined the difficulties many stepfamilies face in blending members from different families, it's hardly surprising others are running into trouble. Often it is the donor's partner who foresees the problems. Nancy, the partner of Justin, the Melbourne IT guy who was donating to two lesbian families, was pregnant with their second child and had major misgivings: "I think it will be harder on me than on him. I'm prepared if there's a person to embrace into our lives but I see it as so many unknowns."

Her concerns increased since their first child: "I had huge reservations a second time." She was nervous about her children's relationship with the half-siblings, who "could be in any sort of emotional state" when they turn up. "It's an innate protective thing concerning my family." Some of her disquiet may stem from her background: her parents divorced, her father remarried then devoted himself to his new family.

Ken Daniels, professor of social work at New Zealand's University of Canterbury, spent almost three decades studying the social impact of DI and has been instrumental in pushing his country towards increasing openness. In 2004 New Zealand enacted legislation requiring people seeking DI to inform their children about the nature of their conception; at that time New Zealand clinics hadn't used anonymous sperm for more than 15 years and children were increasingly having contact with donors, even from a young age — all moves which Daniels applauded. But he acknowledged that family dynamics aren't always easy. In Australia, this was highlighted by the 2002 family law tragedy involving Patrick, a young boy whose lesbian mother killed both herself and the child when his donor father was awarded regular contact.

Melbourne hotel manager Peter Spark, 33, was once in regular contact with the son conceived by a lesbian woman using his sperm six years earlier. But after the first year, the lesbian couple decided "they didn't want a male in their lives" and Spark hadn't seen the child since. He had a far more positive experience with two children born to another lesbian couple. The older child, nearly four, had started asking to see Spark more often and he was gradually being allowed more contact.

These are tenuous bonds, easily broken at the whim of adults making decisions about their own lives. It's a constant risk with DI, especially via the Internet. Adults become consumed by their own wishes and desires: infertile couples wanting to pretend the child is all their own; lesbian and single women not wanting a man in their lives; well-meaning donors who don't give a toss about the children conceived through their benevolence. As Ken Daniels warns: "The interests of children are often forgotten or downplayed in the rush to satisfy one's own needs."

To add a few words of update to that 2002 article, three years ago the Justice for Men and Boys organisation in the UK reported that through a Freedom of Information Act request, that the UK Child Support Agency had for many years known of over 500 cases (annually) of paternity fraud that are committed in relation to child support claims.[87]

The most famous case in Australia went right to the High Court, which in April 2006 heard Magill vs. Magill, where Liam Magill lodged a case against Meredith Magill whom he had married in 1988, and with whom he thought he had fathered three children. He paid child support for all three children until 1999. In the year 2000, DNA testing proved he was not the father of the two youngest children. Mr Magill was initially awarded $70,000 in damages however, this was later overturned by the High court. The Court ruled that there is no obligation on the part of a wife to tell the truth about the paternity or possible paternity of any child to whom she gives birth.

The proceedings centred on the fact that Ms Magill gave Mr Magill birth registration forms to sign. These named Mr Magill as the father — despite Ms Magill having doubts about Mr Magill being the biological father. Mr Magill claim that this act constituted a false representation by the wife. It was on this basis he sued Ms Magill for deceit. The High Court concluded that while an action for deceit is available to be pursued against a spouse or former spouse in certain circumstances, it does not apply to false representations made during the course of a marriage about paternity because the Family Law Act is not concerned with fault nor morality.

The Magill case and related concerns around paternity fraud have become a flashpoint of debate within the Men's Rights movement both nationally and internationally. In relation to the Magill case, there is deeper concern in that both the Federal Government and the state Victorian Government, through the agency of the Victorian Women's Legal Service, gave partisan, exclusive financial support to Ms Magill in this case whose legal cost must have run into hundreds of thousands of dollars, yet the same financial support was not extended to Mr Magill, the actual victim in the case.

CHAPTER 31

Whose sperm is it, anyway? Deceived into fatherhood

First published 2001

It became the hit story of the silly season. Boris Becker's defence against his 2001 paternity suit was so unlikely that it made news around the world. He claimed he'd never had intercourse with the Russian model who alleged she'd had his child. Initially all he'd admit to was oral sex in the broom cupboard, arguing the sperm must have somehow been kept and recycled. But finally, the story changed, with Becker accepting paternity of the child.

Surprisingly, the unlikely early Becker defence also had a run in the Australian courts. Just before Christmas, a NSW man learnt he'd failed to convince the Family Court that his sperm had been similarly stolen and used for conception. This time the deed didn't take place in the dark depths of a cupboard. Far from it. In the NSW case of J and D there was a witness. J's mate, S, gave evidence that both of them received oral sex from D, when she and a friend entertained them during their motorcycle tour of central NSW. What's more, the two men claimed they were using condoms at the time. J alleged that following the act, D dashed off to the bathroom carrying his used condom and conceived a child using the contents.

Sadly for J, the Family Court chose to believe the mother's story namely that she had intercourse with J and pregnancy resulted from a failure of contraception.

Had J's story been believed, the legal consequences would have been intriguing. The fact that his sperm was used without his consent for artificial conception would mean J would not have been regarded as the father to the child for the purposes of child support. Instead, he would have been in the same legal position as a sperm donor and not liable for child support payments.

The Full Court decision on J and D was simply the latest round in the growing battle over men's reproductive rights. Courts in many countries are struggling with complex paternity cases, with developments in DNA testing now providing decisive answers to age-old questions about who's the daddy. Paternity issues are high on the agenda of men's rights groups both here and overseas, as men challenge their lack of control over reproductive decisions.

"Where's men's right to choose?" asked Sue Price, co-founder of Men's Rights Agency, one of the Australian lobby groups tuned into this groundswell of discontent.

"Men can be tricked into becoming fathers, or be denied the chance to be a father, they are powerless to stop a woman having an abortion and are seen as having no right to ask her to have one.

"Men's reproductive choices don't exist. They all depend on women's whim."

The issue at the heart of the J and D case — the question of whether J could have been tricked into paternity — is attracting particular attention. The role of fraud in paternity has already had a run in the United States, in a 1981 case involving Frank Serpico, the New York policeman made famous through a movie on his role as whistle-blower calling out corruption in the city's police department. Serpico claimed in a New York State family court that he should not have to pay child support because he could prove his child's mother had deceived him into pregnancy.

A friend of the mother testified that the mother, an ex-girlfriend of Serpico, decided to seduce Serpico in order to get pregnant. She told the friend that she had stopped taking birth control pills but had assured Serpico she was doing so. The judge in the family court ruled in Serpico's favour. The mother's "planned and intentional deceit barred her from any financial benefit at the father's expense", she wrote. But Serpico lost on appeal when higher courts ruled charges of fraud were irrelevant since the only consideration in child support was "the best interests of the child".

An interesting twist on this case was that one of Serpico's lawyers was Karen DeCrow[88], a former director of the National Organization for Women. DeCrow attracted considerable critical attention for supporting Serpico's cause. She told the court: "Autonomous women making independent decisions about their lives should not expect men to finance their choice." It seems unlikely men will gain that right in the near future[89] [90]. In fact, the impact on men of women's decisions to choose to become single mothers, with or without deception, as yet hardly registers in the public consciousness.

In the year 2000 there was a fascinating public debate on single women and IVF. A recurring theme in the debate was the benefits of enabling such women to conceive in medically safe circumstances. "No one is going to stop single women having children if they want to and I would far prefer to treat them medically with properly treated sperm, rather than forcing them to have one-night stands to get pregnant," said Gab Kovacs, the medical director of Monash IVF.

"It's much more honest than tricking a man into fatherhood," said one such mother who was quoted in *New Idea* promoting the benefits of donor-inseminated conception. In the entire debate, not one word was raised about the consequences for men being "tricked into fatherhood". Indeed, there was a widespread assumption that deceiving men into paternity is a far from unacceptable course.

During the 15 years I answered a *Cleo* advice column, I had many letters from women who were considering doing just that and wrote seeking my approval for staging a "supposed accident".

It seems unlikely that a successful legal challenge can be mounted using fraud to overturn a father's requirement to pay child support. However, it may be possible to pay the child support and then sue the mother for damages. Lawyers at this time see this as a long shot. Even if you could find a mother with the capacity to pay damages, it may be that no Australian court would be willing to accept the case. Sydney law professor Patrick Parkinson put it this way: "It would raise a novel point of law. An Australian court may be reluctant to allow a remedy because it would mean that there is a court judgment saying the child was born as a result of deception. The court would want to protect the child from that."

So duped men are legally required to pay, but Australian courts have produced judgments which appear to question the morality of this situation.

Sydney lawyer Robert Benjamin[91] mentioned a case about 20 years earlier where he represented a man who was stunned to discover his girlfriend was pregnant despite the fact that he'd been using condoms. Witnesses gave evidence that the woman had boasted she had removed the used condoms from the bin where he had deposited them and used the contents. The magistrate was clearly sympathetic and the client was asked to pay a mere $5 a week in child support.

Jeremy, a Melbourne engineer, had a similar victory. He'd fought a 15-year battle to maintain contact with a child who was conceived deceitfully. The mother was a woman he'd only known for a few weeks who'd assured him she was using contraception. "Thanks very much. You needn't worry, you won't need to be around," she told him when gleefully announcing the pregnancy. That was before she discovered she had to name the father in order to receive welfare benefits.

Jeremy refused to be shut out of his son's life. "'You are not going to walk away,' I told her and insisted the child was going to know me."

He then fought for regular contact and always provided some financial support for the child but resisted the Child Support Agency's efforts to determine what he should pay. "I dispute the right of this woman to surrogate me to get a sole parent's benefit." Recently he appeared before a magistrate who gave him a sympathetic hearing.

"I can't let you win in this case because it would set a precedent that would change Federal law," she told him. But while the fraud was not a ground for departure from the child-support formula, it appears to have influenced her decision to accept the income figures he presented in his application for reduced payments.

She lowered his child support to $15 a week and worked out an extremely favourable payment schedule. "I got virtually all I asked for," said Jeremy. Since the child's mother comes from a wealthy family Jeremy was considering mounting a damages case against the woman.

Parkinson believes the Federal law should be changed to give judges and magistrates some leeway for making decisions in such difficult cases. "The Government should amend the child support legislation to allow the court to exempt a parent from paying child support in exceptional circumstances," he suggested[92].

Apart from fraud, there's another paternity issue which could well be regarded as an exceptional circumstance and that's the question of the responsibility of minors.

Two years ago, a young Sydney man received a bravery award for dragging a stranger from a burning car. The local newspaper showed the handsome twenty-five-year-old smiling modestly as he displayed his award — the very model of a decent, upright citizen. Yet Andrew spent the past decade suffering the consequences of a youthful mistake which has placed him centre stage in the political battle to recognise the role of fraud in denying men's reproductive choice.

Andrew was a cheerful, confident 16-year-old when he first received flattering attention from Sheryl, the good-looking older girl who attended the same school. Pleased to be singled out by a girl a full year older than himself, he quickly found himself embarking on his first sexual relationship despite his sheltered Catholic upbringing. Sheryl assured Andrew that she was on the pill and they discussed abortion as the best solution to unwanted pregnancy.

He now berates himself for not listening more closely

when she talked about her fervent desire for children — her sister was already a single mother. A few months later Sheryl announced her pregnancy. Andrew was stunned by her obvious delight. "She was elated, as if it was the best thing that could have happened to her. When I reminded her of our previous conversation about abortion, she told me to f... off. 'I'm having it and I don't want you in my life!'" she said.

Andrew's paternity became hot news when Sheryl brought the child to show to friends at school. "What was that, Dad?" teased a teacher when Andrew asked a question in class. His previously solid academic record declined rapidly, and he withdrew from school activities (he'd been a star athlete). Ten years later he's finally back on track towards his long-held goal of studying medicine but it has been a long struggle through periods of intense depression.

"I've been so worried about him. Whenever we didn't know where he was I'd worry that he might have done something terrible to himself," says his care-worn mother. Andrew's parents are currently paying their son's monthly $320 bill for child support to enable him to resume his medical studies. "Andrew's been a victim for long enough," says his father, a retired air force officer who is conducting a public campaign to draw attention to issues of fraud and responsibilities of minors with regard to child support.

Andrew's story points to the fact that traditional parental concern for a daughter regarding the hazards of youthful sex could well be misplaced. At least daughters have choices, however difficult, in dealing with unwanted pregnancy. But a son, unless he insists on taking sole responsibility for contraception, may be given no alternative to starting his adult life facing up to 18 years of paying child support.

Under NSW law, as a 16-year-old male, Andrew was of age to consent to sex and so liable to pay child support. This is not the case for a boy two years younger. The bizarre consequences of such anomalies in the law are seen in a series of extraordinary US legal cases involving minors: A 34-year-old single mother in San Francisco was convicted of statutory rape after having sex with the 15-year-old boy she was babysitting. The boy, Nathaniel J, was required to pay child support for the child born as a result of their illegal union. "Victims have rights. Here, the victim also has responsibilities," wrote the judge.

In Kansas, 16-year-old Colleen Hermesmann was charged as a juvenile offender for a sexual relationship which started when Shane Seyer was 12 years old. Although Shane was still legally underage to consent to intercourse, the court determined he was liable for child support when their child was conceived two years later. "If voluntary intercourse results in parenthood, then for purposes of child support, the parenthood is voluntary. This is true even if a 15-year-old boy's parenthood resulted from a sexual assault upon him," said the court.

Doesn't make sense? Perhaps not, but we shouldn't expect the law to always be logical, says Bond University Law professor John Wade. "The world is not logical. We are living in a world where there is a bunch of conflicting interests which have to be balanced. Does the taxpayer pay for the child or does the taxpayer mitigate damages by asking someone else to chip in?"

Wade made the point that the balance struck at any point in time is subject to an ideology which serves to "push the balance one way or another from one decade to another". At this stage in history, the taxpayers' interests are predominant, the balance tipped by public alarm at the rising welfare bill and anger that, in the past, so few men paid to support children after divorce. Currently the rights of individual men get short shrift.

Wade summed up: "The view is that who cares that he couldn't consent when he was 15 or 16? He's older now, he's got a job and so he should pay."

In a few years' time, the balance could well be different and there are many people working very hard to ensure this is the case. While the rights of children need generally to be given priority, it hardly makes for a just society when women are given licence to exploit and deceive men in order to pursue their reproductive choices.

DeCrow was determined to see this change. "Because of Roe v Wade, women have the right to choose to be parents. Men, too, should have that right," the feminist lawyer proclaimed.

CHAPTER 32

Are Mums Killing Football? Boys no longer boys

First published 2008

NSW rugby league players had a busy year, dominating the sports headlines with their loutish behaviour — urinating out of windows, exposing themselves to young women, groping women's breasts in nightclubs, boozing, brawling.

And every time it happened, Max Groll, the then NSW Manager for coaching and development with the Soccer Federation, rubbed his hands with glee. "The rugby league culture does us a lot of favours. The publicity is just great for us in terms of recruitment," he said cheerfully.

It was all about the "mother factor" — according to Ian Holmes, general manager of the NSW Amateur Soccer Federation. Holmes was convinced that the violence on and off field in Rugby League was alienating mothers from the game. And the new power of mothers to determine their sons sporting habits was swelling the numbers of boys playing soccer.

"I have a bit of a laugh when League runs ads which emphasise the brutality of their sport. Every time they do it, I think 'There's another little Johnny whose mother will be switching her kids across to soccer,'" says Holmes.

Of course, with the small boys, the under 12s, soccer has long had the numbers. Nationally, 16 per cent of boys aged

5-14 play soccer, as compared to 14 per cent playing AFL, eight per cent league and two per cent rugby union — according to Australian Bureau of Statistics figures.

But in NSW, soccer had long been experiencing strong growth in the younger age groups, whilst league was struggling to maintain their numbers. Rugby union participation was increasing, with the game showing an overall growth in school numbers. At the time I wrote this article, many boys were still asserting their independence as teenagers by coming back to rugby union, even after starting off in soccer, whilst for League the teenage boys were dropping off[93].

But all Rugby officials were well aware that mothers were lining up to discourage their sons from the game. And since many mothers fail to distinguish between the two rugby codes, the antagonism towards league was rubbing off on union. A 1997 Herald-AGB poll found a high level of concern about the level of violence in football, with predominantly women reporting they had discouraged their sons from playing the game. "The mothers are driving the push for soccer," says David Gibson, NSW Rugby Development Manager.

Remember all the talk about targeting the "Soccer Moms" in the US presidential elections? Victorian University of Technology sports management lecturer Bob Stewart reported all the talk at American sports conferences was of mothers dissuading sons from playing football. "Soccer is booming in the US because mothers see soccer as far more acceptable in terms of the feminist notion of what they want their young boys to be like."

I spent a Saturday morning talking to parents who were watching their little boys playing soccer. Some of the boys had dads who'd played the game, particularly those from ethnic communities. But there were also many others where rugby was the family tradition yet the mothers had convinced their sons to follow a different code.

The mums lined up to express their low opinion of rugby. "I'd never let him play rugby. It's an animals game." "I call it 'Thugball'." "Rugby players are meatheads." "My image of a man who plays rugby is of a drunken yobbo who's totally out of control."

Women's rejection of the rugby culture was clearly part of the story but it was the safety issue which was most telling in their decision to discourage their sons from playing the game. The mothers were convinced that rugby was an extremely dangerous sport, a sport unsuited for slighter boys, particularly boys with long thin necks. It was touching how often slender necks came up in the conversations — scrawny necks clearly loom large when it comes to mother's protective instincts.

It's all due to Dr John Yeo, who as head of the Spinal Unit at North Shore Hospital, lead the push in the 1980s to reduce the risks of rugby spinal injuries by encouraging both rugby codes to modify their rules for younger players. Yeo started the talk about those long thin necks: "We promoted that idea of making sure boys are trained for the position for which they are chosen, suggesting boys with long thin necks should not play in the front row of the scrum."

Yeo told me he was delighted with the success of this campaign: "As a result of these modifications to the game, such as de-powering of the scrum, we've seen a marked reduction in major accidents like neck or brain injuries in rugby league and union." Yeo said that as a result of the significant changes made to the game, spinal cord injuries in schoolboy rugby dropped from 10 or 15 a year to less than one or two per year. He said he'd never seen a documented case of such an injury in a boy under 12.

The injury issue has certainly been oversold, said Mathew Reid, Chief executive of Sports Medicine Australia, who stressed that playing any organised sport is still safer than playing in the back yard. In the younger age groups, rugby doesn't result in serious injuries. "Kids are smarter than adults — they don't run into each other as hard," says Reid.

And even though in the older age groups rugby shows higher injury rates than other sports, soccer does have substantial rates of lower limb injuries. "Soccer has done a great con job on mothers by telling them soccer is safe and rugby's not," commented David Gibson.

But it's not just that mothers are afraid of their sons being hurt. In the minds of many mothers, football has come to epitomise everything they dislike about traditional masculinity: "I think a lot of women feel that if they can stop their boy playing football they'll have a better chance of stopping him becoming hardened, brutish and unfeeling," said Jane Ewins, from the Good Beginnings parenting programme.

Yet in focussing only on the violence and brutality, many women are blinded to the real appeal of rugby, particularly for young boys. The essence of the game is body contact, manly rough and tumble — precisely the kind of male behaviour which leaves most women cold.

Yet boys love it. Watch any group of boys gathered in a school playground and they'll be at it. Rough housing, wrestling, jumping all over each other. It's classic male play not only amongst boys but between fathers and sons. In his book *Manhood*, Steve Biddulph talks about the rough and tumble which fathers so typically enjoy with their children and notes the difficulty mothers have in dealing with it. (I recently included in my YouTube videos, a conversation about the benefits for children of roughhousing with their dads, between celebrated Canadian clinical psychology professor, Jordan Peterson and Warren Farrell, the well-known author of many books about men[94].)

I spent years watching my teenage son playing rugby and was struck by the boys' obvious delight in physical connection, in sweaty bodies locked together. I wondered how much this pleasure was heightened perhaps by the long period of physical isolation experienced by many boys, from the time their parents stop cuddling them, until the day they first enjoy intimacy with a girlfriend.

But for many women this type of male behaviour is secret men's business — totally unfathomable. And hence rugby, the sport which celebrates all this tumbling and grunting, meets with utter female rejection. "Mindless bum-sniffling barbarism", commented Tasmanian academic Margaret Lindley, summing up women's bewilderment at male attraction to rugby.

Women just don't get it. And when it comes to their sons indulging in this alien male behaviour, many are now determined to try to prevent it. There have always been women who hated the game but until recently mothers were loath to speak out, said Babette Smith, who surveyed generations of mothers for her book *Mothers and Sons*.

"Back in the 1950s the whole subject of football was a no-go area for women. If they had expressed a view, it would have been disparaged. The mother who dared to interfere in the choice of her son's sport was accused of making him into a mummy's boy, or worse, a homosexual."

The fact that so many women are now actually determining what their sons play, speaks not only to women's new confidence but to the changing balance of power in family relations. University of Queensland psychology professor Matthew Saunders reports research showing the increasing influence of wives in family decision making. "Women are more assertive about expressing their viewpoint about a whole variety of things that in the past they weren't prepared to tackle head-on."

But as far as rugby is concerned, Saunders isn't convinced that women have it right. A former rugby coach, Saunders fears mothers are inadvertently cutting off fathers from a rewarding activity which would promote more engagement with their sons. "It's garbage to suggest you can't be a football player and still be sensitive and look at gender issues in a favourable light."

Saunders finds real tension in some families over the issue. "As a clinical psychologist I get asked all the time, 'Should he play rugby?'", he says, reporting many men are uncertain how to defend their old sport in the face of new female hostility.

Owen Pershouse, a Brisbane clinical psychologist, suggests men flounder when it comes to defending such traditional masculine behaviour. "Dads are not very good at articulating their needs and desires. Women are usually better able to express their concerns and in the face of attack some men default to the power thing — 'He's my son and that's what he's going to play!' — whilst the rest end up giving in, 'Oh well, maybe she's right about this stuff'."

Of course there are also men who always hated rugby and are relieved that their sons can now avoid it. Others find many of the values promoted by rugby unappealing. Sydney account manager Daryl Sturgess wasn't keen on his son playing rugby. "I felt it was encouraging qualities that weren't necessarily going to be useful in today's world — like switching off to your own pain."

In fact, there's a new crop of academics, many of them male, now joining with feminist scholars in expressing concerns about the model of masculinity fostered by the football culture. "Where the Boys Are" was a 1998 collection of papers on masculinity, sports and education published by the Deakin Centre for Education and Change. Many of the authors express concerns about the promotion of the "warrior body", which celebrates toughness and the ability to withstand pain and injury, the linking of masculinity with warlike violence and competitiveness, the endorsement of questionable moral values when football authorities overlook instances of anti-social and sexually predatory behaviour.

Education lecturer Lindsay Fitzclarence, one of the book's editors, found himself coaching an Australian football under 15 club team after local mothers heard a lecture he gave on the dubious masculine values celebrated in AFL and promoted his appointment at the local club. Despite the popularity of AFL with female audiences, Fitzclarence reported a growing group of Melbourne mothers determined to keep their sons away from the objectionable aspects of the footy culture. "I wouldn't be surprised if AFL is facing a groundswell problem," he said.

Surprisingly, in NSW rather than suffering as a result of the mother factor, Australian Football has been given a boost. Like soccer, AFL managed to convince some mothers that AFL is a less violent sport than rugby and, as a result, AFL received a steady stream of enquires from mums keen for their boys to play the game. (Rugby injuries are certainly more common but AFL is very concerned about a significant injury rate amongst high school players — rugby may cause more head injuries, but with AFL they are more severe[95].)

Although mother power has yet to really make much of a dent on football participation in Australia, the authorities are right to be concerned. Talk to football officials and they'll tell you how hard they are working to clean up their act and gain female support. All codes are slowly starting to impose stiffer penalties on loutish behaviour of their stars, coaches are being encouraged to step back from the traditional killer mentality, growing numbers of girls are now playing the sport, with women brought in as coaches and recruiting officers.

It's all good sense but there are signs that efforts to please mothers might just be going a little too far. Rugby union has cut out all tackling from Walla rugby — the under eights version of the game. John Searl, acknowledged the reason was "PR aimed at the mums", but the boys are complaining. "The feedback we get from coaches is kids want the tackles. They want to grab hold and have a wrestle in the way they would in fun play," says Searl. Boys still want to be boys but will their mothers let them?

SECTION SEVEN

The tricky world of modern dating

CHAPTER 33

Why women lose out in the dating game

First published 2015

Where are all the good men? That's all the women's magazines seem to talk about these days. The number of wonderful single women in their 30s who can't find any men. Women astonished that men don't seem to be around when they decide it is time to settle down. Women telling men to "man up" and stop shying away from commitment.

But there is another conversation going on — a fascinating exchange about what is happening from the male point of view. Much of it thrives on the Internet, in YouTube vlogs or in the so-called "manosphere". Here you will find men cheerfully, even triumphantly, blogging about their experience. They have cause for celebration, you see. They've discovered a profound change has taken place in the mating game and, to their surprise, they are the winners.

Dalrock (dalrock.wordpress.com) is typical: "Today's unmarried 20-something women have given men an ultimatum: I'll marry when I'm ready, take it or leave it. This is of course their right. But ultimatums are a risky thing, because there is always a possibility the other side will decide to leave it. In the next decade we will witness the end result of this game of marriage chicken."

The end game Dalrock warns about is already in play for hordes of unmarried professional women — the well-coiffed lawyers, bankers and other success stories. Many thought they could put off marriage and families until their 30s, having devoted their 20s to education, establishing careers and playing the field. But was their decade of dating a strategic mistake?

The crisis for single women in this age group seeking a mate is very real. About a quarter of women in their 30s don't have a partner, according to the latest 2016 census statistics. The challenge is greatest for high-achieving women in their 30s looking for equally successful men. Some years back sociologist Genevieve Heard, then working at Monash University, revealed that almost one in four of all degree-educated women aged in their 30s will miss out on same age well-educated men.

And the gap keeps widening. Over 40 per cent of females aged 25-34 now have degrees, compared to 29 per cent of males — up 11 per cent for women and seven per cent for men since 2006.

So there aren't enough men with degrees to go around and many of the other available men fall far short of what these well-educated women have come to expect. Although there are similar numbers of single 30s males and females — many of the available men have only high school education, earn low incomes or are unemployed.

The high expectations of these professional women are a big part of the story. Many high-achieving women simply are not interested in Mr Average. They've swallowed the L'Oreal line: "Because you're worth it!" These women want Alpha males, men who are just as successful as they are and ideally tall and handsome as well.

The problem, according to the male commentators, is many of these women are used to sharing the attention of the most highly desirable men. During their 20s women compete for Mr Big, many readily sharing a bed with the sporty, attractive, confident men while ordinary men miss out. As "Whiskey" puts it at whiskeys-place.blogspot.com.au: "Joe Average Beta Male is about as desirable to women as a cold bowl of oatmeal."

There's some research from American college campuses showing 20 per cent of males — the most attractive ones — get 80 per cent of the sex, according to an analysis by Susan Walsh — a former management consultant who wrote about the issue on her dating website (www.hookingupsmart.com).

That leaves a lot of Beta men spending their 20s out in the cold. Greg, a 38-year-old writer from Melbourne, started adult life shy and lonely. "In my 20s, the women had the total upper hand. They could make or break you with one look in a club or bar. They had the choice of men, sex was on tap and guys like me went home alone, red-faced, defeated and embarrassed. The girls only wanted to go for the cool guys, good looks, outgoing personalities, money, sporty types, the kind of guys who owned the room, while us quiet ones got ignored."

He barely had a date through much of his 20s and gave up on women. But then he spent time overseas, gained more confidence, learnt how to dress well and hit his early 30s. "I suddenly started to get asked out by women, aged 19 through to 40. The floodgates burst open for me. I actually dated five women at once, amazing my flatmates by often bedding three to four of my casual dates each week. It is a great time as a male in your 30s, when you start getting more female attention and sex than you could ever have dreamt of in your 20s."

It's not surprising that men in this situation will take advantage of the bounty on offer. Here's a comment on one of the online chat sites from Take Greenlander, an apparently extremely successful engineer in his late 30s. In his early adult life, he was unable to "get the time of day from women". Now he's only interested in women under 27.

"The women I know in their early 30s are just delusional," he says. "I sometimes seduce them and sleep with them just because I know how to play them so well. It's just too easy. They're tired of the cock carousel, and they see a guy like me as the perfect Beta to settle down with before their eggs dry out … when I get tired of them I just delete their numbers from my cell phone and stop taking their calls … It doesn't really hurt them that much: at this point they're used to pump and dump!"

Greenlander's analysis is echoed by Australian singles, both male and female, who report many of the unattached males are simply interested in playing the field. "It's wall-to wall arseholes out there," reports Penny, a 31-year-old lawyer. She is stunned by how hard it is meet suitable men willing to commit. "I'm horrified by the number of gorgeous, independent and successful women my age who can't meet a decent man."

Penny acknowledges part of the problem is her own expectations — her generation of women was brought up wanting too much. "We were told we were special, we could do anything and the world was our oyster." And having spent her 20s dating Alpha males, she expected them to be still around when she finally decided to get serious.

But these men go fast, with many fishing outside their pond, some choosing younger women and others partners who offer something other than career success. Some doctors still marry nurses, and lawyers their secretaries. The most attractive, successful men can take their pick from women their own age or younger women who are happy to settle early. Almost one in three degree-educated 35-year-old men marry or live with women aged 30 or under, according to ABS statistics.

"I can't believe how many men my age are only interested in younger women," wailed Gail, a 34-year-old advertising executive reporting on her first search through men's profiles on the RSVP Internet dating site. She was shocked to find many mid-30s men have even set-up their profiles to refuse mail from women their own age. The choice makes sense for a man who doesn't want to be pressured into immediately starting a family — a likely scenario if he pairs up with a woman of his own age — or is rightly nervously of getting involved in IVF with all the stress that brings to a relationship. Younger woman offer him more breathing space to make sure it is the right relationship before starting a family.

But talking to women like Gail, it's intriguing how many look back on past relationships where they let good men get away because at the time they weren't ready. The American journalist Kate Bolick wrote in *The Atlantic* about breaking off her three-year relationship with a man she described as "intelligent, good-looking, loyal and kind". She acknowledged that "there was no good reason to end things" yet at the time she was convinced something was missing. That was 11 years before she wrote her article by which time she was 39 and facing grim choices.

"We arrived at the top of the staircase," she wrote, "finally ready to start our lives, only to discover a cavernous room at the tail end of a party, most of the men gone already, some having never shown up — and those who remain are leering by the cheese table, or are, you know, the ones you don't want to go out with."

Many women are missing out on their fairy tale ending, their assumption that when the time was right the dream man would be waiting. The 30s are worrying years for high-achieving women who long for marriage and children — of course, not all do — as they face their rapidly closing reproductive window surrounded by men who see no rush to settle down. Of course many women eventually find a mate, often ending up with divorced men. The complications of that second marriage market, where men come complete with ex-wives and sometimes stepchildren, was not what they expected. That was never part of the plan.

Many really struggle with the fact that they aren't in a position to be too choosy. American author Lori Gottlieb gave a painfully honest account of that process in her book *Marry Him — The Case for Settling for Mr Good Enough*.

"Maybe we need to get over ourselves," she writes. The 40-year-old single mother enlisted a team of advisers who helped her see that while she was conducting her long search for the perfect man — Prince Charming or nobody — her market value had dropped through the floor.

"Our generation of women is constantly told to have high self-esteem, but it seems that the women themselves are at risk of ego-tripping themselves out of romantic connection," she wrote. She acknowledged she made a mistake not looking for a spouse in her 20s, when she was most desirable. She advised 30-something women to look for Mr Good Enough before they have even less choice. "They are with an 8 but they want a 10.

But then suddenly they're 40 and can only get a five!"

That's a five judged by her own unrealistic expectations about the type of man she hoped to attract.

Her point hits home, highlighting the problem when women delay too long their search for a serious relationship. That delay has set up a very different dating and marriage market, with delighted men very much the beneficiaries. Many single men in their 30s can't believe their good luck.

Jamie, 30, a Sydney barrister, finds himself spoilt for choice. Like many of his friends he's finding women actively pursuing him, asking him out, cooking him elaborate meals, buying him presents. "Oh, you're a *barrister*," they say with eyes sparkling.

While many of his mates are playing the field, determined to enjoy this unexpected attention, Jamie is ready to settle down. He's very wary of the *Sex and the City*-type girls convinced that they are so special but he's confident he will soon find someone with her feet on the ground. "I'm lucky to be in a buyer's market," he says smugly.

CHAPTER 34

Marginal Men – missing out on marriage

First published 1998

Mark Peel has fond memories of Elizabeth, the tough working-class suburb in Adelaide where he spent his early years. A few years ago, the Monash University historian revisited the suburb to find out how the working-class community was changing. Over many months he conducted hundreds of interviews, not only in Elizabeth but in struggling suburbs elsewhere: Melbourne's Broadmeadows, Brisbane's Inala and Sydney's Mount Druitt.

When he arrived in each place, he noticed something strange.

"If you drive through the poorer areas, you get the impression that no men live there. The public space — the streets and shopping centres — are filled with women and children. The men are all sitting at home waiting to work again."

These are all suburbs containing pockets, housing estates, where adult male unemployment hits 30, 50 or even 60 per cent. Robbed of their role as providers, the married men in these communities struggle to maintain their place in their families. But there was another group of men Peel came across — men on the fringe. "There was the story about the 32-year-old still living with his mum. No money, no job, nowhere to go. Stories about young single men on their own who end up committing suicide because there's no future. And, most of all, young men blocked from becoming real men, family men, because they can't get work. Many of these young men are ending up on their own. They have no path, no way in."

Mark Peel discovered a group of men who are being locked out. Excluded from family life, from settled relationships and marriage. Men whose lack of economic resources are now sentencing them to life as outsiders.

They are a rapidly growing breed according to Dr Bob Birrell and Virginia Rapson, from Monash University's Centre for Population and Urban Research, whose 1998 report *A Not So Perfect Match* showed dramatic shifts occurring in partnering patterns in Australia.

Their research showed that between 1986 and 1996 there was been a substantial increase in unattached males. For men aged 30 to 34 the percentage unpartnered increased from 29 to 37 per cent, while the increase for 35 to 39-year-olds was from 21 to 29 per cent. At an age when traditionally men were raising young families — their early 30s — it was startling to discover only half of all men were married, with a further 10 per cent in de facto relationships. Almost one in four men in their 40s was unpartnered[96].

It was mainly the poorer men who were being left out. In 1996 only half of men aged 30 to 34 earning less than $15,600 were in couple relationships compared with 76 per cent of men earning $52,000 or more. By the of age 40 to 44 the proportion of partnered men in this poorer group rose to 65 per cent, while 87 per cent of the high earners had partners. We're not talking here about some tiny minority of the population. Massive numbers were being affected by these changes —

19 per cent of men aged 25 to 44 earned less than $15,600 in 1996 according to Birrell's analysis.

These men were hit hard by the deterioration in the male labour market in Australia, which led to a seven per cent drop in full-time work over the previous decade. A striking 30 per cent of men in their 30s were not in full-time employment. There was clear evidence that this dramatic drop in men's capacity as breadwinners meant many were unable to maintain stable relationships. Bob Birrell found men in full-time work were far more likely to be partnered than those in casual or part-time employment. Linking occupation with men's partnership status, he showed that men in high-status jobs, such as managers, were far more likely to be married or in de facto relationships than unemployed men or men in low-status jobs. So, for men aged 35 to 39 in 1996, 82 per cent of managers were in couple relationships compared with only 54 per cent of unemployed men and 66 per cent of men in labouring and similar jobs.

This strong trend for such a large sector of our male population to remain unpartnered is well known to those working in disadvantaged communities. John Embling, founder of Melbourne's Families in Distress Foundation, has been working with low-income families for many decades. He has long been aware of this growing group of unpartnered men. He refers to them as "floaters", drifting at the edges of society.

"Since the '80s I've started seeing more and more of these blokes," he said. "It's become a real phenomenon. These itinerant men float around, sometimes trying to find an old girlfriend in the hope she'll put them up for a few nights, or going back to Mum, if she'll have them. They come and go from pretty second-rate rental situations, caravan parks, boarding houses. Many of them end up as pretty pathetic characters, broken down and sometimes into pretty serious addictions. No one wants them, no one knows what to do with them."

The Birrell data showed surprisingly high numbers of low-income men end up living at home with their parents. For the low-income men aged 30 to 34, 15 per cent were still at home with their mums or dads.

So what's going on here? Bob Birrell's explanation as to the plight of these men lies in what's called "resource" theory, the notion that low-income males fail to make lasting relationships because they haven't the goods to attract and support women.

Birrell referred to the substantial literature on the plight of American black men who have become increasing detached from family life — most black children are now being brought up by sole mothers. Many American commentators believe a major factor contributing to this trend is the low economic resources of the black man, which reduce the economic gains from marriage and hence increase marital disruption and the likelihood that sole mothers remain unattached.

Birrell's finding that a similar pattern was emerging in Australia has big cost implications for this country. The deteriorating mental and physical health of this male population is well documented. But Birrell also suggested a link between male detachment and the growing numbers of single mothers and consequent rise in the welfare bill.

Compounding the problem is the sheer impossibility of extracting child support payments from impoverished fathers who form a significant part of this population.

"The damage that has been done to the male workforce

through the economic restructuring is now coming back to haunt us," Birrell said. "There's a very strong connection between the economic circumstances of these men and the increasing numbers of poor single mothers supporting children on their own."

It wasn't hard to find Australian men in this plight but far harder to persuade them to talk about it. This 40-year-old man — I'll call him "James" — preferred to remain anonymous. He was reluctant to be named because he had been unemployed or in part-time jobs for most of his adult life but had just scored a decent job and was nervous that publicity may jeopardise his hard-won situation.

For James, the link between his lack of resources and his unpartnered status was obvious: "I've had women interested in me and then when they found out I didn't have a job, or when they found out where I lived, they didn't want to know me anymore." He was living in a room in a boarding house in Marrickville. It was pretty basic, but better than some of the other dives in which he had lived. He went home to his mother for a while but she couldn't handle his being out of work, so he moved into his present place and was staying there until he managed to get a little more firmly on his feet.

But he was very conscious that his rough abode doesn't help when it comes to the ladies. "I wouldn't bring any woman back here," he said. "When people ask where I live, I just lie."

Not that James was holding his breath expecting some great new romance. He'd been on his own much of his adult life, apart from a few casual relationships and a period in his 20s when he lived with a woman. She was a uni student, he was unemployed but then was pretty active in various political causes such as the men's movement. All was fine until she graduated — soon after, she moved out. Since then he'd been through a decade or so of women making it clear that they are not interested. James sums up what he's learnt about women. "If you are a woman and you want a man, it's not so much what he's like; it's 'Does he have the car? Does he have the clothes? The money?' It's a big part of women's culture to go after the bloke with the money. Women who don't think they can make it on their own want to latch onto a guy who's making it so their own lives will be easier."

Even though he was, at the time of the interview, better placed, James wasn't optimistic about his chances of settling down. "In some ways I have given up. I'm not feeling too confident about myself."

I talked to Paul Whyte, a Sydney counsellor who often worked with unemployed, low-income males. He was well-aware of their social isolation. "These men often have a sense of complete hopelessness and worthlessness," Whyte said. "They internalise their economic position. As far as women are concerned, they don't want these men around. They see them as just too dribbly, needy, useless. 'No, thank you!'"

In trying to help these men gain some sense of self-worth, Whyte found he was pushing upstream. His conversations with these men revealed they were all too aware of how they were seen by women. "They are treated with such open disrespect, like the women who roll their eyes when they are around. It's seen as all their fault for being such a failure as a male."

This was an important theme that emerged in Mark Peel's historical analysis of the changes occurring in working-class suburbs. Males in these communities are usually the most traditional of men, whose sense of masculinity is utterly bound up in their role as providers. "That's what it meant to be a man in the working class," Peel said. "Men earned a wage and brought it home. Work provided the momentum of their lives."

In such a context, unemployed or a failure to find full-time work hits very hard indeed. And as any welfare worker will tell you, the psychological consequences for these men are all too apparent, ranging from anger and depression, through to substance abuse and even suicide.

"They are emotional basket cases," says Margana Smith, 22, from Mount Gambia in South Australia. Smith had had her share of unemployed boyfriends but found them heavy going. "They carry all their shit with them. They become too emotionally dependent on you because they have so many problems of their own."

But what was happening to the women? If there were so many men remaining unattached, surely this must have left large numbers of women on their own, particularly in these disadvantaged suburbs.

The Birrell figures showed there were indeed plenty of unattached women, but comparatively fewer in the younger age groups (25 to 34) where there was a surplus of more than 90,000 unattached males. (Younger men tend to be in surplus because of the sex imbalance at birth, plus the fact that women usually marry older men.)

By the age of 35, the numbers reversed, with more unpartnered women than men. This is particularly true in lower-income suburbs — for men and women in their 40s in 1996, there were over 35,000 more unattached females than males, with the unattached female surplus significantly higher in the groups lacking post-school qualifications. By the early 40s, most of the unattached females (37 per cent) and 55 per cent of the males were divorced. Theories abound to explain this overall trend towards delaying marriage or avoiding permanent partnerships. Certainly, in the more affluent, better-educated population, women's increasing economic independence was encouraging them to explore the benefits of such options. Equally, it may be that more affluent men were showing some fear of commitment with the costs of divorce so loaded against them.

But at the other end of the income scale, more traditional values were still holding sway and marriage remained women's best hope of improving their situation. But complicating the mating game with this group is the fact that large numbers of unpartnered women are single mothers. By the age of 35, more than half of all unattached women had children, with the proportion of single mothers far higher in lower-income groups.

While most of these single mums in the older age groups were divorcees, particularly in low-income suburbs, there also had been a rapid increase in the number of unmarried young women having children on their own. Twenty-seven per cent of Australian children were born out of wedlock and more than half of these ex-nuptial births were to women under 25.

By 1996, there were 101,224 female sole parents aged 15 to 29, up from 75,533 in 1986. Of these women, 71 per cent had never married in 1996 compared with 53.5 per cent in 1986. Three-quarters of never-married lone mothers were on welfare.

Many working with disadvantaged communities believe that the declining breadwinning capacity of the low-income males is contributing to this trend because they are unable to entice single mothers into permanent partnerships.

Andrew Humphreys was a social worker operating in the Dandenong area of Melbourne. His research work on male suicide gave him insight into the troubles of low-income males — Dandenong has the highest suicide rate in Victoria and one of the highest in the world. He found that when they are young, the women in his area were happy to be with low-income males. "At 20, it's whether he has a car, or is good looking or has a nice haircut." But once they are older, and more often than not have a child or two in tow, then their priorities were different.

Said Humphreys: "She'll then be hoping to marry out of her situation. You are not going to marry a lemon. You are not going to marry someone who is in the same boat as you are. You want the guy with the job and the Commodore."

But there just aren't enough guys with jobs to go around. Not only are many of the men Humphreys came across unemployed but most were pretty unemployable. "In this group you'll find a huge over-representation of men who can't read or write" — a result that Humphreys attributed squarely to the failure of the education system to address critical issues affecting boys' education.

According to Humphreys, this was having a big impact on the marriage market in such areas. "This is the first generation of young women who'll be largely picking their husbands from men who earn less than they do, men who are less educated, less employable and often coping less well than they are."

This was a strong theme to emerge from conversations with welfare workers — they have a strong sense that the women in their communities are coming out on top. Some are benefiting from efforts being made to improve girls' education but others gain maturity through becoming single mothers.

John Embling, of Melbourne's Families in Distress Foundation, said: "The single mums had a pretty rough and ready education in the mechanics of survival; they've learnt how the system works, become involved in re-education schemes with the schools. It all brings them back into the mainstream, re-socialises them, and they end up quite robust, strong. The last thing they want is a broken-down guy who can't hold down a job."

As the Birrell research showed, while the male workforce was contracting, women's participation was improving significantly. Over the previous decade there had been roughly a seven per cent improvement in the proportion of women aged 25 to 44 in employment — although mainly in part-time work.

Humphreys said women in his community had noticed the score. "They are angry at what's happened to their potential partners. They are aware that their group of guys is impaired in some ways. That the pond they are fishing from is not a very good pond."

But for those women who do have children, there were also are other issues — such as welfare payments. For a woman on a lone-parent's pension there can be real financial penalties associated with taking on a low-income male. If she acknowledges living with a male, she must then give up the lone parent's benefit, (now known as the "parenting payment") but the couple could still receive welfare support if their combined income remained sufficiently low.

This means that even if the man is unemployed, their combined welfare payments would exceed her previous pension.

For instance, a sole parent with a 10-year-old child would have a disposable income of $247 a week from her pension. Living with a man on unemployment benefits, their combined disposable income would be $342.00 — a significant advance[97].

Yet most single mothers didn't see it that way. As Deb Pedretti, a welfare worker in Moe in Victoria, and herself a single mother, explained: "You are going from having your own income, and knowing what's coming into your bank account, to all the hassles about who is going to divvy up what, not knowing if he'll spend the pay cheque before you see it. Most of these women have been down this path before. They've learnt to cope on their own and they don't want to go back to all that."

It may well be that part of the explanation for the increases in unattached males and females showing up in census figures lay in the conditions governing these welfare provisions.

Sole mothers were allowed to have defactos stay overnight three times a week before having to shift to couple status but Deb Pedretti acknowledged many single mothers stretch the rules. "There's heaps of it going on. There are plenty of people I know are cohabiting but still they'll come to me wanting help with forms for sole-parent's benefits."

But there are many others whose economic circumstances presented genuine obstacles to re-partnering. A substantial proportion of the unattached low-income males, particularly in the older age groups, had in fact already been married. But many of these divorced men were so badly hit by the financial consequences of the marriage break-up that they had little hope of forming stable new partnerships.

The Birrell data showed that men in the lower-income

groups were far more likely to remain divorced or separated than higher-income men. For example, of the ever-married men aged 35 to 39, 24 per cent of men earning less than $15,600 were divorced or separated in 1996 compared with just 10 per cent of those in the $52,000 income group. Over the previous decade the proportion of men remaining unattached after divorce in low-income suburbs increased dramatically but remained stable with more prosperous men.

A study conducted at the Research School of Social Sciences at the Australian National University showed that many of these low-income divorced men could barely afford to support themselves, let alone pay child support. The research showed that men earning under $15,000 a year were required to pay about half their disposable income (excluding a minimal self-support component) in child support.

The Birrell research included an intriguing new analysis of Child Support Agency figures which showed that 46.2 per cent of men registered with the agency reported incomes of less than $16,000. It's true that some of these men may have been involved in income minimisation and others deliberately cut back on their earnings to avoid paying what they should. But the ANU research showed many were simply not in any position to support their children.

Steve Carroll was a nurse/educator working at Long Bay Jail in Sydney. He came across plenty of prisoners who are in jail for defaulting on paying child support. They were usually males who have been struggling on very low incomes, living from day to day. "They couldn't have paid in a fit, they are so chaotic and disorganised."

It's hardly surprising that many of the low-income divorced

men were bitter at the obstacles they face in finding new relationships. For instance, there was a very nasty little surprise for any sole mother who decided to live with a man paying child support. The way the system was set up, the calculation of the new family's entitlement to the family payment was then based on their combined household income but this income test failed to take account of the fact that he could lose substantial amounts through child support. So, her welfare payments could be reduced significantly, yet they don't even have access to the income he was assumed to provide.

Greg Holmes was eating banana sandwiches three weeks out of four in order to afford food for his four children when they stayed with him a week every month. He was a farm labourer living in a weatherboard shack near Coffs Harbour, a shack with no electricity or running water, and the dunny was a pit up the back.

The area was doing it tough, with unemployment about 30 per cent, but Holmes wasn't prepared to move away from his kids so he survived on casual work, mainly on banana plantations. For the previous two years, his income had been about $11,000 a year.

Greg was not optimistic about his chances of finding a permanent relationship. "The only way it would work would be if the lady had a good job and she'd end up supporting us while I supported my kids. Why would she want to do that? She'd be far better off having me as a boyfriend rather than any sort of live-in relationship." In fact, Greg was involved with a woman, Susan Foster, 36, a single mother with four children. Foster was supporting her family on a pension plus a little casual work. She knew it would be many years before she had any hope of living with Greg.

"There's just no way you can move in with your partner if he's on a low wage or on the dole. It just puts so much stress on the relationship to have that financial crisis where he's supporting another family and you're losing some of your pension because he's also expected to support you."

Like many thousands of others, the couple was on hold, awaiting the economic miracle that would make it possible for them to be together. Meanwhile the community has to support them.

These alarming trends are costing us plenty, not only in growing welfare payments but the long-term social consequences of children being raised in poor single-parent families and many thousands of lonely men living on the fringes of society.

With youth employment reaching new heights, new generations are headed in the same sad direction.

The message to government and society is clear — we simply cannot afford to ignore the drastic need for more targeted education and training for these large numbers of working class boys and young men. We cannot leave them with no hope of a decent job. By depriving them of these fundamentals, we sentence them to a fringe existence, excluded from the comforts of family and community — a tragedy in a society that prides itself on giving everyone a fair go.

CHAPTER 35

Leaping back in the saddle – older singles and sex

First published 2015

It's not how women in their 60s are expected to behave. George, 68, was a good catch, a retired Sydney lawyer, chatty, charming and well-read. When he first tentatively entered the online dating world three years ago, he was stunned by provocative sexual behaviour from women in his own age group.

From the first meeting some women made their intentions clear. Massaging his crotch whilst standing at the bar ordering their first drink. Rubbing his thigh under the coffee table. Tongue kissing to say a first "hello". Brushing a braless breast repeatedly up against him. Finding an excuse to ask him home and then undressing before the front door had even closed.

"I certainly didn't expect women to come on so strong," says George, explaining that after some indulging in the bounties on offer, the novelty wore off. He's now in a happy relationship with a somewhat more reticent woman he met online.

His experience isn't unusual. The current generation of seniors is no blushing bunch of old fogies ready to hang up their spurs. This is the baby boomer generation which came of age during the sexual revolution so it's hardly surprising that when large numbers found themselves over fifty and unattached, many revelled in new opportunities provided by online dating to leap back into the saddle.

The large numbers work in men's favour. According to the 2011 Census figures there are over 386,000 more unattached women than men aged 55-74 — about 528,000 men compared to over 915,000 women. That's a huge pool of older singles and many are enjoying having the Internet to bring them together. According to 2014 Nielsen research conducted for RSVP most over-50 singles (53 per cent) have tried or would consider trying online dating.

In the face of this stiff competition women have become far more active. When RSVP started in 1997 males outnumbered females almost two to one — but gradually more women, particularly older women, have joined various sites and are participating with enthusiasm. And for some that means not just approaching men but putting the hard word on them when it suits them.

I've been working as an online dating coach for the past four years and amongst my clients are some very lusty women happy to acknowledge that whilst they are ultimately looking for a relationship they aren't adverse to just a roll in the cot.

"If I meet someone I find attractive, I'd rather just jump into bed quickly and get the preliminaries over and done with. Chatting in bed has always been much easier than stiffly conversing over a cup of coffee," says Andrea, a 66-year-old Melbourne woman who is revelling in such pleasures following a long sexual hibernation after becoming a widow.

"It is all a big adventure. As long as I am up front with myself and my partners, I reckon I can do what feels good and have a ball. No more fears of pregnancy, no more of those crazy messages like 'He'll think you're a slut' or 'He'll think you are too easy'. What a load of rubbish all that was."

Whilst these women usually find plenty of prospective partners keen to indulge with them, the ageing male body isn't always up to it. When one of my older female clients contacts me with glad tidings — she's met a lovely man and giving up dating to enjoy their new relationship — often she gets back in touch some months later to say they are struggling with an erection problem. That's hardly surprising — with men in their 50s one man in two has some erectile dysfunction. By the 60s the numbers hit 60 per cent, 70 per cent for 70-year-olds. These are big numbers which means that lovemaking in this age group can often be a very bumpy road.

Making matters worse is men often don't want to talk about the problem. I've had a number of clients who have gone out for long periods with men who never touched them. A man may have good reason to take things slowly — an older father who still has youngish children may be just taking care not to get too quickly involved, given the high stakes for his family.

There are also older men who just aren't very interested in sex or who believe in waiting until the right person comes along — all sort of possible reasons why a man might not want to rush into a sexual relationship. But the erection issue looms large for many who prefer to avoid sex altogether than risk having sex and failing. The good thing is there are now very effective treatments available to help a man in this situation but it isn't so easy for a woman to negotiate this with her new lover.

"It was all so hard, not wanting to pressure him into thinking I needed him to have a stiff dick. That was never the issue. He was the most generous and skilled lover and you don't need an erection for giving pleasure. But I hated the fact he was feeling a failure and wanted to help him find a solution so he didn't beat himself up over the issue," commented one woman I helped through this difficult phase in their new relationship.

So while some older online daters are enjoying all sorts of erotic adventures, many prefer to take it slow. The RSVP 2014 Nielsen research shows online dating is doing a good job helping these over-50 singles connect — 53 per cent report it's led to a short-term relationship or new friendship whilst 12 per cent end up married or in long term relationships.

The research showed roughly a third of singles over 50 have slept with someone they met online. A similar proportion typically have sex on the third date but another third wait for five to ten dates or longer. Eleven per cent have sex on the first date.

When couples take it slowly often it is the women putting on the breaks. George mentions a number of dates who refused a goodnight kiss even after the fourth or fifth date. "I didn't want a refrigerator," he said scathingly.

Another man reports he's had women pronounce that sex was never to be on the agenda. "I've grown out of *that*," said one woman firmly. It's baffling for men meeting so many women who want to just be friends. "If you find the person physically attractive I guess you always expect others to feel as you do," explains a Sydney widower, 65. With research showing large numbers of older women with low sex drive it's hardly surprising that men encountered many women who are only seeking companionship. But divorced men emerging from often sexless marriages are rightly wary.

Women can be equally confused, as this Sydney woman, 59, explains: "I want sex in a relationship that will last. I can't do one-night stands because I'm only interested in sex if there is chemistry and if there's that spark it means I will want to see them again. Sometimes men seem to want you to be prim and proper and so if you have flirted they think that all you want is sex. And then there are men who are all over you like a rash, sucking your tonsils on your very first kiss. It's just not that easy."

It's true these early sexual negotiations can be tricky territory but for women still open to a sexual relationship it pays to make that clear. I've found it works wonders to hint in an older woman's profile that she hasn't shut up shop. There's nothing like a subtle, sexy touch to stand out from the crowd.

For the last year Melbourne physiotherapist Patricia, 62, has been doing very well online with her lively, entertaining profile which amongst details of her interesting life mentions the fact she enjoys being "ravished". Yes, she finds it attracts some inappropriate male attention but also the intelligent, respectful, professional men she chooses to date. "Sometimes I have sex but that is my choice and I've learnt to accept the consequences if it doesn't work out," she explains. She finds that going to bed with someone she doesn't see as a prospective partner is a "hollow experience" so she avoids that. But overall her experience is very positive. "I have never felt pressured — just gently seduced," she says.

It's the age-old problem for women — wanting sex to be the start of something wonderful and being bitterly disappointed if it turns out he just wanted sex. But there are many lively boomers handling negotiations over sex with confidence and self-knowledge. Andrea mentions the old Kris Kristofferson lyric — "Freedom's just another word for nothing left to lose." Given their history, it is natural for this boomer generation to still take risks, enjoy sexual freedom and live with the consequences.

Finally, speaking of risks, what about all those media linking online dating to increased risk of sexually transmitted infections?

Professor Basil Donovan from the Kirby Institute, University of New South Wales, says the risks are often overblown. Online dating has meant older singles are having more sex which has pushed rates of STIs up a little — but that's compared to very low rates in a generation where sex with new partners used to be less common.

"We know that people over 50 have poor knowledge of STIs and are less likely to use condoms but, although it pays to be careful, in reality the risks aren't very high," explains Donovan. He points out that some of the worst threats to younger generations don't apply to this age group:

- Hardly any women over 50 contract chlamydia and there's no risks for fertility for this age group. According to 2015 National Notifiable Diseases figures, 195 cases of chlamydia have been reported this year in women over 50 compared to over 12,000 for women aged 15-25.

- People who've had herpes for many years are very unlikely to spread it.

- The HIV, syphilis, or gonorrhoea risk is almost entirely confined to gay or bisexual men or people who've been sexually active in high prevalence countries in parts of Asia, Africa and the Americas.

"The safe sex talk is still a good idea but if you pick your partners carefully this is not as big an issue for the over 50s," says Donovan, "But seeing your GP for a check-up after an exotic holiday seems like a good idea."

So that's not such a huge issue but the tricky business of getting naked with someone new remains a real challenge for older folk navigating the dating game. Yet the rewards can be remarkable, unexpected pleasure and long-forgotten delight. That's well worth the many disappointments and odd embarrassing moment.

CHAPTER 36

Desperate and dateless – broke, older divorced men

First published 2012

Harry is an impressive man. Jolly face, plenty of hair and slim. That's what comes from getting about without a car. He's living with his red setter in a rented Sydney terrace, studying and doing some university coaching. It's a far cry from his life a few years back when he was married, settled in a large house in Palm Beach, earning $250,000 plus as an executive for international corporations, running expensive cars, and with children in costly boarding schools.

It was the demands of his job that led to it all coming unstuck, he says. "Often the male partner has been working hard to support this lifestyle. The female views this as not paying enough attention to her, so she initiates divorce. She has little to lose, so why not? In my case, this is exactly what happened."

Soon after that his share portfolio was wiped out, a major client refused to pay a bill and Harry couldn't afford the legal fight to obtain the money owed. As he struggles to re-establish himself, he's using online dating to look for a new partner.

It should be easy. How often do we read that there's a glut of single older women, a dearth of appealing unattached men?

But Harry is wilting under women's scrutiny. "Many women I meet regard me as a hopeless failure because I can no longer afford holidays in Europe every year and don't own a car or a house in the Eastern Suburbs.

"You see the judgment in their eyes, in their body language when they discover you are a renter. There's little signposts that they are summing you up and finding you wanting. It's as if you come from a totally different social milieu."

He finds the contempt unbearable and generally prefers to be on his own. That's the sad surprise awaiting all those intrepid older women who've moved on from their marriages and set forth into the tough world of online dating. They keep meeting men like Harry.

Harry should be in a buyer's market. There are many more older single women than men in Australia — 2006 census figures show 68,000 more single women than men in their 50s. Only 13 per cent of these men have degrees, less than half the number of tertiary educated women in that age group. But the trouble with men like Harry — and it turns out there are many like him — is that they simply can't meet women's reserve price.

For contrary to common assumptions, older divorced women are on average more financially secure than older divorced men. Many of these women are professionals earning a good income and with their own homes. They prefer a man who can match their assets, but there simply aren't enough to go around.

At the time I wrote this article, I was working as an online dating coach, mainly offering advice to older women about how to improve their chances in this difficult market. I heard all the time from my clients that they kept meeting men who were struggling financially. "All the men are broke!" they moaned, as they worried about protecting their nest eggs.

It turned out they were right — older divorced women are often better off than divorced men in their age group. In 2007, David de Vaus and colleagues from the Australian Institute of Family Studies used data from HILDA (the Household, Income and Labour Dynamics in Australia survey) to compare divorced women and men aged 55 to 74 and found half the women owned a house compared with 41 per cent of the men.

The average household income of the women was also higher and just under half of the older divorced men were renting compared with about a third of the women. Superannuation was the one area where men's assets outstripped the women — the sorry state of older women's super is a story that attracts constant attention.

Yes, there are many single, older women doing it tough, just as there are men. But the constant attention on women at the bottom means a big story is overlooked: the financial mismatch at the upper end of the dating market for older people.

That's the problem facing women like Sharon, an attractive 61-year-old Perth doctor. "I have no intention of being a nurse or purse to any man," she says. Her long marriage to a successful businessman left her with a prime piece of real estate overlooking the Swan River.

She has been Internet dating for about eight years, met about 50 men, had relationships or sometimes just sex with about a dozen. She says she is brutally honest with the men she meets, declaring she's not interested in anyone who doesn't match her financially. She grills them about their solvency. "I just about ask them for their tax returns."

Sharon does missions for Medecins Sans Frontieres in hot spots all over the developing world, in the toughest bits of

Asia and Africa. "Such work is sad, dangerous, difficult and stressful," she says, "so in my down time I want to be able to enjoy travelling with a bit of luxury.

"I am neither rich enough nor willing to pay for a man to join me. If I have spare dollars, I'd rather take my children."

She has decided she is almost ready to give up on finding her future partner and travelling companion. "I cannot find anyone who comes within a bull's roar of what I want. Nearly all the men I have met have been utterly hopeless and devoid of any real spark, [they're] broke, needy ... I can only assume the good ones get snapped up quickly and have no need to look around."

Sharon may be right about that. There is a pool of mature aged single men with deep pockets out there — but they are rarely single for long. Dr Genevieve Heard from Monash's School of Social and Political Inquiry studied 2011 Census data and found there are more divorced men than women aged 50 to 70 in the top household income bracket ($104,000 or more a year): 17,100 men compared with 10,400 women. But these men are often snapped up as soon as they hit the market. Their friends usually have swarms of single women lining up to meet them.

The surprise, though, is that in every income bracket below this one, older women outnumber men. Heard's analysis shows there are 82,300 divorced women and only 67,400 divorced men aged 50–70 with a yearly household income of between $52,000 and $104,000.

The data also shows a huge gap in the numbers of divorced women and men aged 50 to 70 who own or are paying off a house: 291,000 women compared with 195,100 men.

That's almost 100,000 more women than men. The financial gap is real and there are repercussions in the dating world. Women's concern about protecting their assets makes them hyperalert to any hint of an impecunious man, like reticence to pay for that first drink or coffee. "If a man doesn't pay, it's a very bad sign," says one 49-year-old divorcee.

Many women complain about men's lack of generosity. "They are often really tight arsed, rarely taking out their wallet until you say, 'It's OK, I'll pay'," says another divorced woman. A third tells the story of a man who turned up with a nice bottle of wine for their first dinner. When it came time to pay the bill, he readily accepted her offer to split it and then deducted the cost of the wine from his share. Needless to say, that was their only date.

Men say that their lack of generosity results from irritation that even very affluent women are often reluctant to put their hands in their pockets. "They are as tight as buggery," says an underemployed architect who simply can't afford to shout expensive dinners.

Most men are very conscious of being financially screened from the very first meeting; a financial consultant mentions the unseemly eagerness of one date to escape as soon as he mentioned how tough it was getting new work. Another man — an editor now living in what he describes as "genteel poverty" — commented that some women react well to his circumstances but others "become sneering and offensive almost immediately".

I'm struck by a comment from a 49-year-old divorcee who told me: "If a man is broke, it says something about them. We should all be financially sorted by now." She's a woman whose husband "chewed through most of the savings" she brought into the marriage, so her viewpoint is understandable.

Yet it's so easy to assume that a man who doesn't shape up financially must be a loser. How often does it occur to women — myself included — that maybe we might have something to do with the plight of these older men?

Divorce is a growing hazard for older married men. The percentage of divorces involving men over 50 more than doubled between 1985 and 2010 — leaping from 11 to 22 per cent for men in their 50s and four to 10 per cent for men aged 60 and over. A Family Court study by Pauline Presland and Helen Gluckstern in 1993 showed it was women who made the decision to leave in two-thirds of mature-aged marital separations. Australian National University professor Matthew Gray, a former deputy director of the Australian Institute of Family Studies, says this is most likely still the case: "Research from around the world shows women make the decision in most, around two-thirds of marital separations."

After a long working life of building up their financial security, many rightly grumpy older men end up losing 60 per cent to 70 per cent of the joint assets; homemaker wives or those on low incomes will often receive an extra 10 or 20 per cent above an even split because it's assumed a high-earning man will gain more from future earnings.

But as prominent Sydney family law practitioner John Barkus says, this takes for granted that the man's high income will continue. "That doesn't always happen. It's a dog-eat-dog world when a professional or executive is over 50. Openings have to be made for younger people in the business and so it's bye-bye to the older person. That's the reality," he says.

According to 2002 research by Melbourne Law School researcher Grania Sheehan, divorced Australian wives end up with two-thirds of the domestic assets — the home and its contents — plus another quarter of nondomestic assets such as superannuation. Women from low-asset marriages receive a majority share overall, found Sheehan, but this is of relatively low value, while high-asset marriages result in women receiving a more equal share, worth far more.

Sheehan says women living alone, including single mothers and older women from long-term marriages, are particularly likely to be financially disadvantaged by divorce, but so, too, are men living alone. Men's share of the assets is often in super, which Sheehan says "can't be relied on to meet housing and other more immediate day-to-day financial needs" except in high-asset marriages.

Patricia Frost has spent 25 years as chief executive of the Inner West Skill Centre in Sydney. She sees a steady stream of these men in the centre which finds jobs for unemployed people. She says divorce is often the start of a slippery slope which can lead to well-established, professional men ending up on the skids.

The global financial crisis was another major factor that decimated the savings of many formerly affluent men. And high-salaried older men are also very vulnerable when companies downsize. Frost's organisation has had unemployed barristers, ex-university lecturers, men formerly in executive management positions and ex-creative directors on its books. "It's very, very difficult for these to step back to the level they were beforehand," she says.

And that's when the men, once successful and sought after

by women, start running into disdain. Harry fears the women he dates will chat to others about his finances; he mentions the excruciating humiliation of knowing women often share personal information. He says that men are more protective about their financial situation: "That's their vulnerability vis-a-vis other men."

This quietly spoken, sophisticated man finds it hard to even talk about the shame he feels. But he nails the hypocrisy of women who label him a failure when, as far as he can see, they are well-situated as a result of ending a marriage. "'I'm the queen bee and who is this scum?' I'd like to say, 'Hang on a moment. Stand back and look at yourself!'"

On the other hand, women do have reason to be cautious about men who disguise their finances. Imagine the shock for Laura, 55, when she discovered her very eligible suitor wasn't what he seemed. The Melbourne physiotherapist shared half the assets in a divorce 12 years ago but has worked hard all her adult life and looks forward to a financially comfortable retirement.

The man she met through online dating had all the trappings: an Audi, club memberships, expensive clothes, family silver, a country retreat. "He's a businessman and right from the start I felt intimidated by him when it came to discussing money," she says.

So, when he vaguely mentioned a "financial arrangement" when he sold his house, planning to move in with her, she didn't like to push him. Alarms sounded only when a mate's reaction to the house sale was: "Where's my cheque?" Now, two years later, Laura has learnt (from papers he left on her dining room table) that her partner has massive loans on his house, maxed-out credit cards and significant debts. He's "working" from an office in her garage, still hoping to move in with her but, she says, he's contributing nothing — and stalling on giving her all the details of his finances.

What to do? She's undecided. "Do I accept the lifestyle limitations this relationship imposes on me, such as he can't afford to travel, which I really love? Also, the risk that he would, because we're in a de facto relationship, have a legal claim to my assets? But then, he's very decent, presentable, doesn't mess around with other women and really wants me. That's something and it is not as if there are many other options out there."

Women rightly fear deception but what is surprising is how few women are willing to contemplate taking on a less prosperous mate. Most of my dating clients are scathing when I suggest financial status isn't always that important.

Divorced Sydneysider Michele Waterlow, 50, is different. She earns big money in the IT industry but has no problem with dating men who are less well off. Recently she met a builder who caught her fancy. He made it clear he was financially strapped but she was still keen to see him. Her girlfriends tried to put her off. "He's punching above his weight," one told her.

Yvonne, a 54-year-old Perth academic, is another who doesn't judge a man by his financial status. "If I was really attracted, money would not matter. Some men with very few assets are still very generous in that they give of their time, their body, their mind — and their handyman skills!"

The attitude of women like Michele and Yvonne is just what James is banking upon. A retired accountant who once worked for Citibank, he isn't interested in deceiving women. He's upfront about the fact he's looking for a woman to support him. He has it all worked out. He needs about $9,000 a year to subsidise his pension and make him a suitable partner for one of the well-established professional women he meets through the Internet. Plus, he plans to move in with her; at present he keeps a roof over his head by housesitting.

He's convinced he has plenty to offer. "Most of the girls say I am streets ahead of most of the guys they meet." He looks pretty good for an older man. Dark hair, cheeky smile with fetching laugh lines. According to his Internet profile, he's an "educated, fun, retired professional; cultured, active and sophisticated." He mentions his accounting and finance career and his six months sailing in the Caribbean while the share-market features among his retirement activities.

James has had a few women circle but once they've listened to their girlfriends, they knock back his offer. "Their friends put them off. They don't understand these women might be better off trying the arrangement rather than being alone for the rest of their lives." He's even offering a legal contract which would give a woman the right to back out, assets intact, at any stage.

Fancy his chances? Judging by the almost universal shudder that greets this story whenever I tell it, it's clear that any man seeking financial support is up against it. The trick for James will be to find a woman who doesn't resent how hard she has sweated to achieve her current financial security. Despite the windfall many receive through divorce, most women are cautious with money. Many are managing their finances for the first time and are perhaps overly afraid, thanks to the media, of ending up as a homeless bag lady.

Michele Waterlow can see the worry from that viewpoint.

"At this age, looking for someone to share one's life is very scary," she says. "You don't want to be starting off with a struggle again. You're done with stretching your finances to pay off a mortgage or meet your grocery bills. You don't want to end up back there."

Helen, 57, a Sydneysider proudly earning $80,000 after years of low earnings while her kids were at school, says: "I want a man who can manage to live his life on his own and is not looking for a life-support system."

Her marriage fell apart after six years of supporting her husband, who had become unemployed. "Although he subsequently got work and we started to gain ground again, it wasn't enough. I'd had the upper hand and all the responsibility for too long." With honesty, she says she feels the concern about a man's finances is hardwired. "I think we haven't evolved far enough for financial strength not to be attractive to women. We're still turned on by a man who has more than we have."

That may be so but perhaps men are right in calling women to task for our unwillingness to move on. Phillip, 59, is a charming, funny Sunshine Coast engineer who readily admits his current financial crisis is due not just to his two divorces but his casual approach to running his previously extremely successful business.

The taxman eventually caught up with him. He's online dating and quite open about the fact that his new retirement plan involves finding a woman with a house ready to take him on: "I have already married two paupers who lived in fine state for many years. Is it unfair to expect that it is my turn?"

Endnotes

1. https://www.youtube.com/watch?v=mE1HM0RQSFE

2. Bruce Baird's son Mike later became Premier of NSW.

3. https://mentoo.com.au/notafeminist

4. https://mentoo.com.au/far-enough

5. https://www.youtube.com/watch?v=pVx_SOxM78A&t=562s

6. https://www.youtube.com/watch?v=3LT44DzC-MQ

7. https://www.youtube.com/watch?v=sF7K5bsj7mk

8. Also known as "The Australian Study of Health and Relationships" (ASHR1), first published in 2003.

9. Latest ABS Personal Safety Survey figures show that during the 12 months prior to the 2016 survey. Almost half the persons who experienced emotional abuse by a partner were male (45.8 per cent).

(47.7 per cent of persons who experienced it by a current partner and 43.4 per cent by a previous partner). https://mentoo.com.au/ABS-2016-PSS

10. pp 104-5 of the Children's Rights Report 2015 by the National Children's Commissioner found that "children comprised the second most frequent group of victims of family and domestic homicides (21 per cent) after intimate partner homicides (56 per cent)." And "while males accounted for the majority of offenders in domestic/family homicides, in cases of filicides, offenders were slightly more likely to be female (52 per cent) than male (48 per cent)." https://mentoo.com.au/Childrens-Rights-2015

11. https://mentoo.com.au/DomesticViolenceResearch

12. Flood is now at QUT https://mentoo.com.au/Staff-profiles-Michael-Flood

13. The proportion of males has gone up since then — in 2016 the ABS Personal Safety Survey found that 35.3 per cent of persons who had experienced violence by an intimate partner in the last 12 months were male. https://mentoo.com.au/one-in-three-infographics

14. The 2016 ABS Personal Safety Survey found that 42 per cent of men aged 18 years and over had experienced violence of some kind since the age of 15. https://mentoo.com.au/ABS-2016-PSS

15. https://mentoo.com.au/violence-against-women-in-australia

16. https://mentoo.com.au/false-claims-undermine-good-causes

17. https://mentoo.com.au/WAstatistics-child-maltreatment

18. https://www.youtube.com/watch?v=0CX_jFlP1oM

https://www.youtube.com/watch?v=tldOXwc0dh8

19. The study also determined mother's violence was not carried out in self-defence.

20. In 2016 the proportion was still 0.8 per cent.

21. By 2016, physical violence from ex-partners had dropped to 0.5 per cent.

22. Australia was recently named the safest country in the world for women, according to analysis by consultancy New World Wealth in its 2018 Global Wealth Migration Review.

23. ABS Personal Safety Survey data shows this increased to 1.18 per cent in 2016, a minimal change.

24. https://mentoo.com.au/violence-against-women-in-australia

25. That dropped to around 40 per cent in 2016.

26. The latest Institute of Criminology figures report that there were 99 female victims of intimate partner homicide over a two-year period in 2012 — 2014. A man is now killed by his partner every 27 days, 27 over the 2-year period 2012-14.

27. More recent statistics suggest that 21.4 per cent of intimate partner homicide victims are male.

28. When the latest, 2012-2014 figures are included, the drop isn't so dramatic. There's been a 24 per cent decrease over the period. https://mentoo.com.au/homicide-in-australia

29. Victims of Domestic or Family Homicide: https://mentoo.com.au/victims-of-domestic-or-family-homicide

30. See the video I made talking to the brave Augusto Zimmermann about his work. https://www.youtube.com/watch?v=xLai47ieB08&t=834s

31. The 2016 Personal Safety Survey showed that figure had increased further, with men accounting for almost 40 per cent of victims of current partner violence over the 12 month period and 47.7 per cent of victims of current partner emotional abuse.

32. In 2016, 2.62 per cent of male deaths and 0.93 per cent of female deaths were attributed to suicide.

33. My video — Monstrous Lies about Domestic Violence — includes an extract from the SBS television show, featuring Terrie Moffit speaking about this research. https://www.youtube.com/watch?v=-1-I8AttyDc&t=8s

34. https://mentoo.com.au/change-the-story

35. Despite Miller's and Ogloff's witness statements, the rhetoric in the Royal Commission report exposes a strong feminist bias. The report endorses the prioritisation of female and child victims (p.1), includes 'gender inequality' and 'attitudes towards women' that are 'rooted in power imbalances' and 'reinforced by gender norms and stereotypes' as key causes of family violence (p.2) and reveals an acute disproportion of female perspectives in the commission's investigative processes (p.4).
https://mentoo.com.au/Victorian-Royal-Commission

36. https://mentoo.com.au/Ken-Arenson-paper

37. Of even greater concern, Arenson referred in his ICMI speech to further radical recommendations made by this academic that will undoubtedly be pushed by strident feminists in the future. One example is the push for enthusiastic consent laws, a reform which is currently being pursued by Minister Pru Goward in NSW. See my recent video discussing these proposed laws with Murdoch University law lecturer, Lorraine Finlay.
https://www.youtube.com/watch?v=ADrKfnVWvXA&t=87s

38. https://www.youtube.com/watch?v=061f7xO8ni0

39. Daisy Cousens is now appearing regularly on Andrew Bolt's programme on Sky News.

40. https://youtu.be/vp8tToFv-bA

41. https://www.youtube.com/watch?v=4r7wHMg5Yjg

42. The AHRC survey instrument included questions about participants' experiences of "sexually suggestive comments or jokes that made you feel offended", "repeated or inappropriate invitations to go out on dates" and "intrusive questions about your private life or physical appearance that could be offensive" (p.209). Such a broad and subjective style of questioning can easily explain the alarming results that were subsequently circulated, such as the finding that '1 in 5 university students were sexually harassed in a university setting in 2016.' https://mentoo.com.au/AHRC-change-the-course

43. Indeed, currently there is a concerted push to do just that in New South Wales, with Pru Goward, the Minister for the Prevention of Domestic Violence and Sexual Assault advocating for this model, and the NSW Law Reform Commission reviewing the laws around consent in relation to sexual assaults.

44. The AHRC survey report briefly acknowledges this sampling problem on page 226.

45. 'BME' stands for 'black or minority ethnic'.

46. https://www.youtube.com/watch?v=oDmYW8TW6nI

47. https://mentoo.com.au/victim-centered-practices

48. The 'Start by Believing' campaign has also spread to Canada, and similar concerns are being expressed. Last year an Ontario Superior Court Justice wrote that the slogan Believe the Victim 'has no place in a criminal trial' as it 'is the equivalent of imposing a presumption of guilt on the person accused of sexual assault'. https://mentoo.com.au/Nyznik-2017

49. https://mentoo.com.au/clementine-ford-petition

50. https://mentoo.com.au/clementine-ford-removed

51. https://mentoo.com.au/mission-australia-fails-children

52.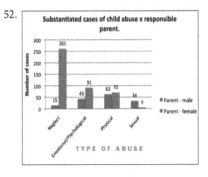

53. Also known as the Australian Study of Health and Relationships ASHR1, published in 2003. https://mentoo.com.au/ASHR1

54. Also known as the Australian Study of Health and Relationships ASHR2 (2014). https://mentoo.com.au/ASHR2

55. Also known as the Australian Study of Health and Relationships ASHR2 (2014.)

56. Also known as the Australian Study of Health and Relationships ASHR2 (2014). https://mentoo.com.au/ASHR2

57. Also known as the Australian Study of Health and Relationships ASHR1 (2003). https://mentoo.com.au/ASHR1

58. Also known as the Australian Study of Health and Relationships ASHR1 (2003).

59. In the most recent survey ASHR2 (2014), 57 per cent of men and 71 per cent of women reported having discussed expectations of sexual fidelity with their partner.

60. https://mentoo.com.au/mens-health-melbourne

61. Research conducted since this article was published has shown variable results for penile rehabilitation — it helps some patients far more than others. But even men who fail to regain their natural functioning can have erections using injection therapy or by having a prosthesis and hence resume a normal sex life.

62. The proportion of divorces involving children has, however, been steadily declining. Since 1977, the proportion of divorces involving children under 18 declined from 63 per cent to 47 per cent in 2016. https://mentoo.com.au/ABS-2016-marriages-and-divorces

63. By 2016, the crude marriage rate was down even further 4.9 per cent https://mentoo.com.au/ABS-2016-marriages-and-divorces

64. In 2016, ex-nuptial births represented almost 34 per cent of all births in Australia. https://mentoo.com.au/ABS-2016-births

65. Between 1996 and 2011, single-mother families increased from three per cent to four per cent while single father families remained static at one per cent. During that period, 75 per cent of Australian children who had a natural parent living elsewhere were living in one-parent homes. The vast majority (79 per cent) of these children were living with their mother. https://mentoo.com.au/families-in-australia

66. More recently, in 2014, the ABC ran a fact check on the then Social Services Minister Kevin Andrews' claim that de facto relationships had a higher incidence of break up than marriages. The verdict was that couples who never married were six times more likely to break up than couples who married https://mentoo.com.au/defacto-fact-check. It is very difficult to get updated data specifically on de facto couples with children.

67. More recent statistics show that in 2011 only 57 per cent of single mothers were in paid employment, however that is still an increase of 13 percentage points since 1991 https://mentoo.com.au/parents-working-out-work. Today, even a single parent who is employed can still qualify for the parenting payment so long as their income is sufficiently small. (To receive full payment, a mother of two needs to earn less than $213.20 per fortnight, but partial payment is possible if she earns more than that.) https://mentoo.com.au/parenting-payment

68. ABS data from 2016 confirms that this pattern still holds.

69. In 2018, the Workplace Gender Equality Agency reports that Australian women earn 84.7 cents for each dollar a man earns. https://mentoo.com.au/pay-gap-australia

70. At that time Pru Goward was very fair and told the truth about many controversial gender issues. However, since she took on her current position as a Minister in the NSW government she seems to have been totally captured, promoting feminist ideology. See chapter 8, Fox Guarding the Henhouse.

71. Researchers J.D. Baron and D. A. Cobb-Clark studied the source of the wage gap across the Australian public and private sectors between 2001 and 2006. They found that the wage gap among low-paid Australian workers was thoroughly explained by differences in wage-related characteristics but postulated a 'glass ceiling' effect in high-wage occupations. Gender differences were found to advantage women in all but high-paid jobs. Disparities in educational qualifications and demographic characteristics did not account for the gender wage gap, while disparities in labour-market experience explained much of the differences in private sector wages. (Occupational Segregation and the Gender Wage Gap in Private and Public Sector Employment: A Distributional Analysis 2010)

72. More recent comparisons show a similarly stubborn trend, for example in January 2000, 28.8 per cent of Australian women above the age of 15 were working full-time https://mentoo.com.au/labour-force-ABS-2000, and in January 2017 the figure was still only 28.9 per cent. https://mentoo.com.au/labour-force-ABS-2017

73. More recently on the Freakonomics podcast episode 'The True Story of the Gender Pay Gap' (2016), Harvard Economist Claudia Goldin also discusses the overwhelming evidence that men and women in the same occupation tend to start out on similar wages immediately after graduating from college, and that differences in their pay emerge over the subsequent 10-15 years.

74. Research from Denmark, one of the world's most egalitarian societies, identifies 'child penalties' as the main factor explaining the persisting gender wage gap. The arrival of children negatively impacts the earnings of mothers more than fathers, and accounted for approximately 80 per cent of gender wage inequality in Denmark in 2013 (Children and Gender Inequality: Evidence from Denmark H. J. Kleven, C. Landais, J. E. Sogaard 2017).

75. Statistics from the Australian Institute of Health and Welfare report that the overall average weekly hours worked by male medical practitioners in 2015 was 44.9 for men and 38.6 for women. The proportion of men who worked 50 or more hours per week was almost twice that of women (35.0 per cent of men and 19.6 per cent of women), whereas twice as many women (25.3 per cent women to 10.5 per cent men) worked between 20 and 34 hours a week. https://mentoo.com.au/AIHW-medical-practitioners

76. Harvard economist Claudia Goldin suggests that women's incomes are heavily penalised by their preference for temporal flexibility in working hours, that is, the freedom to choose which hours they work and on what days (Freakonomics Radio, 'The True Story of the Gender Pay Gap' 2016).

77. Even temporal flexibility does not always offer a path to pay equality, as demonstrated by women's performance as Uber drivers. In the 2018 Freakonomics podcast episode 'What Can Uber Teach Us About the Gender Pay Gap?', U.S researchers reported their analysis of the seven per cent hourly wage advantage experienced by male Uber drivers. Discrimination could not account for the wage gap, as Uber sets work assignments using a gender-blind algorithm and pay is determined strictly by output without negotiation. The team discovered three factors that accounted for the pay discrepancy: the time and location of trips, the amount of experience that the drivers had accumulated (men were more likely to stay in the job and work more hours per week), and humorously, the faster average speed at which men drove, allowing them to complete more trips per hour.

78. Warshak has published an update of this article confirming the earlier results: https://mentoo.com.au/Whitehall-article-1

79. Professor Whitehall's most recent article 'Experimenting on Gender Dysphoris Kids' further explains that "medical history has confirmed dangers in unsubstantiated interventions, despite all the good will in the world". https://mentoo.com.au/Whitehall-article-2

80. Paediatric Professor Quentin Van Meter also addresses unethical transgender medicine involving children. In this YouTube video I introduce a talk he gave in Sydney: https://mentoo.com.au/Quentin-Van-Meter

81. Policies that normalise non-binary gender identities are being advocated by Australian governments who are increasingly under pressure from some members of the LGBT community. The Tasmanian Labor party has called for gender markers to be optional on birth certificates https://mentoo.com.au/Tasmanian-Birth-Certificates. A discussion paper by WA's Law Reform Commission makes similar recommendations: https://mentoo.com.au/WA-law-reform. Queenslanders are no longer required to display gender on their driver's licenses: https://mentoo.com.au/QLD-licences. The Queensland government recently commissioned a discussion paper to address the failure of the Births, Deaths and Marriages Registration Act (2003) to adequately recognise sex and gender diverse people: https://mentoo.com.au/BDMRA-Qld-discussion. One could be forgiven for thinking that existing government policies were inclusive enough — the South Australian BDMRA (1996) 'Record a Change of Sex or Gender Identity' application form advises readers that they can change their gender identity "once in a 12 month period and three times in your lifetime..." https://mentoo.com.au/South-Australia-sex-change.

82. https://mentoo.com.au/Warshak-article

83. Laws have since been passed in Victoria, Western Australia, South Australia and New South Wales that provide varying degrees of access to information. Since 2005 the National Health and Medical Research Council (NHMRC) guidelines have recognised that donor-conceived children have an entitlement to information.

84. https://mentoo.com.au/NHMRC-ethical-guidelines

85. Tragically Narelle Grech met her biological father six weeks before she passed away of bowel cancer. A bill was introduced into the Victorian parliament to mandate the registration of donors' names and birthdates so that donor details could be released to biological children regardless of consent, the bill entered into parliament was named after Narelle. https://mentoo.com.au/donor-conception-support-groups

86. Justice for Men and Boys general election manifesto 2015, Published 28 Dec. 2014. p. 52-54.

87. https://mentoo.com.au/2015-manifesto-J4mb

88. Karen DeCrow died of Melanoma 6 June 2014.

89. The concept of a 'man's right to choose' or opt out of his obligations and rights was put to the test in the US case of Dubay v. Wells in 2000 and was rejected by the court. In Australia the Magill vs Magill High Court case considered whether such obligations (namely child support) could be discharged in light of paternity fraud. This case was also ultimately unsuccessful and the father was required to meet the financial obligations despite not being the biological father of two children and being unaware of this fact when the children were born.

90. In the 2012 US case of Hodge v. Craig, intentional misrepresentation of paternity was recognised by a unanimous Tennesse Supreme Court and damages were awarded in compensation for child support paid for 15 years. There have also been successful cases in the UK: Gerard Bradbury recovered child support payments of £30,000 (plus interest) made through the Child support Agency over seven years, and a Mr A successfully recovered £22,000 in damages for the emotional hurt of discovering that he was not a genetic father.

91. Robert Benjamin is now a Family Court judge.

92. More recently in Australia there was the Hallis and Fielder 2017 case where, following a DNA test, a mother was ordered to repay $4,142.73 in child support and pay a further $5,000 in costs to the father.

93. By 2017 government statistics showed soccer and AFL were far more popular sports for boys. The breakdown of the different football creeds in schoolboy sports was as follows: 29.8 per cent, football/soccer 21.9 per cent), AFL (14.6 per cent), Rugby League 5.7 per cent and Rugby Union 3.2 per cent https://mentoo.com.au/australian-sports-commission

94. https://www.youtube.com/watch?v=ryVSS0q2FCM

95. "The most statistically dangerous sports in Australia in terms of hospitalisations, adjusted for the number of participants, include Australian Rules football, soccer, motorsports, cycling, rugby and water sports, in roughly that order. https://mentoo.com.au/sports-injuries-australia

96. The 2016 figures (% unpartnered) are slightly lower than in 1996 for men aged 30-34 (34 per cent) and 35-39 (26 per cent). However, by age 40-44, a quarter of men (25 per cent) remain unpartnered.

97. The pension is now called the 'Parenting Payment' and currently offers a maximum pay-out of $762.40 per fortnight for a single principal carer or $492.80 per fortnight for a principal carer cohabiting with a partner. So an unemployed single mother on the parenting payment who begins to cohabitate with an unemployed partner on a Centrelink pension lower than $290 per fortnight, or a partner who earns a low income of less than $269 a fortnight, will similarly find that their combined income amounts to be less than the maximum parenting payment she could receive without a partner. However, the maximum $492.80 payment for couples is still available if the principal carer earns a small supplementary income lower than $104 per fortnight, and the partner's income amounts to less than $964 per fortnight. https://mentoo.com.au/parenting-payment-income-and-assets

Acknowledgements

My passion for writing about men's issues hasn't endeared me to many of my friends and has made life tough for my grown children who sometimes find themselves cast in the role of reluctant defender. I know they'd far prefer a mother who toed the line a little more.

But I can always count on loving support from Ian, my splendid partner, who copes so well with my frenetic life and knows exactly how to calm me down when my latest crusade has my mind racing in the wee hours and fragile the next morning. Luckily, he gets why it matters so much to me and cheerfully applauds from the sidelines.

I've had an amazing few years since I decided to give up my other activities to concentrate on men's business. It's been so heartening to find myself attracting a growing team of volunteers keen to do their bit. Like the brilliant, patient Scott Korman, whose IT and multi-media expertise proved a godsend, particularly when he foolishly agreed to produce my YouTube videos. The ever-versatile Irene Komen is always digging up amazing research and helping make things happen, now including video production. And Hobart graphic designer, Fraser Hopwood, at Naughtee.com, who comes up with smashing thumbnail images which liven up my video collection. And there's Greg Andresen, Senior Researcher for the One in Three Campaign who has devoted many hours to ensuring my domestic violence statistics are totally accurate.

There's a huge bunch of other helpful souls, some of whom need to keep their identities private since they still have careers to protect. Like brilliant young Emma who is handling my social media, and Bruce Chambers, a most methodical researcher and editor. Luckily, I found many people willing to help with the onerous task of updating the many articles we've included in this collection: John Stevens, Armando Miotti, Ray Lewis, Caroline Riley, and Tom Alexander.

Most of the pieces included here were first published in The Australian which is one of the very few local mainstream media sources willing to challenge the feminist narrative. I'd like to thank all the editors who have supported my writing, particularly Jennifer Campbell. More recently I've enjoyed writing for *The Spectator Australia*, where editor Rowan Dean is always interested in contrary views.

I was so happy with the surprisingly flattering cover image, taken by a talented young photographer Katherine Griffiths, who'd worked with me for many years taking profile shots of my online dating clients – quite a challenging business.

Lastly thanks to the thousands of men who have poured their hearts out to me over the last few decades. I'm in awe of their stoicism and outraged by their stories as they seek to survive in our increasingly hostile, male-bashing society. I'm rooting for you all.